THE MEANING OF THREE
THE MASK

SANDY SELA-SMITH, Ph.D.

authorHOUSE®

AuthorHouse™
1663 Liberty Drive, Suite 200
Bloomington, IN 47403
www.authorhouse.com
Phone: 1-800-839-8640

This book is a work of non-fiction. Unless otherwise noted, the author and the publisher make no explicit guarantees as to the accuracy of the information contained in this book and in some cases, names of people and places have been altered to protect their privacy.

First published by AuthorHouse 12/11/2008

ISBN: 978-1-4389-0370-5 (sc)

Printed in the United States of America
Bloomington, Indiana

This book is printed on acid-free paper.

Photo of Prisoner eyeglasses at Auschwitz # 14877 (1943) is reprinted by permission of the United States Holocaust Memorial Museum.

Information related to Alanza Sote and the reading that constitutes the context for the writing in this format as included herein is with her permission (11-21-07)

Table of Contents

DEDICATION

I dedicate this book to David
...A name that means the beloved...

In my personal journey to discover who I was under the mask, I was gifted with a plethora of Davids. Each one has been a mystical part of my life and my transformation. And each one holds a place in my heart that can be filled by no other.

Seattle David, I will be eternally grateful to you for daring to reveal your shamanic healing powers letting me know I possessed them as well; for in your courage, you taught me that we are all healers, a message that I pass along to all who are open to read *The Meaning of Three* and find this truth within. You, also, opened my eyes to understand that we humans are far more complex—so much more multi layered and multi-dimensional—than we were taught to believe, perhaps, one of the most challenging and transforming thoughts in my life. This understanding of who we are is a core concept in this book.

Oregon David, there are only unspoken heart words that can convey the love that I feel for you in being my true friend, for your standing beside me and reflecting to me the strength that I possess, a strength that exists in all of us if we would but look within. You were willing to see who I am in all of my light and my shadows, and accept all of me before I came to know myself, which made it so much easier for me to learn to accept me as you had already done.

China David, you were a needed and dear friend, when I was surrounded by strangers in a strange land, and you let me know that I am never alone, even if I feel like I am. This, too, is a message that is embedded in the pages of this book. You taught me to believe in my own power to create what I believe. In living this truth, you showed me by what you have demonstrated in your living that we are all the powerful creators of our lives, as well.

Connecticut David, you have trusted me with your vulnerability and your deepest truths and you have taught me to not be afraid of speaking my truth, by you speaking yours. There can be no greater gifts for any of us to give to each other than our vulnerability and our truth, for in the giving, not only we, but also humanity can grow into its most authentic self. Because of your courage, I have learned courage to be vulnerable and truthful, something I can now share with those who read what I have written, and, perhaps, they can find that same courage in their own selves, as well.

Clearwater David, you guided me in my connection with alternate realities and universes, as well as parts of myself from whom I had long been disconnected. You helped me accept my magical self on the deepest levels. As I pass along your gift to others, I honor your special gifts and acknowledge your contribution to the awakening of so many.

St. Pete David, you saw in me what I wasn't sure others could see, and you opened to a friendship with me by sharing the everyday things of your life, teaching me the value of those grounded life-events that touch our hearts so deeply.

Indiana David, you provided the reflection and care that I needed to believe that what I had to say was worthy of being heard. You used your wisdom and your skill to guide me in the publication of *The Meaning of Three: The Mask,* and perhaps most importantly, you continued to believe in me when I began to doubt myself and stayed in touch with me, reminding me of my purpose when I lost contact. For this, I am deeply grateful.

I dedicate this book to all these Davids, and to the beloved in all of us, in you and in me…because we all possess the amazing gifts that these special Davids embody and have given to me, if we would but look beneath the masks that most all of us have worn too long, and finally know our true selves.

So, David, the beloved, I dedicate this book to you. Without you, it would not have been written.

Sandy Sela-Smith, Ph.D.

7-31-2008
3:33 PM MT

ACKNOWLEDGMENTS

The removal of a mask is a profoundly delicate process that requires patience, love, honor, and respect for the frightened and vulnerable part of the self who first believed that the mask was necessary and has been hiding behind it for years, if not decades. And it requires having the same love, honor, and respect for that part of us that has identified with the mask and wants so much for others to look only at the mask and not behind it. I would like to acknowledge many fine healers and friends, who provided that patience, love, honor, and respect for my masked self and for the me that was under the mask.

Heartfelt thanks to all the Davids, scattered across the country, who are my forever friends, and to Michael in Bellingham, Washington; Carol Ann, Harvey, Lisa, Mary Ann, Reed, and Tim in Clearwater, Florida; and Cynde, Doug, and Harmony in Denver—all magnificent practitioners of body therapies—each with unique and powerful skills in their various methods of body-mind healing. And thanks to Bill in Atlanta and Anne in Seattle, both friends and gifted psycho-spiritual healers, whose support adds significantly to this book. And I have great appreciation for Steven in Seattle, Ben in Clearwater, and Laura in Denver, all psychotherapists who knew to stay present during intricate and difficult uncovering experiences.

I offer a special thanks to two beautiful friends, Esther Klein and Terry Waters, who contributed much to what I have learned about my true self, and to the Manitou Springs psychic, Alanza, who did her job with such connection that it became the catalyst for the writing of this book.

I acknowledge Saybrook Graduate School and Research Center, an exceptional institution of higher learning in San Francisco in the fields of psychology, human science, and organizational systems. Without the unique training offered, I would not have been able to articulate what I have learned to the degree that I have. And a special thanks to Don Cooper who, for me, kept everything together as Dean of students and then Director of Alumni Affairs. I offer special appreciation to professors who supported me in my process, including: Drs. Jeanne Achterberg, Thomas Greening, Eugene Taylor, Ruth-Inge Heinze, Tony Stigliano, John Wagener, and Barney Chin-Shong, and to Dr. Maureen O'hara, a world renown humanistic psychologist who was president of Saybrook during the majority of time I was in attendance.

A deeply felt and special acknowledgment goes to Dr. Stanley Krippner who graciously agreed to write the forward to this book. He was my mentor while I attended Saybrook and masterfully chaired both my masters and doctoral committees. His dedication to his graduate students is surpassed by none, and now that I am teaching graduate students at the same institution, I find myself asking, "What would Stanley do?" when confronted with an issue or concern, and that is what I do. His commitment to inquiry into non-ordinary reality has contributed to the expansion of consciousness around the world. I can think of no other person who has had such a great influence on my academic life and no one who is a more beloved model of excellence.

Much appreciation to Frank Lawlis, who endorsed my book at a time when he was deeply involved in writing his own book, a man who gave so much of himself to shamanic healing of others, as well as to me.

To Jeremy Geffen, MD, board certified oncologist, friend, and co-worker in the field of bringing healing to the whole person, who trusted me to work with the psycho-spiritual healing of his cancer patients, I offer my gratitude, as we sought to move beyond anecdotal evidence to collect verifiable data relating healing of emotional wounds to physical healing of the body.

To Matthew Manning, world-known healer from London who first introduced me to conscious healing, I wish to offer my prayerful thanks. And to Author, John Chilton Pearce, who dared to teach what he knew was true in a time when telling such truth was not celebrated, I want to express my gratitude for your willingness to stepping out of the box. Thank you for teaching me to accept that I could venture into unknown waters and teach about my adventures before most of the world would be ready to understand. By being courageous, you both gave me courage.

I offer my deepest gratitude to the gifted Pinellas County, Florida Drs. Sultenfuss and Lapolla, and all of their staff members for their kind and superior treatment of me when I really needed their wisdom and support, as I faced cancer concerns.

With great appreciation, I would like to acknowledge the Staff of Authorhouse. With special thanks for the dedicated work of Erin Watson who turned my manuscript into a work of art.

And finally, I want to acknowledge my eldest sister, Kathryn, the woman who literally saved my life in the darkest time of my adult life and Kathy, the child who lived with me in a dangerous and life-threatening world. She provided protection when the adults in our world offered little. I would not have been here to learn or to write what is contained in *The Meaning of Three: The Mask* had she and the Universe not decided that she would come into the world when she did. To her, my heart will be eternally grateful.

FOREWORD

By Stanley Krippner, Ph.D.

A few years after his death, comments made by Joseph Campbell (1904-1987) regarding what he called "the Mystery" were quoted in *Pathways to Bliss: Mythology and Personal Transformation:*

> As early as the eighth century, B.C. the Chandogya Upanisad explicitly states the key idea—*tat tvam asi*—"You are it." The whole sense of these religions—Hinduism, Jainism, Taoism, and Buddhism—is to evoke in the individual the experience of identity with the universal mystery, the mystery of being. You are it. Not the "you," however, that you cherish. Not the "you" that you distinguish from the other. p. 40

This was the mystery that he *found moving in him* when Campbell brought together his writings to create his 1972 book, *Myths to Live By.* His ordinary conscious self thought that he and his ideas had changed and progressed over the years, but when he looked at what he wrote, Campbell found that he had been writing about the same thing all those years. Something in him that he did not know was expressing the same thought, year after year, although his experience was that the message in his writing had changed. Whatever it is that moves within us, despite our lack of awareness of what it might be, is what he calls *the mystery.* He suggested that Jesus' statement that "I and the Father are one" alluded to the same mystery. This is even more clear in Jesus' pre-crucifixion prayer as recorded in the New Testament's book of John, 17:21, when Jesus is reported to have asked his heavenly father to let his followers know that just as Jesus is in the father and the father is in Jesus, so they are in the father and son.

While Campbell noticed the mystery in himself and studied the mystery through the myths expressed in the writings, the art, and the religions of the world, Sandy Sela-Smith, as revealed in this book, *The Meaning of Three: The Mask,* studied the mystery through her personal myths using a method she calls heuristic-self-search inquiry, which has led to her own understandings of what moves in her, something she identifies as the authentic self, the "you" under the mask. The authentic self may well be the "you" that Campbell alludes to when he says, "You are it" but not the "you" that you cherish, with the cherished you being what Sela-Smith call's the false self. Sela-Smith believes that the mystery, which is in union with the authentic self, is the "you" under the mask. But the masked, or false self, is what most of us believe we are.

For most of us, this mask is the image, which we identify as being who we are—especially if we have some special contribution that we can look to that is our mark in the world—or it might be our "best-foot-forward self" that we want others to recognize and honor as who we are. Some of us might know that who we pretend to be is false and struggle with knowing what other people believe about us is not true or we do what we can to make them believe it as a way to get what we want, while holding on to the secret that who we are is hidden. Still others believe that the mask is who they want to be, and they spend their lives trying to force themselves to work towards it and live it into reality.

According to Sela-Smith this false self—this mask, along with what we keep hidden—from others or from ourselves behind the mask—must be released, if we are to experience reconnection with the mystery of our authentic self. If we remain without awareness of the mystery or if we continue with a feeling of disconnection from it, the false self feels empty and goes through life feeling that something deeply important is missing. Her conclusion is the unique being that you are, "the eternal essence that flows in each of us, unfettered by fear, free to be and free to express that being, is both the mystery and the reflection of the mystery in the union of the physical and the spiritual," in each of us, and this is your true self.

I met Sandy Sela-Smith in the fall of 1994, when she attended her first residential conference as a new graduate student at Saybrook Graduate School and Research Center, where I have been a professor of psychology since 1973. For the next 7 years, I worked with her in coursework, and was her committee chair for both her master's thesis and her dissertation. She focused her studies on internal inquiry and was honest and frank when dealing with her own life; she articulated her process of self-discovery quite well. Her doctoral work used a heuristic method, with the addition of a final step in the process, which acknowledged resistance to the very inquiry that we make into the self. I now require that Saybrook students using this method review Dr. Sela-Smith's dissertation and include the final self-reflective step that she added in their work.

She dedicated herself to her spiritual studies at Saybrook, which included taking Personal Mythology and Dream Work with me. It was clear that she took her emersion into consciousness and spirituality with extreme seriousness. She went beyond her course work to study with some of the finest teachers of our time including Dr. Jeanne Achterberg, foremost researcher and innovator in imagery and healing, which Sela-Smith applied to her own work with cancer patients, assisting them to find healing in the midst of their disease. She studied with Montague Ullman, MD, world renown researcher in dreams and psychic experiences, and applied Dream Appreciation in her personal work as well as her with clients to help them find entry into the hidden aspects of their unconscious. She studied breathwork with Stanislav Grof, MD, Ph.D. known internationally for his Jungian based work in accessing the hidden aspects of the human experience and expanded her understanding of shamanic practices with Michael Harner, as well as many other practitioners around the world.

One could not be in Sandy's presence very long, without discovering that she holds views of life that are not commonly held in the Western culture. Her extensive work with dreams, with internal inquiry, and shamanic journeying has led her to accept beliefs in reincarnation; in the existence of non-ordinary reality; and in the mystery that weaves together the ordinary and non-ordinary realities in unexplainable synchronous events; and she holds the understanding that the Mystery, also called Spirit, God, The One, is not external to humans, but is integral to our being.

She has expressed a belief that an aspect of human nature seems to draw wounding into our experience, usually very early in a person's life, so painful that it feels too overwhelming for us to contain, or even remember. This original wounding in each human life, she believes, is a replication of a universal wounding that occurred when life first arose, eons ago. In the current life, the wounding event causes the child to separate from the authentic self, and to begin a life-long pattern of becoming a false self, a condition she believes occurs for nearly every human, if not all of us, often prior to the development of language. She, also, holds a belief in the innate multiplicity of all humans, not just a condition in those who experienced some kind of extreme abuse, and that multiplicity creates the internal conflicts that are an integral part of most all of our lives.

Though most humans, with great effort, try to believe that they know themselves, Sela-Smith contends that most have no clue as to who they really are. And they spend decades of their lives using anything they can to distract themselves from thinking about not knowing. Many try to pretend that they know, and may have even convinced themselves that they are the roles they play or the masks they wear, but for many, something in them senses there is a problem, whether they admit it or not.

Jungian, humanistic, and transpersonal theorists would easily recognize aspects of their principles embedded in *The Mask,* but though it contains these principles, this is not a theoretical treatise, it is a personal story of a woman who risked letting go of who she tried to be to find who she was under her mask. In an unusual style of writing, Sela-Smith tells the story of her life in puzzle pieces that reveal themselves throughout the course of her book, and finally, come together, both for herself and for the reader, as *The Mask* comes to an end.

Though the perspective that Sandy presents is not new, there are significant contributions to philosophy that she makes in this work. She takes the concept of Karma and personalizes it by tracing her relationship with her former husband through lifetimes, a journey that explains behavior patterns she accepted that otherwise made no sense. She presents the intricate inter-workings of the past that spin the stories of our lives, showing that much of what we live is from patterns, rather than from spontaneous, authentic living. She, also, presents a concept of the original trauma of the human species as originating from a major misinterpretation made at cell-level consciousness that we are separate and is replicated in individual lives over and over again. She proposes that this misinterpretation has caused all the conflicts between and among people throughout human history, but she, also, provides a solution that offers hope.

The Mask reflects a process that most people undergo, one that drains away their individuality, hampers their creativity, and limits their options and choices. Dr. Sela-Smith's lucid rendering of her own story, and her description of the hazards that wearing a "mask" entails will have a therapeutic effect upon many readers. It will not take the place of psychological therapy, but will help resolve long-standing issues with which readers have been grappling, often for decades.

As a result of interacting with *The Meaning of Three: The Mask,* like with any piece of authentic human artistic expression, the reader is given the opportunity to be transformed by what is presented here between the covers and behind the mask.

Stanley Krippner, Ph.D.
2-2008

Chapter One
THE BEGINNING

From the dawn to the dusk of our lives, all of us—with the possible exception of the saints and those who are completely innocent— wear masks at least some of the time, even if we don't believe we do. Many of us wear them almost all of the time and come to believe that we are the masks.

A very long time ago—it seems like lifetimes ago—when I was a little girl, I used to listen to *Dragnet*, a radio show that later became a popular television program. Every Thursday night, each episode began with words something like, "*This is the city; Los Angeles California. There are a million stories out there, and this is just one of them.*" And like that prologue to the archetypal police drama, I am beginning *The Meaning of Three: The Mask*, with a 50-year update to the words:

> **This is the matrix; the world in which we all live and experience our lives; it contains our pasts, our presents, and our futures and all the meanings we have attached to them…There are billions of stories out there, and the one I am going to tell is just one of them. But on some mystical level, this story you are about to read contains all the stories—all the billions of stories that could be told, including yours—all connected into one profoundly magnificent human story unfolding in us and through us…all present in what is written here, revealing what is in me, and what is in you, this very moment.**

On the surface, my story could be like anyone else's, including a birth, a childhood, an education, a marriage, a career, a mid-life crisis to find myself, a divorce, and a transformation of my life into the one I am living now. I have my own particular details that might be close to a few other people's lives, though not exactly the same…*but*…this is not a story of the surface; it is a story that goes much deeper, and though the details of it are mine, it touches all of us.

Like many other people in their middle years, in my 40s I became aware of a gnawing, emptiness that made me feel as if something very important was missing. In my search for whatever that was, I discovered that what was missing was my connection to my *true self,* and as I searched for reconnection, it became clear that I had been deeply unhappy for years. No longer able to live with the unhappiness, I made the decision to get a divorce, which meant ending a 23-year marriage. Soon thereafter, I left the US to live in China for a couple of years, an experience that helped me see the universe, even our little planet, as much more diverse than I had imagined. When I returned to the States, I moved to Florida, and then completed training as a clinical hypnotherapist in New Zealand, and began working as a therapist while completing a Ph.D. in psychology.

I built a reputation for being a non-traditional psycho-spiritual practitioner, who worked with the energy fields of the mind and body using depth psychology and shamanic practices to facilitate soul healing. This work led to my giving lectures and workshops around the country and in a few other countries, as well. I wrote a book and contributed many articles to journals and became an adjunct professor of psychology, but in spite of my discovery and all the changes in my life, I still felt as if something important was missing. In 2006, I uprooted myself again, as I had done 20 years earlier, and began another quest that led me to where I am in this moment, in a rustic mountain retreat in Colorado, on sabbatical to write books; the first I completed is, *The Meaning of Three: The Mask,* the one you are reading this very moment.

This book might appear, on the surface, to be a paintbrush picture of a life—the written version of an autobiography—but you will discover that this, like any biography, is really a "Mask" that covers up a deeper story, and it is the deeper story that I want to tell. The details of my life are important only because they act as an indicator of that more deeply hidden story that exists in me, told in such a way for you to more clearly see your deeper story and what exists in you. You will learn how the life most all of us lead is actually a "mask" that hides, not just what we think are the most unacceptable aspects of ourselves, but also, the true essence of who we are. Your details will differ from mine, but when we release the masks that hide us and let go of the details of our stories, the truth of what we all possess—of what is in us…of what *is* us—remains. And that mystery in us, the true self that we can spend decades or even lifetimes getting to know, keeps calling out to us to move past what we have kept hidden and to reconnect with who we truly are.

Among other intentions, there are three primary goals of this book. One is for you to learn that there is a mask you are wearing that you may never have known you were wearing, although it has been there for far too long; and the second is for you to really understand that this mask is *not* you, though you may have come to believe that it is and everyone else may identify you with it, as well. The third goal is that you will consider the possibility that under the mask there is your *true self,* waiting for you to acknowledge its existence, reconnect with it, and live from this connection.

***

In the very early days of living our life-stories, something shattering happened to all of us, usually when we were very young, before we had words to explain what the "shattering thing" was. This event that we interpreted as frightening because it caused us to believe we were not safe or not loved, resulted in a shift of our attention from experiencing the magical mystery in us, to focusing outside ourselves to recreate a sense of safety and wholeness, as well as to find the way to reconnect with the love we believed we lost. In attempting to be what we believed the outside wanted from us, we began a life-long pattern of becoming someone other than ourselves. This is not a flaw in the cosmos, or even a flaw in humans, but is truly a part of being human. And part of being human is the healing of this break from the mystical truth of our connection as we release the masks.

We put on "masks" to cover up the parts of ourselves that didn't feel acceptable only to discover, in time, the acceptance that our masked selves received from others felt inauthentic. For most of us, we kept searching for ways until we found what seemed like the way to please the ones we believed would help us feel safe again and loved again, or we became too angry or too depressed to keep trying when we couldn't find a way to please them. Neither the pleasing nor the struggle to please felt satisfying, and in time, many of us learned how to use myriad distractions, some socially acceptable and many unacceptable, to keep us from feeling or knowing that something was wrong.

We might have discovered that our mask—chosen to increase our appeal—began to feel inauthentic, yet, wearing it felt absolutely necessary. In time, we came to accept the inauthentic feelings we received from the outside as real. We lost conscious awareness that we were even wearing any masks at all. But in accepting the inauthentic as real, we lost the ability to feel *real* love, whatever safety we tried to create did not really feel safe, and we lost even more connection with the authentic being on the inside that is us …a being far more amazing than our masked selves could even imagine.

Our earliest years were about collecting the patterns that our masked selves would use, usually for our entire lifetime, and these became our personalities. When we were teenagers, some of us began to become consciously aware of the difference between what we appeared to be to others and that ineffable *something* we sensed was in us, some internal mystery that felt illusive and at that time, we started to wonder who we really are. For some, this wondering happened without awareness, but nonetheless, it was our first time of questioning. However, during our teen and young adult years many of us got caught up in the whirlwind of finding a place in the world, and we dreamed of making a name for ourselves instead of being ourselves. Then, we became absorbed by the need to fulfill the social customs of marriage, family, and career, or we struggled to survive and may not have had the luxury of time to have those quiet moments for revisiting the question regarding our true self. Sometimes this question comes back, exploding into our consciousness, especially if we are faced with a major life-trauma that shakes us from our normal patterned way of living. The question of who we are might come back for us to pondered in later years when there is more time. But for others of us, we move through all the stages of our lives and never again revisit the question.

Dr. Carl Jung, one of the founders of modern psychiatry and psychology, wrote a great deal about the second time of questioning, a time that he called the mid-life crisis that usually takes place in our 40s. At this time, some of us become willing to step away from everything that seems false to begin the search for what is real. But those of us who don't step away almost always try to fill those empty places with more of what didn't work before, or we try to find new challenges that can distract us for a little longer, hopefully, we think, just long enough to ease the feeling in our heart or our gut, that something isn't right. Our heroic efforts to prove our worth in the post teen years or mid-life years might cause us to win fortune and fame, and we may be acclaimed for our success or our great contributions to the world, but it doesn't take long to discover that even these successes or accolades don't fill up the emptiness as we had hoped.

If we failed to begin that inner journey to find ourselves in our teens or 20s during the first time of questioning or later in our 30s or 40s at the second time, and are among the fortunate, we might, just might, get another chance sometime in our 50s 60s, 70s, or even later, a chance to recognize that we have been wearing masks all of our lives…and if we have the courage, we will discover how to remove the masks and look deep inside to find out who we are underneath the mask.

It is difficult and maybe unlikely for us to find ourselves without help and inspiration or guidance, because our culture supports the illusion that masks are necessary to cover up our flaws, and from early on, we learned that if our flaws showed, we would be rejected, living out our greatest fears of being left behind, lost, and alone. It is my hope that the story of my life can influence your life by improving how soon and how easily you can discover your masks and most importantly, the perfection of your truth and the wonder of who you truly are.

This story is about overcoming fears of letting go of the familiar mask, or doing so regardless of fear. This is a story about learning that you don't have to get to the end of your life, however soon or far away it is, having missed becoming real. It doesn't matter how much time we have left; we may have many decades, a few decades, or even just a few years or months; whatever time we have can be a time of magnificent fulfillment that can only come when we have connected to who we are under the mask and live from that place. Choosing now to find your true self, in spite of the courage it may take to face pain and make changes is far, far better than waiting until this life is finished and never experiencing your true self.

Part of the story is about discovering what is the real self and what are masks. Through my story you will begin to accept that humanness is about masks and it's about learning to remove masks and discover the real self. It's about learning that being human is more than what is pretended today. And it's more than about pretending, something so many of us have become too good at doing.

You don't have to remain hidden behind masks pretending to be who you are not, stuck in the past, unable to feel alive in the present, and frightened of the future. You don't have to live your life feeling confined and limited, trapped by the way you always have lived, the way your families always lived, or the way most humans live. You will learn that you don't have to live with empty, gnawing places inside, desperately trying to numb them or attempting to fill them with people or things that eventually leave you still feeling empty. You can learn from my story that you don't have to live separated or feel fear as you approach either the middle or the end of your life, still haunted by an unquenchable mournful sadness that you missed something so important in life, and failed to discover whatever it was that you came here to experience. You can learn how to safely explore the mysteries inside your self without derailing your life until—and only if—you want to.

You can live and explore the great questions even while living the life you are living. You can discover that there is a void inside without being devastated by that discovery. For without finding out that you can survive your own woundedness, you can't discover that you can heal it. Without forgiveness of your flaws, you cannot discover what they really are.

My hope is that you can learn to risk what once might have felt like losing all that you thought you were, and all that you tried to be, or maybe even all that you thought was important in order to discover your authentic self—that part of you that you disconnected from when you were too young to know what you were doing. From my story you can realize that it is not the huge risk you once thought it to be. It will become an acceptable risk, or it might come to feel like really no risk at all. You can discover that by exploring and embracing your real self—you give yourself the greatest gift you could ever receive, no matter what your age may be.

Whether we take that risk in our teens, our 20s, our 40s, our 60s, our 80s, any time in between, or even later, we have the opportunity of finding what was so painfully missing. And this discovery can lead to transforming our being as we experience—likely for the first time—the joyous gift of finding what we have been looking for our whole lives and finally living from the authenticity of our soul's purpose, perhaps very different from the purpose we created for ourselves when we were wearing masks.

***

Though what is written here is grounded in principles of Jungian-based depth psychology, humanistic psychology, and transpersonal psychology, this book grew more from my personal process of taking that most terrifying risk of letting go of the person I tried to be, to find who I was under my mask.

From the time I was a small child and at various times in my life, I knew I had understandings that seemed to be not the same as others, something that terrified me, because, more than anything, I wanted to fit in or at least to blend in and not be noticed as different. But from the beginning, I was different. It took me years of struggle to finally accept my differences that I spent far to many years hiding under my mask. It took decades for me to acknowledge to myself that I am a shaman, not in the more traditional understanding of the word where the shaman is a recognized member of a tribal community to whom others come for healing and not in the more modern sense where people take training classes in shamanism and conduct shamanic rituals as an adjunct to the other things they do in the world. There are many meanings to the word. It is a word that resides in all languages of all peoples of all times. A commonality in all languages is that a shaman is a person who operates in more than one reality, more than one universe, maybe many. And from this ability to operate in multiple worlds, the shaman is able to bring healing to those who come for it. And it is from my shaman nature that I write *The Meaning of Three: The Mask.*

A shaman becomes a guide by having been a scout into unknown lands, offering the insight gained in exploration as guidance to others entering new territory. This does not mean those accepting the guidance will be following the path of the shaman. It is about each person finding his or her own path. What you will read in the chapters that follow is about the path of a particular shaman, one who wore a mask most of her life and then made the decision to release the mask and become herself. Your reading of the story and following along with my journey can help you on your own journey no matter who you are or where you are going. I realize that my path is not the path of the typical person, but then, the authentic path that each of us follows is not typical; each one is unique.

This book is written to the extraordinary that is inside every person; whether you are typical, below average, above average, or exceptional. This is not a book written for you to follow me. This is a book written to lead you on your own path to your self. As a shaman, I do not claim to be an example of how you should lead your life. I do not claim my life is an ideal life for you or, sometimes, even for me. However, as a shaman, I do believe and know that I can contribute to the quality of your life if you are willing to work and/or play along with me.

***

The *Meaning of Three* is a literally a labor of love, the result of a 20-year journey to find the Sandy under the mask. My journey took me into some very unusual places—unusual only from the perspective of the limited, materially based Western culture that has cut us off from so much of who we are as humans—and these places are a significant part of what I share with you. Your own path may not share the extreme experiences of my life, or it may. But your following the experiences of my path as I write about them here has the potential to expand your path. My search took me into my hidden past, into what I have interpreted as past lives, and into the future, as well as beyond the physical world into the farthest reaches of the universe, and there is a possibility that your path could lead you into similar places.

I discovered, through experience—not simply as a thought or theory—that we are far, far more than we have been taught to believe that we are. I have come to understand that we are all creators, and we create our lives by building them from what we believe. I have written *The Meaning of Three: The Mask* as a way to provide those who have realized or are coming to realize that something is missing and want to understand more, to see how one person navigated the waters on what often felt like the treacherous journey within to find what was under her mask. And it is my hope that you can learn from my experiences in your own life.

The Meaning of Three, though at times reads like a novel, is a non-fiction reflective autobiography that expands beyond the details of the life history of one person into the deeper realms of human experience. It is spiritual, mythical, psychological, magical, and often mysterious, even to me who lived it. My intention in writing this is to take you on a journey to uncover the profound complexities of your own life, normally not seen or understood. I want to reveal the mask that acts as a hiding place for fears and covers up your authentic self. I have weaved my explanation of a multi-dimensional tapestry of life with a style of writing that uses one story to tell another, which opens, yet, to another, and in the process, my writing presents an interpretation of the meaning of three—on one level the explanation of the meaning of three is the mask, what is behind the mask, and what is under the mask. But there is even more to the meaning of three than this.

This story that I have written winds along a path that moves back and forth between past and present, sometimes taking what seems like detours, that are, in fact, significant to the journey. The path, also, finds its way into futures not experienced in ordinary reality. While interpreted by some as fiction, at least by those who hold the Western worldview, my perspective embraces the possibility that past, present, and future are not three separate events, but instead, may well be simultaneous experiences, though not available to ordinary awareness.

I have come to believe that when you connect to the mystery that is under the mask, the mystery that has drawn you to read this book, you will discover so much more about the human consciousness you possess. This consciousness, this mystery in you, is not confined to your brain, but permeates you and is non-local; with it, you are capable of retrieving information far beyond your five senses, if you would only let yourself access all of you. And you are far more than you think you are. There are readers who might not be ready to accept this idea just yet, but some will.

I have, also, come to understand that time does not move only in one direction, but future can impact the present and the present can impact the past. You will learn that this three-dimensional, time structured reality is only a small part of multiple dimensions of your life and who you are. And all of this can be accessed when you choose to let go of the fear that attaches you to one way of experiencing the world to become aware of how much more there is to this universe, and to yourself underneath the mask.

This story is personal; but it is about humanness. It is the record of how I overcame the darkness of my beginning and in doing so discovered what I have come to believe is the truth of life as reflected in the multiple meanings of 3, including the interconnectedness of past, present, and future; the oneness of the underworld, the material world, and the spiritual world; the unity of mind, body, and spirit; the non-separateness of you, me, and us; and more. You will learn that I, also, believe that embedded in the metaphoric DNA of this story is not just my experience, but may well contain both the history and the future of us all. My purpose in writing is to present to you a way of looking at the world that offers hope for you and for the future of the human race at a time when so much is happening to us, individually, nationally, and globally that can cause despair.

In the chapters that follow, I begin with the story of an unplanned visit to a psychic—a woman who peers into my future, as well as my past—and I weave this encounter into a multi-dimensional platform from which I collect and share the stories from my past that move you through a non-sequential unfolding of my life story. This platform, along with my life story, provides a way to present to you my perception of the human story, a perception that has grown out of the evolution of my individual journey. You are invited to suspend judgment by allowing yourself to move through the unfolding of the stories and reflections upon them to decide how what I have concluded about who I truly am—and about who you are under the mask—resonates with you. If you let yourself do that, you will learn and you will discover more than you can imagine. You may well find it is safe enough to take the risk.

And, with all that said, the story begins…

Chapter Two
THE TATTOOED LADY

Life is the playing field that exists in the present and is nestled between the past and the future. In the present we can decide to release the tornadoes and storms created by the unresolved challenges of the past, which may well continue to distort the experience of our lives. When we garner the courage, we can unwrap our-selves from the constraints of the past to become more alive in present and we can learn to surrender to the unfolding of the future... if we choose.

Swirling paisley-shaped tattoos covered her forearms, and a large teardrop tattoo in gray tones adorned her cheekbone just below her right eye. Beneath the silver rings on her fingers were more tattoos that wrapped themselves around each digit, connecting one winding shape to the next. The soft pink, cotton knit shirt that draped loosely around her body offset her thick black hair that dropped in gentle waves to her shoulders, and silver hoop earrings rocked back and forth with each movement of her head.

She could have been an actress on a film set, playing the roll of a fortune-teller—a mesmerizing matriarchal gypsy, part nurturing earth-mother, part charlatan, and part magical mystic—who predicts the future by casting spells or giving the evil-eye to make her predictions come true. But she was not playing a part for a movie, except maybe the one in my head; she was on her own life-stage doing her work in a most perfect, quaintly furnished storefront shop on Manitou Avenue, the main street in the picturesque Colorado town of Manitou Springs. This town at the base of the 14,110 foot Pike's Peak makes visitors feel as if they have stepped through a time-space portal into a Swiss mountain village of the early 1900s.

The dark-haired woman seated behind an oval shaped hardwood table invited us to sit down on the padded high back wooden chairs that were across from her. I don't recall that she introduced herself, by name, though she might have, as she asked my friend and I what we wanted.

Esther told her we were interested in a future reading and wanted to know if we could sit in on each other's sessions. The psychic said she was willing to combine the reading for both of us since it was very clear to her that we were close and had much in common, not just friendship in this lifetime, but likely as mother and daughter or sisters in many previous lifetimes, something that was not a surprise to either of us.

Over the past 15 years, Esther and I have become very dear friends. She is one of those ageless beauties; a tall, slender woman, who carries her age and herself like royalty, so very dignified and always dresses as if she just stepped away from a catalog cover shoot. Yet, she is a most earthy woman, a true humanist, who has been fighting for the rights of women, children, and the downtrodden, from the 1960s era to the present. Flower child at heart, she is sensitive to what is wrong in this world and has spent her life doing what she can to contribute right-ness.

***

The medium directed her first comments to my friend, and what didn't fit for Esther, she assumed, was something coming through for me. She talked with Esther about a man who would be entering into her life, and about people from the *other side* who were making contact. After about 10 minutes or so, the fortuneteller turned to me and began a more focused reading about my future. After a time, perhaps 10 minutes or so into my reading, she looked directly into my eyes and with an almost staccato emphasis, asked, "What does the number 3 mean?"

Before that most emphatic question, the fortune telling psychic, who goes by the name Alanza and calls herself a natural clairvoyant and clairaudient, had been giving me all the usual messages that palm readers and tellers seem to give to women without wedding or engagement rings, predictions about finding a rich man and living in a large house with huge windows that overlook the water...East Coast, not West...and that I would be relocating from where I am now, to a place probably near my friend. She said the rich man I would be meeting in the coming year, would be an unlikely someone, a big teddy bear of a man who would adore me and defend me against anything that might feel threatening. She thought he would be probably about 45 years old, and at first, would appear to be a mechanic or some kind of a laborer who worked with machines, but she advised me to not dismiss him as someone I wouldn't be interested in because there was far more to him than would meet the eye. In fact, she said, he would be the owner of some very large enterprise involving machines and would be the love of my life. I would meet him in a line, like at a bank or a grocery store, and we would start talking...we would have the sense that we met before without really knowing where. We would exchange cards and a relationship would soon bloom. She suggested that I might marry him. She continued with the reading saying that this relationship would bring joy and spontaneity back into my life.

***

Alanza paused for a moment; her energy shifted and, then, with furrowed brow, she said, *"It is like somebody stole your childhood, your young years. Your ability to play and have fun was taken, stolen, and this is the time you will take this all back."* Her comments about my past touched a very deep cord inside me, because she was right about the theft of my childhood, my teen years, really the theft of a very big piece of my life, and when my childhood was stolen, too much of the joy of life had been taken, as well. For most of my life, happiness and joy were present only in bits and spurts and I wanted to reclaim the depth of those feelings.

A very distressed look came over her face as she told me she couldn't look much into what she was seeing of my past because it was too disturbing to her; however, she assured me that the people who did those things to me would have to pay. They would suffer for what they had done, if not in this life, then in a future lifetime. I had a feeling that her intensity had more to do with her response to what she was seeing than to my need to feel that justice had been done. I have long since released attachment to punishment of the perpetrators and have let go of the need for vengeance.

Years of spiritual searching, multiple therapies, and what feels like decades of journaling, have taught me so many lessons about how my world works, how my life works, and what I need to feel peace. All the work I have done with myself helped me understand that I have no need to focus on the lives of those who participated in the darkness of my childhood. I just needed to reclaim what is mine.

Though the past does return in wisps and flashes, mostly to help me understand something in the present, I don't live in the past, at least not consciously. My present world is not defined by as many of the unconscious beliefs that used to direct my life, although I am aware that there is always more to learn, more to release, and more to embrace. I am usually grateful for the understanding that these little wispy snippets of information offer. As I become aware of the residue of old beliefs that can subtly control my life in ways that I didn't know before, beliefs not in my best interest, I do what I can to dismantle them.

I have long since come to recognize that the very dark beginning of my life—a story that will be told in greater detail later on—contained a hidden gift; and without all that happened and all the understandings that emerged from a very long healing path, I would not have come to be the person I am and I would not know what I have come to know. On some level, I can thank those who were so damaged that they were capable of passing on that damage to such a degree that it cracked me open enough to discover what I might never have known without it. … And that was the Sandy under the mask.

Chapter Three
I WAS NEVER REALLY MARRIED

Our lives are replete with messengers from myriad realities bringing information that holds the power to open our eyes to what we have not allowed ourselves to see before, and when we listen to the messages, our paths can finally move toward our bliss, which is our soul's ultimate journey.

Alanza looked up for a moment, as if she heard something that Esther and I couldn't hear, and then she looked back at me and asked another question in the form of a statement, *"You have never been married!"* I assured her that I had been, and without missing a beat, she said, *"No, you weren't; not really. You might have been legally married, but you were not really married."*

Her comment caused my thoughts to slip back to a conversation I had with a stranger on a bus in Washington DC, easily 20 years before Esther and I paid a visit to the tattooed psychic in Manitou Springs.

From the early to mid 1980s, I worked part-time in Washington, DC as a state coordinator for a non-profit organization, a job that took me to the Capitol City several times a year. On one of those trips, I had the afternoon off from my work and decided to use the free time to visit the Holocaust Museum. I wanted to see a famous photo exhibit I had heard about and felt very drawn to experience it. I got onto a city bus to find only one available seat left at the front, so I sat down next to a very ordinary looking man. I don't recall what caused us to begin a conversation, but as I turned my head to speak, something in me knew that despite his appearance, he was not ordinary; although, I couldn't tell you how I knew. He was tall and slender; he had clear blue eyes that appeared to glow from the inside out, and to my astonishment, this stranger seemed to know everything about me, about my childhood, my marriage, my life in the present and even my life in the future; some of the things he spoke about, no one could have known, but me.

In the conversation, he told me that though I was married, *I really wasn't married,* words so very similar to Alanza's words two decades later. He explained that my husband and I had a contract that had been completed and I would be leaving him to create a new life for myself that would be one I could not even imagine in that moment. His words seemed totally absurd to me because I believed that marriage was 'til death do us part." How could a perfect stranger tell me these things with such absolute certainty? Somehow in all of the ins and outs of the conversation, we touched on the subjects of, previous lives, other universes, and alternate realities, though I was unable to remember much of that part of the conversation, since these subjects were completely unfamiliar to me at the time, and I am sure I resisted opening to the information.

He asked me if I had more time and offered to take me to lunch and, surprisingly, against all my better judgment, I told him I would accept his invitation. We got off the bus together and found an outdoors restaurant near one of the museums. We talked for what I thought was about a half hour and then he wished me a good life; he got up, stepped back from the table, and said good-bye. I glanced at my watch to see how much time had actually passed to make sure that I would still have time to see the photo exhibit, but when I looked back up to thank him for talking with me, he had disappeared. But he couldn't have melted into the crowd, because there was no crowd; the area was nearly empty of people. He was simply gone and I have never seen him since, at least not that I know.

I continued my journey to the Holocaust Museum to see the photography exhibit of Concentration Camps from World War II. The presentation was powerful, but when I stepped in front of one large photograph of a mound of eyeglasses, taken from Jewish people before their executions, I became violently sick, I had to leave the museum and could not return to view the rest of the photographs on display. That image has remained with me and so often when it came into my mind, it would cause me to momentarily freeze and become nauseously sick. At the time, I had no idea why that photo had such a profound impact on me. That information came much later.

***

After telling me that I had not been married, Alanza paused and then her brow furrowed again as she exclaimed, "You were a dart board! That was not a marriage; he hurt you and he didn't know how to adore you. This teddy bear man will give you a true marriage."

Alanza couldn't have selected a better metaphor to describe how I felt treated in the relationship with Jake. After Esther and I returned home, I looked up dartboards on the Internet, and discovered that they are made from fibers that were once alive and free flowing, but are cut down and compressed under tons of pressure to turn them into a tight circle, kept together and locked into place by steel bands and all is bonded to a non-warping backboard to prevent any movement.

In retrospect, it is easy to see how my marriage became a bond that locked me in place and prevented any natural movement in all the fibers of my being. And there is no question that I felt controlled and imprisoned by my husband's will that figuratively compressed me into a form that he wanted me to take. It took many years for me to discover that I, too, had contributed to pushing myself down and compressing myself to be in the form I believed he wanted. Similar to the dartboard whose surface is sanded smooth, until there are no unacceptable protrusions, my identity had been sanded away, as well.

After all the identifying features of the fiber are gone, the last stage in turning the once free fibers into a dartboard is to screen print it with a design that covers any last remnant of the fibers underneath. Like a screen-printed design, I wore a mask to cover up anything that didn't match the role I took on when I became Jake's wife.

Looking more deeply at the metaphor, I became an object that participated in a game with Jake by being completely passive and receptive to his sharp darts that pierced into the fibers of my being. His darts were in the form of emotional zings, psychological cuts, physical force, and experiences, which felt to me like sexual assaults that allowed him to maintain control and win. Over time, I learned to accept the pain of what he threw in my direction and the wounding from the holes his darts left in my soul. All the while Jake seemed unconcerned for who I was inside. I had no idea there was any other Sandy beside the mask that I wore, and I didn't even recognize I was wearing a mask.

On the unconscious level, dartboard people believe that the only way to survive is to allow the other to have complete control, and the game they play together is explicitly about the needs and desires of the active player, not about the passive one. For over two decades, the life we two lived was about Jake, and everybody, including me, believed that what Jake wanted was what Sandy wanted; our masked life was his game.

In the Western culture, it is more common for the woman to be the dartboard, and the man to be the darts player, but these roles can be reversed. It, also, is possible for both partners in a relationship to shift between being the dartboard and the darts player. When one becomes too aggressive, the other may find ways to throw darts, while pretending that they were not intended to be darts, or might finally explode and become outright aggressive, throwing the darts with an intention of hurting the other. Whenever a couple engages in dartboard games, the relationship becomes one of control instead of love. As much as I loved Jake, my interaction with him became a game of survival, trying to do whatever I could to let him win so I would hurt less. Unfortunately, though it might seem to at the time, that strategy never works.

The deeper truth was that I had been a dartboard person long before I met Jake; it started back when my childhood was stolen. For years, the difficulty I had in acknowledging dartboard status in my adult relation-ship was that I knew a person can't become a dartboard without consent. What I hadn't, yet, learned was that it is not uncommon for children, who have already been compressed and had their identity sanded off in their family of origin, to become people who take on dartboard status in their adult relationships. In cases like this, the dartboard seems to be all that is left with which to enter into an adult relationship.

The loss of identity in childhood opens the way for the adult partner, who might begin the relationship with the best of intentions to love, honor, and support, in sickness and in health, to feel robbed when he or she discovers the one with whom they have entered into a relationship is presenting just a mask. As a result of not getting what was expected, the new partner might easily begin treating the masked person like an object to supply his or her needs, because there seems to be no one there under the mask with needs. Or maybe, the partner believes that if enough hurt is inflicted, the person underneath the mask will come out and will finally have a real partner. What the aggressive one can't see is that he or she is wearing a mask, too; it is just less obvious.

Because of being sanded down so much, even the dartboard person might not know what his or her needs are. The needs of the dartboard partner, even though they are generally unconscious, remain unexpressed. In this kind of relationship there is no part of self in either partner that is strong enough to require respect and honor for self or for the other, and both become deeply disappointed in the relationship, blaming the other for the loss. And that was the way it became with Jake and me, though it didn't start out that way.

***

I met Jake when we were both juniors in high school. I was exceedingly shy and at 5'7" I was tall for a girl back in the 60s. I was slender with long, thick light brown hair that dropped below my waist. I had light brown eyes that I always kept down to avoid eye contact and connection with anyone. The one expressive thing I did was to sing in the school choir, and even there, I could hide among the 80 other voices. In most of my classes I was the teacher's assistant and became a hall monitor between classes, a human "object" standing in the middle of the corridor like a post in a fence to make sure that students going in one direction didn't flood into the other side of the hall, blocking students going in the other direction. As a fence post, I was invisible as a person, and those who moved didn't talk with those who monitored their movement.

I could be counted on to answer questions from the teacher but seldom talked to my fellow students. I would have been on the top honor roll, but for a time in my first year of high school, I was out for several hours each day for a number of weeks having all sorts of medical tests and procedures done to find out why I had headaches and bouts of blindness, the causes of which were never discovered. My grades in the morning classes suffered badly that first year, and I was never able to make up for the difficult beginning because the low grades of the first year were averaged with the high ones of the last years.

The only close friend I had in school was one of my sisters, three days short of one year older than I; and though I was acquainted with a few of her friends, I barely knew anyone in my class. I would be surprised if anyone in my class even knew my name. I was a pretty girl but didn't know it back then, likely because I never even thought about that sort of thing. Except for a short time in 9th grade, I didn't date until my last year of high school. Dating meant being walked home from school or meeting my boyfriend at the movies on Saturday afternoon, accompanied by my younger sister or brother and on occasion going to the school dance with my older sisters. I seldom participated in school events, and never was invited to classmates' parties. My entire focus was on my studies and my only dream was to go to college to become a teacher.

Jake and I were in the same history class for our entire junior year, but I didn't know he was there. He was a quiet boy who didn't have school as his top priority. Since he wasn't one of the few students with whom I competed for the highest scores, I didn't notice him. Our class was held in one of those old-fashioned rooms with plank wood flooring and long rows of wooden desks, connected by wrought iron sled-like rails that were bolted to the floor to keep the rows straight. The room looked like it was constructed in the 1920s, and it even had a wood burning stove in the corner near the front of the room. Most of the students kept their books in the compartment under the writing surface of the desk that you'd access by lifting up the top, so when I began to search for anyone who had a physics book, there were few whose books were visible. I scanned the entire room, and there, on the top of a boy's desk a couple of rows away from me, was the faded tan and green cloth-bound physics book.

Completely abandoning my usual shy way of being, I asked the boy if he was taking physics, and when he said, yes, I asked if he could explain the principle of electricity related to batteries and transformers. For some reason, I just couldn't understand where the higher volts went when they were turned into lower ones and if that was asked on the final exam, my score could drop from an A to a B, which, for me, would have meant failure.

While we walked from history class to physics, Jake explained the principle so simply that I was sure I could remember what he told me if the question were on the test. It was on the exam, and I knew I got it right. After class, Jake was waiting for me in the hall to find out how I had done and I thanked him for being my physics lifesaver. That was the beginning of the relationship of a lifetime. By our senior year, we were considered one of the "couples" in the school, even though my parents controlled my dating very closely and I was seldom allowed to be alone with him.

***

From the beginning, I liked Jake, but he won my heart the first Christmas we were together when he came to my family home bearing gifts. I answered the doorbell to find him standing on the front porch wearing his long tweed winter coat that had that 1920s look, when men wore long coats and had hats that they tipped to the side, looking so in charge…and he looked so very much a man in charge, in spite of the fact that he was only 17 and came without the advantage of a hat. Jake was tall and slender, standing 6'3" with strong shoulders and the long, powerful, sleek legs of a track star. He was generally quiet and acted very shy most of the time; at least he was shy around me.

It was a chilly winter's night that Christmas Eve of our senior year in high school when I stepped out of the house to greet my unexpected guest. The small porch light illuminated his blue eyes as he stood in front of me with a beautiful smile on his face. From where I stood, it looked as if he was on a magnificent stage with the backdrop being an unobstructed panorama of Seattle's skyline, sparkling with city lights, all silhouetted against the night sky. This spectacular post-card view was visible from my family's home that overlooked Elliot Bay, Seattle, and the majestic Cascade Mountains in the far distance. Even though it was Christmas Eve, and not Christmas day when my family usually opened presents, Jake wanted me to open the big gift he had brought for me, right then. The gift was in a large box wrapped with shiny silver paper and tied with a wide, red satin ribbon.

I had never seen a package that was so beautifully wrapped, and part of me wanted to save the opening at least until Christmas day, so that I could gaze upon it for a time before unwrapping it, prolonging the excitement that comes from not knowing what might be in such a magnificent gift. However, since he asked, I carefully removed the bow and loosened the tape on the sides of the box. Whatever was underneath was covered with several carefully placed layers of white paper. I lifted the covering and saw that inside was an electric blanket. It was very soft, and so, so beautifully sky blue. I had never felt my heart as full as it was that moment. Jake whispered that he bought it because I was always sick and since he couldn't keep me warm at night, he wanted to give me something else to protect me from the cold. Feeling both excited and embarrassed by his comment about keeping me warm, I fell in love.

I had never had someone buy such a special gift just for me. The whole experience was overwhelming, and though I really appreciated the blanket, it was not the gift that impressed me as deeply as the idea that the gift represented. I knew he must have actually thought about me in order to buy it. He was all of the goodness, the thoughtfulness, and the caring that felt missing in my life. He was my *Knight in a Tweed Coat*, the one that had come to rescue me from all that was not good in my family home. I felt loved. So when he asked me to marry him a few months later, the only possible answer from my heart was, "Yes!" But as the years passed, both my life and my Knight moved beyond that Christmas Eve moment.

The events that spun into my mind, that I include here and in the chapters that follow, though they seemed random at the time that I was remembering them, were in fact little puzzle pieces of a much larger picture that I was not able to see until *The Mask* was nearly finished. In retrospect, everything that I wrote about needed to be included for the whole picture to be seen, though I am getting a bit ahead of myself by saying that.

***

The two statements, Alanza had made—one that I was a dart board for my husband, and the other that I had never been married, not really—seemed to touch deeper and certainly more painful memories from my past. In only a microsecond after she made those comments, I was no longer in Colorado sitting beside Esther listening to the words of the tattooed lady; I was in Seattle experiencing events that had been exceedingly difficult to live. I slipped into and out of those times, one after another, reliving the pain and sadness of being treated as an inanimate object, a dartboard that didn't matter.

I remembered an event when I was almost 19, not even two years after Jake had stood on my porch bearing his gift in the shiny silver box. I was in the process of transferring to the University of Washington from another university I had attended my first year of college and needed to get a physical examination as part of the admittance requirements. After the exam was over, Jake asked me to tell him every detail about the visit to the doctor's office. It felt a bit awkward sharing such personal details about my body; but he was going to be my husband, so I figured that made his questioning acceptable, despite my uncomfortable feelings. I told him almost everything that happened, leaving out information about a pelvic exam that had embarrassed me and ended my report with an explanation that I wouldn't get the blood test or pap results for a little while. And then I added that the doctor said everything looked good. My words seemed to stun him. His expression shifted from curiosity to an almost seething anger, but he wouldn't tell me what was wrong. After a couple of months of silent dates and a significant reduction in telephone calls, he invited me to his parents' home for dinner.

Earlier in the day of our special mid December date, Jake planned a meal, had gone shopping, and cleaned up the recreation room in the daylight basement of his parents' home. He had even put up the Christmas decorations including the traditional tiny town figures and spun cotton on the fireplace mantle. My father dropped me off at Jake's in the early evening and when I walked in, the scent of pot roast and baking potatoes from the upstairs kitchen mixed with the wonderful aroma of the freshly cut and decorated pine tree. Jake lit a fire in the fireplace to welcome me and seemed truly pleased that I was there. He showed me everything he had done to prepare for my visit, including telling me how his little brother had nearly burned down the house when part of the tiny town spun cotton got too close to the fire some years before.

But something about Jake seemed different than he had ever been before. He seemed awkward, and a little distant, like someone trying to impress another, sort of odd behavior for a boy I had known for two years. While we stood in front of the crackling flames he pulled me toward him and began to kiss me in a way that felt too forceful. I didn't feel comfortable with what was happening and attempted to move away. This made him tighten his hold on me and then he tried to force me to the floor, which was a familiar feeling from my childhood.

But at 19, I was stronger than I was as a little child. I broke loose from his hold and ran to the door that exited into a garage on the daylight side of the basement. When I turned the knob, I found that the door was locked, and something happened inside me that I couldn't explain; I didn't know how to open the door. In retrospect, it should have been a very easy thing to do. Sounding more like a child than a young woman, I began to cry and almost whispered through my tears *"I want to go home. I want to go home."* But for me to go, his mother would have to drive me. Even though I was in my second year of college, my parents didn't allow me to ride in Jake's car and he knew I was obedient about that sort of thing. If I asked to go home before dinner, his mother would wonder why I wanted to leave, and Jake didn't want to have to tell her. Sounding more like a frightened little boy than a young man, he pleaded with me not to say anything.

With my hand still clutching the doorknob, I pressed my body against the locked door and would not look at him. He kept repeating that he was sorry, and begged me to stay. If he tried to get too close to me or touch me, I pressed myself harder against the door, and continued my whispered plea to let me go home. I remained in that frozen position until his mother called down to us from the main-floor announcing that dinner was ready. Her intervention broke the drama in which her son and I had been trapped for a few minutes, and the two of us climbed the narrow stairway, as if nothing was wrong, to get what had been prepared and bring it down to the basement. As we entered the kitchen, his mother, a dignified woman with jet-black hair and deep piercing eyes, proudly explained how Jake had been the one who planned and cooked the meal and expressed how proud she was that he had done all the cleaning up in the basement without even being told to do it.

After several trips up and down the stairs, we arranged the serving bowls on the linen covered table, and using his best formal manners, Jake invited me to sit down as if nothing had happened. He lit a candle, and the two of us ate dinner in near silence. I don't remember what we talked about following dinner, but I do remember being entranced by the red-orange light and the shadows cast from the roaring fire as they danced on us and on the walls and ceiling as if everything was on fire, and I wondered what Jake had done with my knight in the tweed coat.

My father picked me up at the designated time a couple of hours later. And like so many of the events of my childhood, I forgot what had happened that night. Not quite three years later, I walked down the aisle of Central Lutheran Church to marry the man of my dreams.

I don't remember too much of my wedding day, but I do recall I wore my mother's wedding dress. It was a beautiful form-fitting, ivory satin gown with a long train that stretched out behind me as I walked. My mother had sewn a number of tiny satin leaf appliqués on the front to cover moth holes in the nearly 30–year-old dress, and was able to arrange them so carefully that no one would have ever guessed that they did not belong exactly where they were placed. At the time, I had no idea of the metaphor embedded in that wedding dress for my life and for our relationship that went far deeper and was so much more than I thought it was.

All the guests had arrived and most of them had been seated; the ushers had taken their places next to the 21-year-old groom, as the organist began the prelude to the wedding march. My sisters and soon to be sister-in-law were waiting in the vestibule for me to come up from the church basement, and my father stood by ready to walk down the aisle and give his third daughter away to a young man he barely knew; although Jake and I had been together for five years. Just as I was ready to leave the bridal dressing room to walk upstairs and down the aisle, my mother noticed that the train had wrinkles from the box and wanted to press it before the ceremony began. She found a steam iron in a cupboard, plugged it in and began pressing when a bolt of steamy water flushed out of the bottom of the iron and spewed its rusty contents, spreading a horrible red-orange stain down the back of the gown. I was in shock, but then I simply went into a state of quiet calm and watched what was happening.

My mother helped me remove the dress, and then submerged the train portion of the dress in the bathroom sink to wash as much of the stain out as possible; she found a towel to absorb the remaining rusty water. I don't recall feeling anything about what was happening, though I do remember that she was in a near hysterical panic. All the while, the people in the church were waiting; the groomsmen remained standing in their appointed positions next to Jake, and my sisters and father were still waiting in the vestibule, very likely everyone wondering if the bride had changed her mind. The organist kept playing…and finally, I emerged from the basement, with a pressed, but slightly wet train. The wedding march must have begun and the wedding guests must have stood up as they usually do when the wedding march commences; my sisters must have walked ahead of me, and then my father and I most likely walked down the aisle, as planned, though I don't remember it. Jake and I must have exchanged rings, and promised to forsake all others until death do us part… I am sure we did, but I just don't remember.

***

For our first anniversary, we returned to the Holiday Inn where we had spent the first two days of our honeymoon the previous year. We were getting ready to go out to dinner, which included Jake doing a touch-up shave with his electric razor. But before he started to shave, he called me in to the bathroom. As I entered, he asked me to stick out my tongue. I didn't know why he would ask such a thing, but being obedient to whatever he told me to do, I stuck it out. He was holding his electric razor in one hand and the electric cord that should have plugged into the razor in the other, and in that same moment that I opened my mouth to follow his instruction, he thrust the live end of the cord up against my tongue—or using Alanza's metaphor, I was the dartboard, and cord was his dart. The jolt knocked me down and flipped me against the wall. I began to cry. Between sobs, and with stunned confusion, I asked him why he did that to me. He responded by asking, *"Why were you dumb enough to stick out your tongue?"* Though I had been married to him for a year, I had no idea who the man standing over me was, and I didn't see any light coming from his blue eyes.

I'm not really sure if he intended to hurt me as badly as he did, and I couldn't believe that he wanted to kill me, but I was never able to figure out why he would do something that could have been deadly. As I had done so many times in the past, I packaged the painful memories and put them away to avoid thinking or wondering about them again. But, in the deepest places in my heart and mind, I knew what I must have known when I was 19, that I could not trust him anymore. Though, I do believe the lack of trust showed up a week before I was to marry Jake with a difficult dream and a head-to-toe body rash, both of which were the ways my body and mind tried to communicate with me before my wedding day that getting married to Jake wasn't a good idea.

***

Jake never liked my name and after we were married, he began calling me by other names; among his favorites were *slug-bait* and *dog-faced pig*. After a while his references to me stopped stinging and I rationalized that these names were his way of expressing affection. I decided they were special pet names for me rather than insults. In front of other people, Jake often referred to me as *the wench*, and when his male friends visited us, it was not uncommon for him to order me into the kitchen to get food or drink for them by saying things like, *"Hay wench, Ron wants another coke."* Or, to his friends he would say something like, *"If you want anything, the wench will get it for you."*

So *Slug-Bait* followed the orders she was given, and *Dog-Faced Pig* accepted the role Jake had assigned her as the wench. At least she had a recognized place in Jake's life, despite having a broken heart.

When we went to family gatherings, the meals were often buffet style, and I learned to prove my worthiness as a wife by serving his every need. As his wench, it was my job to fill his plate, giving him only what he liked, and keeping his glass filled with whatever he was drinking. When he finished what I had served, like his attentive maidservant, I would ask if he wanted anything more, and if he did, I would oblige him. The other men always commented about how lucky he was to have a wife who was willing to be at his beck and call, and expressed envy of him for having what they considered such a great catch. Jake seemed to be proud that he had a wife who was willing to serve him, and I felt honored to be the one who made him proud, in spite of the fact that he ordered me around like I was a slave in bondage to impress the other men. Most of the women sent dagger stares at their husbands to make sure it was very clear that these husbands not even attempt to treat them as Jake treated me.

I truly believed I served him because I loved him, and that was partially true, but as I look back, I know that on the unconscious level, the driving force for my service was to create safety for myself by convincing Jake that I was not expendable. If he needed me to supply all the basics, he would not throw me away or leave me. What I didn't know was that *dependency breeds contempt*, and contempt was what I received from him, far more than appreciation. This can be one of the painful side effects of wearing a mask. But not until I worked on this book, did I discover an even deeper reason for being so willing to become Jake's servant, one that went back lifetimes, and I will tell you about that in a later chapter.

***

Jake often told me that it was a good thing for me that he married me, because if he hadn't, no other man would have had me. And in time, I came to believe him, especially when he criticized me for nearly everything I did, or didn't do. Scanning everything before he would come home became an ongoing behavior for me, to see if there was anything not right that he could criticize, but no matter how careful I was, there was always something I hadn't noticed, and that was what he would find.

By that time, I was used to being treated with a lack of respect and very little caring. Though it hurt me, I provided myself with excuses that he was so busy he just didn't have time to be thoughtful by remembering birthdays or anniversaries, and his maltreatment was because he was worried about his work or anything else that might be the focus of his concern. And I continued to serve him.

After seven years of marriage, he decided he needed to move out on his own. He told me it would have been much easier for him if I were an alcoholic or a terrible person because then he could justify his leaving, but he couldn't justify it other than saying he didn't love me, or at least he didn't know if he did. I helped him find furniture for his new apartment, and pack his clothes...and fell apart after he left. When he returned a few months later, we didn't talk about his leaving or his return. I accepted him back without knowing why he returned. I didn't know if he had decided that maybe he did love me or maybe he missed being with me, and I continued serving him for another 13 years.

We had been married for about 10 years or so when I decided to do something for him that was out of the ordinary. While Jake was watching a football game on a Sunday afternoon, I washed and waxed his truck, a vehicle that was his pride and joy, polishing it to make it look showroom ready. At halftime, I told him I had a surprise, and asked him to follow me outside. I don't recall feeling more proud about anything I had done for him because the idea completely came from me; it wasn't something he asked for or told me to do. I stood in front of the dazzling truck, waiting for his response as he walked around it in silence. He stopped on the far side and pointed to a tiny place under the mirror on the driver's side and told me that I had missed a spot, after which he turned and walked back into the house, saying nothing more. My heart contracted in deep pain.

Many years later, after I left him, I asked Jake why he had been so cruel as to not acknowledge the things I had done for him, and I was surprised to find out he didn't interpret his behavior as cruel but saw it as an attempt to make me a better person. He believed the goal of anything we do ought to be perfection, and anything short of perfection didn't deserve recognition. Jake truly believed his purpose was to point out my imperfections, to keep me improving by reaching for the unreachable.

At one point, perhaps 17 or 18 years into our marriage, when we were having a particularly difficult time, Jake told me that I wasn't a virgin when we married because a doctor had seen me for that pap test when I was almost 19, and I had been fitted for a diaphragm at 21 for birth control before we were married. His words tore deeply into my soul because my virginity was the only thing I believed I had to offer him at the time we were married, and my fidelity during all our years together was a continuation of that gift. When he seemingly rejected my gifts of virginity and fidelity as worthless, I felt as if I had no value at all. I had completely accepted his interpretation of who I was and what I was worth…or not worth. An angry and deeply hurt part of me wondered that if he didn't value my virginity, then why would I value it…and if he didn't value my fidelity, what reason was there for continuing to give it to him.

***

Two events seemed to open my eyes as none of the other incidents had done. The first was in early 1986. On the morning of January 28th, an employee came rushing into the office in near hysteria, and asked if the rest of us had heard what had just happened to the Challenger spacecraft. She told us that it had blown up and all the astronauts had died. Everyone collected around the television set; some were in shock and others were crying. When Jake walked into the showroom from the warehouse, he asked what the commotion was about. His office manager told him about the explosion and he shook his head in disbelief. With a voice of unexpected coldness that seemed to say, "*stupid people*" to all of us, he told everybody to get back to work. As he walked into his executive office, he turned to the stunned group of employees and said, *"I don't know what you are getting so shook up about! Nobody twisted their arms to get into the shuttle."* His lack of compassion was demonstrated in front of everyone, not just me, and it was very clear that the others were dismayed by it, something I could not deny. There was no way I could box up my feelings and hide them away as I had done with him since I was 19 because the others had seen it, too.

The other event happened shortly after his public display of callousness. For some reason that I don't know, Jake had become upset with me. I must have questioned his opinion or his authority about something, after which I had gone upstairs to the master suite to take a shower. I was fully wet when he entered the huge walk-in shower and turned off the water. He pulled me out, lifted me in the air, and carried my naked body above his head, through our bedroom and headed down to the main floor despite my protests and tears. I begged him to not take me down the stairs like that. On a previous occasion, when we were play-ing, he accidentally dropped me on the steps and the tumble resulted in a serious neck injury. But he paid no heed to my cries.

After making it down the stairs, he carried me, still above his head, into the kitchen and began to twirl me around using the helicopter spin, a move he had seen in countless wrestling matches. Again, I begged him to stop because I was getting dizzy and sick. He finally dropped me to the floor and said, *"Now you will know who is boss."* As I lay on the floor, still naked, nauseous, and somewhat wet, I looked into the face of a man who appeared to be more like a possessed creature than my husband. Something snapped inside me. He left the kitchen and went into the family room to watch something on television, while I picked myself up off the floor and went back upstairs to dry off and get dressed. I prepared a meal, brought it in to him, and sat down at his feet to ask forgiveness for whatever it was that I had done…but it was only part of me that served him that day. The other part of me, who was connected to the *snap* that had happened on the inside, wanted nothing more to do with a man she had come to hate.

Not long after that experience, I became involved with a man I met at a class reunion that summer, and I left Jake on Christmas Eve of 1986—fifteen years to the day after my *knight in the tweed coat* had given me the powder-blue blanket. It took another three years for me to finally end the marriage in which I played the role of a dartboard and a servant, fulfilling the prediction made by that non-ordinary man on the bus, something I can't explain with any traditional way of explaining things, even to this day. But somehow, all of this entwined together and became the catalyst for me, finally, to leave a broken marriage to heal a broken heart.

***

Just before I actually left my husband, I had a nightmarish dream that became far more important than I could ever have imagined, not only for what was happening at the time, but much later, I discovered that the dream was a significant puzzle piece with meanings whose origins went back much earlier than I could possibly have known at the time.

As the dream began, I noticed that there was a major reconstruction project taking place in the offices of the business my husband and I owned and operated together. Workmen were putting up new walls where none had been before. Sawdust and debris was everywhere as everyone was intently involved in the tasks of the remodel. Jake was leaning over a blueprint and was discussing changes with the contractor. I walked from room to room and noticed that there was no office for me.

After several attempts to communicate with my husband, I finally caught his attention and asked him where I might find my office. He seemed disconnected from me and uninterested in my obvious frustration. Without looking up, he pointed to a set of unfinished stairs in the back of the building, indicating they would lead to my office. I walked up the stairs to an attic room and found an old wooden desk with old files and papers on top of it that looked more like a stack of trash than valuable material. There was not even a chair for me. It seemed that all the items no one knew what to do with were relegated to that upper space. There was no phone, no intercom, no windows—it was a dimly lighted space without a carpet, without any comfort at all. I felt heart broken and discarded. I walked back down to the main floor to tell my husband that the place felt really awful to me. But he didn't hear me.

I stood in the center of the showroom where I could see all our employees in their offices working diligently, and a shock wave surged through me as a dreadful thought entered my mind: there was no place for me there! I felt my throat tighten. Hot tears spilled down my cheeks; I felt as if my heart was breaking. The man with whom I had spent most of my life had no place for me anymore. I turned toward the main entrance and noticed how dark it was outside. I felt distraught by the thought of leaving but still walked to the entrance door and opened it. There, in front of me was the most overwhelmingly frightening darkness. If I left, I believed I would enter a black hole that had absolutely no light in it. I realized I had no idea whether or not there was anything outside to support my step if I should leave, or if in the stepping, I would fall into total nothingness.

I turned my head back toward Jake to reconsider my decision to leave. Everything in me wanted to cry out hoping he would see how terrified I was and recognize the horror of what was happening to me, to us. I had been with him for so long; the thought of leaving was excruciating. But I knew he would not hear me even if I did cry out. In the moment of the turning, I knew in my heart that staying would be too painful, perhaps even more painful than falling into an abyss. I walked to the threshold and I stepped into the total blackness. I woke up in a panic. My heart was racing. My body was drenched in perspiration. I was too frightened to cry and I felt totally alone.

Still in that place, between being asleep and awake, I was aware of the immense feelings in that "dream-moment" of standing between what was known and unknown, I became consciously aware of the painful knowledge that my feeling-self—long dissociated from my thinking self—had known for many years. I was living with a man who had no place for me, and I was working in a business where I did not belong. My dreaming self was facing a moment similar to what Harrison Ford portrayed in the film, The Last Crusade, when the character, Indiana Jones, was chased to the very edge of a cliff and he stood looking down into a vastly deep chasm. His father, played by Sean Connery, the man Jones had come to save if he was to save himself, was on the other side of what looked like a bottomless abyss. The distance to the other side was impossible to jump. He had to suspend his belief in falling and trust that his step would create a bridge to the other side as promised in a message he had received. In the dream, like Jones, I felt such intense fear just before my decision to step into the totally dark space and surrender to trust.

But unlike Jones, I had not received a message promising a bridge; at least I didn't think I had received such a message. In the months that followed, my work in therapy helped me find the internal places where personal beliefs had kept me bound in a marriage that was threatening to kill my soul and kept me working in a business that had never been truly connected to my heart. For the Sandy Smith of 1986, it seemed quite clear what the dream meant, but it was not until the Sandy

Sela-Smith of the present was writing this book, did I understand the meaning that took me to a much deeper level.

***

Without any conscious awareness at the time, I was doing exactly what the man from Washington, DC had said I would do. That man on the bus seemed to be a curious messenger from another dimension who came to give me a very significant message. Although, back then, I was not sure what the message had been. I still have no idea who he was and for some reason, no matter how much I have tried, I cannot remember the many things he told me while we were seated at that outdoor restaurant, yet, everything seemed to be so very important. I do remember he gave me a message that I would be leaving my husband and ending the contract with him…and…the life I was going to have was one I could not even imagine. So perhaps, I did have a message like the one Indiana Jones had, after all, and like him, I trusted it and took the step.

Following the strange encounter on a bus, that non-ordinary man drifted from my mind almost as easily as he drifted into my life and out again on that sunny day in Washington, DC. But, every now and then at the strangest times, thoughts of him return, as they did during Alanza's reading.

Some time after my encounter with the blue-eyed man on the bus, I took that most painful step into the depth of the darkness, and separated from Jake. Three years later, I completed the divorce and began the process of moving on with my life by leaving everything behind and relocating to China for almost two years. The man who had treated me like a dartboard for far too many years was becoming a part of my past.

Chapter Four
SLENDER TO FAT SANDY

The protective armor and its accompanying mask, which we unconsciously chose as a way to keep us safe from what we fear, eventually becomes a sarcophagus that suffocates and destroys what it was intended to protect. Unless we go in search of why we became afraid and buried ourselves, face the fear, and release whatever it was that we believed was so frightening, we will remain entombed in the armor and trapped behind the mask. To remove the armor or take away the mask without facing and releasing the fear, may well lead to the formation of another protection that is, perhaps, more impenetrable and more resistant to removal than the first.

With a single breath, the painful memories of my marriage and thoughts of that event in Washington, DC, so long ago, faded away, and my attention returned to Alanza and the reading in Manitou Springs. The next prediction she made was I would be losing weight, and it would be melting off without my having to do anything to make it happen. She proclaimed that all my years of struggle around gaining and losing weight would come to an end. And nearly under her breath, she whispered she had been struggling with weight all her life, as well. She looked puzzled as she said she couldn't see what I would do to lose the weight, but when I did lose it, I was to let her know how I did it. She reminded me again that my life was about to experience a drastic change. I smiled because somehow deep inside me I knew what she said was true; I had heard this message before, but just couldn't remember where I had heard it.

Just the mention of weight sent me on another journey that in real time was just a microsecond, but in any microsecond, there can be years of information and multitudes of images if strung together, they could circle the globe several times over. The time between Alanza's comments about weight and her next statement about my future was such a microsecond.

***

Although I was a very large woman, meeting the definition of morbidly obese, in July of 2007 as I sat across from the black haired psychic, I was not always heavy. I had been generally unconcerned about my body image in my teen years, as my attention was strictly focused on studies and music, though when I look at photos of myself back then, I now can see that I was an attractive, slender young woman. Near the end of my junior year of high school, I began to date Jake, who five years later became my husband the summer after graduating from college. Sometime in my early college years, when I was around 19, I began to put on weight. I went from 120 pounds in my freshman year to 142 pounds by the time I graduated from college and married at 21. Though I wasn't fat, I was no longer the slender, firm teen I had been when I first met Jake; my body was more of a woman's body, softer, curvier, and a little more full. But by my second wedding anniversary, I weighed 160 pounds and felt extremely concerned about my expanding body size, which from that time on became a major focus in my life.

On his 24th birthday, just two years and two months after we were married, I said good-bye to my young husband as he went off to boot camp and then to Vietnam, and I decided to use the time he would be gone to shed the weight I had gained in the previous years. While Jake was living daily in harms way on the other side of the world, I ate cabbage soup and grapefruit to lose the 40 pounds I had gained since I had met him, and even more.

For the first time since junior high school, I was a size 8, and was so excited to show him how I looked when we met in Hawaii for his

R and R just a few months before his tour of duty was completed. Hundreds of relatives, mostly wives and girlfriends, gathered at the air base in Honolulu as the airplane landed, and like most military reunions, many women were squealing with excitement when they saw their husbands or boyfriends coming through the gates towards them.

Excited and afraid at the same time, I searched the faces of the young men looking for my husband among all the soldiers who looked so alike in their uniforms, not knowing for sure if the man coming through the gate would be the man I had held in my heart for so long. One of the last to come out was Jake, dressed in full uniform looking so, so strikingly handsome. I ran to him and threw my arms around his neck and started to give him a welcome kiss. But instead of receiving my embrace, he held his duffel bag between us and turned away from me. He told me he didn't like public displays of affection. Jake didn't seem very animated about seeing me and barely looked at in my direction as we moved through the crowd of excited people who seemed unconcerned about displaying their affection.

I felt awkward and didn't know how to respond to a man who felt like a stranger as we walked from the army base to the Waikikian Hotel where we would be staying for his short time away from the war. The hotel was one of the last truly Hawaiian hotels left in Honolulu. Made primarily of bamboo, it didn't have air conditioning, but had large sliding doors with bamboo curtains that could open to allow the ocean breeze to flow through the space. Outside the rooms were Tiki Torches that were lighted each night, adding to the romantic atmosphere of the Islands. Fire light and shadows from the torch flames danced among the swaying palm trees and the very large-leaf flowering tropical plants that lined the walkways in front of our room. Hawaiian music could be heard day and night from the lounge that overlooked the lagoon, the sandy beach, and ocean beyond. The smell of sizzling steaks mixed with ocean mist filled the night air, and early each morning, the aroma of tropical flowers floated into the room, creating a sense of waking up in Paradise. He could not have picked a more lovely, magical place for our very short time together.

Jake arranged for the hotel long before our vacation, and seemed pleased it matched the image of what it was advertised to be. When we were finally alone, he pulled me toward him and we undressed each other to make love, and then we showered together, as we often used to do, before the war. He dressed first, while I carefully dried my sunburned body, and then he began to rifle through his duffle bag to find two gifts he had brought me from Vietnam. First he pulled out a pair of toeless and backless red high heels with hand painted flowers on the heels, decorated in that indisputable Asian style, and then he handed me a bathing suit, a tiny bikini that was far too small, even for my now slender body; both gifts looked like they were made for a child rather than a woman. He wanted me to try on the suit for him, but it was hopelessly too small.

In that paradise, which should have held only beautiful memories, another image seared itself deeply in my mind on that first afternoon we were together. After we had made love, Jake got dressed in the civilian clothes I had brought for him and sat on the end of the bed watching television. As he sat there, I took a photo of him to commemorate our first day together in months and without looking away from the television he told me he didn't know if he loved me any more. He said he didn't know what love was. I don't remember how I reacted...I'm sure I was stunned; we might have talked about it though I doubt it, and I don't remember anything but those first painfully stinging words.

We spent six days together, doing all the things people do on vacation, acting as if Jake had never said what he did that first day. We swam in the lovely blue lagoon outside our hotel, walked on the white sandy beach, and went out to eat at the most elegant restaurants. Jake asked me to wear the bikini he had purchased in Saigon, but when it was clear the suit wouldn't fit, he used the tiny scissors, needle, and thread from the hotel welcome package to cut the sides of the suit and extend the ties to make it fit a little better. Even with the extra space, it was really too small, but I wore it anyway to please him. Though I was quite slender, I felt extremely fat.

I remember watching his plane as it departed from the airport; the silvery bullet lifted higher and higher as it headed west, back toward Vietnam and the war…and my focus remained on the plane until it turned into a tiny dot and disappeared in the distant clouds. My own plane left later that afternoon, and I was determined to lose even more weight. I am very sure that someplace inside me, I believed if I could just become slender enough, if I could just fit the image Jake carried in his head of how I was supposed to look, perhaps the size that would have fit in the bikini, he would love me.

Though I didn't think of it until long after we had divorced, I wondered if the woman he wanted, was the slender teenager with whom he had planned to have sex when we were 19, but felt as if he had been robbed of the experience because my beliefs made us wait until we were married, and I would not consider marriage until after I finished college. The few months between the end of our time in Hawaii and his return from Vietnam, and the near starvation diet made me smaller than I had ever been as an adult, probably about the weight I was as a pre-pubescent girl in junior high school, though I had the skeletal form of an adult, not a pre-teen. I anxiously awaited his return and was sure he would be pleased with the body I had created…and just maybe, he would decide that he loved me.

***

Upon his return from Vietnam in September of 1969, Jake slept for nearly 48 hours straight and though he wanted sex in between his waking up and going back to sleep, I don't recall feeling like we made love. He was quiet and spoke nothing of his experiences during his tour of duty in Vietnam, and he didn't speak about his statement that he didn't love me, the first afternoon in the Waikikian hotel. Very soon after his return from the war, Jake went back to work and not long after that he began a relationship with a woman he met at the bank where he was being trained to be a manager; the relationship lasted for the next 17 years, something I suspected on and off, but didn't let myself know for nearly all that time. And over the next couple of years, while he was working more and more, not coming home until late, and becoming more negative towards me, I regained all the weight I had lost the year he was in Vietnam.

During the next decade, I was on every diet that came to my attention, and by my late thirties, I had grown to 205 pounds. The most discouraging experience was after starvation-like diets lasting for months at a time and resulting in significant weight loss, any increase in what I ate, even far below what would be normal calorie consumption, caused me to gain weight again.

My husband appeared to have little compassion for my struggle, often making negative remarks about my body, but at the same time tantalizing me with his foods, while I went back to the horrible cabbage soup diet for several weeks at a time or whatever diet promised results. During the most painful times of suffering, my husband would take a cut of steak or a spoonful of ice cream—whatever he was eating—put it in my face, and ask if maybe I would want just a little bite. Years later, when I asked him why he had done such an unkind thing as that, he explained he wanted to help me increase my will power, but instead, the pain of his behavior added to the growing estrangement between us.

Eventually I signed up with a nationally known weight loss program paying $500 to join, which at that time was a great deal of money and made a commitment to a weekly purchase of packaged food to help me accomplish my goal. I vowed to use the exercise equipment at the program office, which I did, pumping and cycling for at least a couple of hours a day. I often didn't eat the required amounts of food at each meal, hoping to finally win in the weight loss game. I lost 60 pounds in the first four months, almost twice as fast as what was recommended for healthy reduction, and worked harder than I had ever worked with a diet. Finally, I reached the weight I had been in high school. I loved being slender; however, fear of getting heavy again as I had done following all the previous diets haunted me. After reaching my goal, I maintained my weight by taking over-the-counter pills that absorbed fat out of food, which made me feel safe for a while, but when I heard the manufactures were being forced to remove the product from the market, I went into a panic and didn't know what to do.

Then I remembered a paragraph from my 10th grade world history book. The text described bingeing and purging practices of wealthy Romans during daylong banquets a couple of thousand years ago. It seemed like a simple solution to the problem of needing to prevent weight gain while appearing to be normal at business lunches and dinners—dining out was a daily event in my husband's and my life—so I adopted the purging practices of the Romans. To me, any consumption of food felt like a threat that could lead to weight gain. So, during or after every meal, no matter how small, I purged, by practicing the horribly humiliating behavior two or three times a day; I didn't know there was a medical name for what I was doing, and didn't know it was dangerous.

I became adept at finding the right time to slip out of conversations, away from the table, and into the ladies room. My primary focus was on how to look as normal as possible, while not allowing any unwanted food to remain inside me. I left the foods with the least calories for post-purge consumption on my plate, and after returning to the table I would eat what was safe, and join in the conversation as if nothing happened. From my perspective, it seemed I had made myself invisible enough where no one noticed when I left or returned, though I have no idea if they were aware of what was happening, or not. To my knowledge, Jake never noticed. At least he never mentioned it.

A few years into the practice, I read an article in a newspaper that identified self-induced vomiting as connected to a disorder called bulimia. The article described the massive physical damage that can result from this life-threatening practice. After realizing the harm I had been doing, I pledged to myself I would never purge again and instead, I almost completely stopped eating. I found a way to order salads and play with the vegetables appearing to eat when I really wasn't eating.

The fear of regaining weight was so overwhelming I didn't notice what new dangers I was bringing to myself. Anorexic behaviors had caused my body to return to its early teen weight, but also, took its toll on my health. When at home, I prepared full meals for Jake and served them to him on a TV tray as he watched sports programs, but I made nothing for myself. Jake commented only one time about my eating habits, or more accurately, my non-eating habits. Some time into that anorexic period of my life, he said, "You can stop dieting, now." But we never talked.

While all of this "insane" behavior was going on, I became politically active and was asked to run for a state senate seat; I operated a successful business and became the state director for a national education foundation. From all outside appearances I was a total woman—fit, trim, successful, reasonably powerful, very well-dressed, and attractive—living the ideal life with a hard working businessman husband, accumulating a fine financial portfolio, and living in what others would likely have seen as opulence. But my heart was painfully broken.

In spite of how wonderful everything looked from the outside, years of being treated like a "dartboard" had taken a toll, and after Jake told me I was not a virgin, my world was torn apart, causing something to crack inside me. I began to seek relationships that would give me the respect I could not find in my marriage. My relationships were platonic, most of them related to my part-time work in Washington, DC, but after a while, some began to blur the line between casual friendship and more meaningful relationship.

When one relationship did cross the line, the one I began in late 1986 when I met a former classmate at the reunion, my life exploded into a million pieces. Unable to handle the conflicts, I withdrew and went back to my old patterns of putting on weight. After I left Jake that Christmas, the tiny body of my anorexic self began to gain more and more weight over the next two years, until I had become fat Sandy again. I moved out of our house in January of 1987 and experienced nearly three years struggling within myself about ending my marriage. I finally completed the divorce just before Thanksgiving of 1989 and less than three months after the end of my marriage, I was on a plane, headed to China to fulfill a life-long dream, all the while feeling the pinch of a too-tight seatbelt for the 25-hour trip from Seattle to Beijing.

Living in China for nearly two years—riding a bicycle everywhere, and living on a diet, primarily of vegetables, coupled with being away from the emotional conflicts that had raged inside me in the years before —resulted in another significant weight loss. I was nearly back to the size I had been in high school and felt better than I had ever felt in my life, but within weeks of returning to the states, my weight began to climb again.

In the eight years following my return from China, I grew from a size 8 to size 2X. As I tipped the scale at 220 pounds, it seemed like an entire lifetime had separated me from when I was a single digit size. In reality, it had been only a few years since my slender body had fit into the most stylish of petite designer cloths. While it was easy to point to Jake as having something to do with my weight gain, in looking back, it is clear there was something much deeper than Jake at the root of my weight problem, because the climb in weight continued even when I wasn't with him. By June of 1999 when I was about to graduate with a Masters degree in psychology, I had put on so much weight that none of my clothes fit properly.

Just before I was to leave for my graduation, I went to a department store near my home in Clearwater, Florida to buy something special. While I was pulling on and off the dresses I had picked out for myself, my friend Terry, who had come to help me find something spectacular, was searching the racks for more selections. She returned to the dress-ing room with new possibilities, tapped on the curtain, and handed me what she had found. I examined each of the size 2X dresses she had selected. One of them I would not have picked out for myself because it was knee length instead of full length. It was a red and black professional styled dress, with strong business-like lines and attractively placed gold buttons on the front to draw the eye inward to create an illusion of thinness. I closed the curtain, tried it on, and reopened my dressing room to the larger space where I could see myself in the three-paneled mirror.

I really hadn't looked at myself in a full-length mirror for a long time, and was in for a horrible shock. There I stood with legs exposed that were thick and swollen from my ankles to my knees; all 250 pounds of me, in a knee length dress, looking like an elderly fat woman. The dress revealed a body I had tried so hard not to see by wearing the long flowing skirts. At first I was numbed by the shock; then I felt shame that the ugliness of my body had become exposed, even if it was just in front of the mirror, my friend, and my own eyes.

I sat down on the dressing room chair and felt an uncomfortable tightness as the seams of the dress strained against the pressure of my body. I began to rock back and forth, cradling in my hands a watermelon-sized belly, while tears filled my eyes and spilled down my cheeks. *"When did this happen?"* I whispered to myself through the tears. *"When did I turn into grandma? I never imagined I would ever look like this."* Saying these words filled my heart with a mournful cry. Again, a tearful, whispered question fell from my lips: *"How did this happen to me?"* I sat in silence for some time, though I am not sure how long, and slowly rose to close the curtain. Until that moment, I was unaware Terry had been standing out in the hall, simply observing what I was experiencing. I put away the short dress and bought a floor length blue one, and the two of us left the store in silence.

After returning home, I packed the blue dress that fit loose around my grandmother-sized hips, a dress that would cover my large legs and thick ankles, as I prepared for the trip to San Francisco, the Saybrook residential conference, and the graduation ceremony. On June 26, 1999, I walked across the stage at San Francisco State University to be recognized for receiving my Master's degree in Psychology. Over the blue dress, I wore a black floor-length graduation gown that covered a multitude of my body's flaws. The chair of my committee publicly commended my work, praising my thesis, which opened my heart and made me forget about my size. I felt as if I were on top of the world.

Following the ceremony another professor asked me if I would consider writing an article on resistance in heuristic research for a professional journal he edited. One of my fellow students gave me a beautiful rose and many others congratulated me with hugs, while my eldest sister took photographs. It seemed like I was shining from the inside out and I felt happier with myself than I had felt for years, maybe decades. Shortly after I returned to Florida, my sister sent me the graduation photographs she had taken, but when I opened the envelope, I went into shock. I felt so embarrassed to think I could have felt so special on that day when the photographs showed me what all the others at the graduation had seen. I could not see light shining from the round-faced fat woman who was wearing a black tent that didn't cover anything at all…and to make matters worse, the woman in the photo had a stupid grin on her face she did not deserve to have. I went into a depression that lasted several months. By the fall of 1999, I weighed 260 pounds and looked sallow-skinned, and tired. After a trip home to visit my family a few weeks later, I gained another five pounds.

After years of internal work, I was aware my body-mind had connected being fat to being unattractive, as well as to being not seen, since normal sized people—and for that matter, even other obese people—don't look at fat people and really see them. Completely out of conscious awareness was the thought that if fat, I would not only not attract men to me, but I would assure myself I would not even be seen by them, thus, I could feel safe from being hurt as deeply as I had been hurt by my former husband, and on a deeper level, by my father.

But later, I discovered that as much as not wanting to be attractive to men, a deeply hidden reason for gaining weight was to be sure I, myself, did not feel attractive; In part, I believe I was punishing myself for having "crossed the line," which I concluded was the cause for the ending of my marriage many years before, but again, on a deeper level, if I felt ugly, I would not allow my own sexual energy to be expressed, and I would not be the cause of bringing danger or pain to myself like when I was a child.

***

Over the years, I used psychodynamic therapy, many types of body therapy, dream work, as well as shamanic journeys with spontaneous entry into alternative consciousness states, and "past life" experiences to help me make profound connections to the patterns that had been ruling my life. With each discovery of some past event, I brought healing to the wounds related to them. In all the therapeutic work, whether mainstream or "on the edge," the most common factor in any of the healing processes was the use of feelings to enter the places where wounds were buried in order to re-assess, re-evaluate, and reform old patterns into new and healthy patterns with new meanings. And certainly, gaining weight was a significant, long-time pattern from which I wanted to be freed.

Each time I made a powerful emotional connection with deeply buried body awareness, I felt a sense of new hope that the pattern of putting on weight, as a fleshy armor of protection, would finally be released, but the opposite occurred. Over time, I became terrified if I continued to have break-through healing experiences without finding the core problem that seemed to have become more resistant with each discovery, I would grow so large my very life would be at risk.

I began having difficulty breathing; the smallest amount of physical exertion left me breathless and exhausted. My body was filled with pain most the time and no position brought relief; it hurt to sit, to stand, to walk, and even to lie down for any length of time. There were times I was unable to walk. As my physical condition declined, I began to lose hope that I would ever be "normal." I felt devastated and hopeless to change the pattern that threatened my life.

Alanza had not made a mistake when she said I had struggled with weight all my life. Certainly it was one of the most persistent struggles of my life, something I was aware of when I was making a decision regarding the focus for my Ph.D. dissertation research as the 20th century was coming to a close. Hoping if I studied obesity I would finally find the answer to whatever it was that resisted all of my previous efforts to lose weight, I began my dissertation work. However, soon after making that decision, I gained another 10 pounds that pushed me into having to wear size 3X and the blue dress from my Master's graduation no longer fit. I was more than 100 pounds overweight and had given up on diets that seemed to only make matters worse.

Even more than the physical pain that too often was debilitating, there were times the loneliness in my life caused my heart to ache for the marriage I had left more than a dozen years before, and somehow, I knew unresolved pain was connected to my weight. I knew in my head I had made the right decision to end my marriage, but my heart, at least part of it, still grieved. Though my social isolation wasn't as bad as it had been in years past, there were still times I found every excuse imaginable to not have to leave my apartment because I just couldn't contend with "being out there." I lived alone and felt lonely more often than not. But whenever I forced myself to go out in public and socialize, I felt even lonelier than I did when I was alone. As much as I was distressed by all these life-patterns, I wasn't doing whatever it took to change any of these behaviors, and I didn't know why. I wondered, at times, if dying would be less painful than living. Though I didn't want to die, I can't say I truly wanted to live.

Few people could ever have guessed what was happening in my life or would have suspected how I was feeling. I was a master at hiding most everything; even from myself, except, of course, I couldn't hide my weight. But in spite of my obesity, I was good at dressing and carrying myself like a successful professional woman, a psychotherapist who was becoming more and more adept at helping others overcome the difficulties in their lives, in spite of the fact that I could not solve this distress in my own life.

This wasn't what I had wanted for myself. I wanted to *be* happy. I wanted to experience being a part of a loving family. I fantasized about sharing the joy of holidays and the richness of life with a special some-one and with people who loved me. I wanted to feel good; I wanted to feel vital and powerful, to feel sensual and pretty. I wanted a loving relationship and I wanted to wake in the morning excited about what each new day might hold. I wanted to laugh from the inside out, but I didn't know how.

In spite of the profoundly significant breakthroughs in my own therapeutic process I experienced over the previous decade or more, I was still suffering. Things still weren't working and I wanted the life back that had been stolen! I believed if I could release the more than 100 pounds that were weighing me down, I would feel good about myself and I would feel sensual again. Perhaps, then, I would be able to fully love myself and find a partner to love me; maybe then, I could regain my health, restore my vitality, and transform my life. I hoped my dissertation research would help me find a way to contact the part of myself that was resisting weight loss, sabotaging my life, and robbing me of happiness. What I didn't understand at that time was it wasn't losing the weight that would allow me to be happy, it was finding happiness that would allow me to lose weight; but this was a lesson that would take many more years for me to learn.

***

In those difficult years when I was working toward my Ph.D., I knew if I went on another diet, my body would likely do what it had done for over 30 years. I might have been able to loose the weight by overpowering my body and forcing it to do what I wanted it to do, though that was becoming more difficult. I was convinced that as soon as I reached my goal, if I stopped the focused and rigorous control measures, not only would I gain the weight back, but also, I would end up even heavier than before I dieted. I knew even with maintaining strict control measures, it was possible my metabolism could change as it did all those other times, and I might begin the painful process of slow-but-sure weight gain with very little food consumption.

The only way I might possibly be successful in maintaining a lower weight would be to make weight the center of my life and watch everything related to it; to lose control of the focus would mean to regain the weight. I knew it was possible to maintain a low weight, but I might have to eat less and less, until just eating a salad a day would result in weight gain. I wanted to be slender to experience life; I did not want to experience a life that would require me to observe myself and control my every thought and action as if I were a part of the diet police, as well as put a lock on all my feelings about being so rigidly controlled. At 265 pounds, any more weight could be life threatening. I felt so completely stuck.

***

In May of 2000, while I was very blocked in my dissertation, as well as in my attempts to work with weight loss, my mother experienced a massive heart attack on the other side of the country. My sister called to tell me two thirds of our mother's heart had been without oxygen for over two hours, and the situation was grave. If I hoped to see her before she passed, I needed to get home as soon as possible, so I cancelled my plans to go to a conference in Georgia, one I had thought might re-stimulate my focus on my dissertation, and I flew to Seattle the next day.

In the hours that followed, my mother's vital signs had dropped to a critical level. When I arrived, I was surprised to see that in spite of all she had been through, there was an expression of childlike innocence on her face. A soft essence seemed to permeate the whole room as she lay quietly surrounded by the white sterility of the intensive care unit. At 84, there were still hints of red hair in the nearly white curls that fell gently around her head. But her normally strong presence was gone, and her rosy-cheeked face still smooth and soft had taken on the gray-ish white of a person near death. The enzymes present in her blood as revealed in the sample that had been taken when she was first admitted to the hospital, indicated massive, irreparable damage and her attending doctors expressed surprise that she had survived as long as she had. Perhaps she was waiting for all of her children to return to her.

My siblings were exhausted from having spent over 36 hours without any significant sleep, so they took a break and I spent the early morning hours alone with our mother, quietly whispering healing suggestions using hypnotic techniques I had learned in my hypnosis training as ways to access deeper levels of her unconscious mind. My heart opened wide with love as I held her hand, feeling immense sadness for a woman who had lived much of her life in heart-breaking struggle and suffering.

Just as I had married a man who didn't know what love is, so did she, and as my husband had an affair and eventually left me for another woman, so did hers. Both of us had husbands that returned after their encounters and neither of us talked about the leaving or the returning, and both men continued being involved with the other women after they returned. She had five children and I had five miscarriages. She believed life was supposed to be suffering and I was trying to prove it was not, but none-the-less, I suffered as she did. So the third child of a third child of a third child, who wore her mother's wedding dress, had repeated too many of the same patterns. The wedding dress that we both wore, which was supposed to be the symbol of the purity of union, had holes in it like the union that was not a union, a marriage that was not really a marriage for either of us. The appliqués that she had sewn on the dress to cover the holes only made it look as if there were no holes…but they were there, just carefully concealed, not unlike the masks that both of us wore to show to the world that we were happily married, living lives that other people envied. Such irony!

Later in the day, I had the opportunity to be with my mother when a technician conducted an echocardiogram procedure. It was an amazing experience watching the image of my mother's heart beating on the monitor. The movements of the chambers looked like a delicate but powerful dance between two sides of her heart that connected at the valves. During the whole procedure, I sent silent messages of love to her heart cells and to the movement, while asking her heart to experience the dance inside itself. I suggested that her consciousness could expand to a place beyond that particular space and time where it could find the healthiest heart it had ever known and then match the flow of the rhythm of the healthy heart.

Five days later the doctor released our mother from the hospital but could not explain to us how her heart showed so little damage, it actually looked as if there had been no heart attack. There was no medical explanation for the recovery. I have no way to know if the messages and images I sent to my mother while she was nearly unconscious had an effect on the remarkable recovery. Her healing may have been due to the fact that all five of her children had come to her bedside in her time of need and she decided to live; or perhaps, it was both.

I returned to Florida, exhausted from the ordeal but happy I had been able to go. The five days in the Intensive Care Unit with my mother and communicating with my mother's heart felt extremely significant. I would not have chosen to do anything else; yet, it was a digression from my dissertation work on overcoming obesity that remained unfinished. My dissertation, like my victory over obesity, seemed to be slipping farther and farther away.

Chapter Five
A DIGRESSION INTO HEART-FIRE

There are times when it is difficult to tell the difference between our waking life and our dreams. Perhaps, it is because there are times that there is no difference between our walking life and our dreams.

As I began to write *The Meaning of Three*, I mentioned that what you would be reading would be a story within a story within a story. I began with the story of Alanza who told me about my past, my present, and my future, which took me on a journey into a back-and-forth reflection on past incidents in my life especially around my marriage and to struggles related to obesity, a problem that kept eluding me, no matter how hard I tried to overcome it. The weaving of my life experiences has been the second story. Like mine, built into the DNA of anyone's story are not just the myriad patterns, but also, the ways of looking at one's self and the ways of experiencing the world that are subtly embedded in it. And of course the third story is the universal story that belongs to all of us—to you and to me—that you, as the reader, are experiencing as you identify with whatever you find embedded in my story.

At the time I visited the Tattooed Lady, though I thought I knew, I really had no idea how the two situations—my marriage and my struggle with weight—were interconnected, but they were, and it was Alanza who told me this struggle would soon become a problem of the past. As I continue telling the story that arose from the session with the fortuneteller, I left off with my attempt to reconnect with my dissertation after returning from my mother's bedside the end of May of 2000. Instead of finding myself on a path toward understanding obesity, I seemed to be focused on matters of my heart rather than weight, though I was to discover that heart was intertwined with those other two issues of relationship and weight, too.

A journal entry back then, that became a part of my dissertation began with these words: *A digression within a narrative that has just begun may seem to be confusing and represent a departure from the direction a story is supposed to be going, and yet, what seems like a diversion, may well be the main path that leads to the journey's end.*

And in this writing, the story about my weight and about my mother's heart, as well as to what I am about to tell you, might seem like a digression from where we are supposed to be going—to understand the meaning of the mask—but as you will come to see, all of this is really the way we will get there.

***

The events of this heart-fire "departure" that seemed to be taking me away from my dissertation, my graduation, and my hope to reverse the upward climb in my weight, began in the early morning of June 1, 2000, with one of those very important dreams that had significance on many levels. But I didn't know the profoundly significant meaning of this digression until years later, when I was nearly completed with this writing.

In the dream, I was on a hike with my former husband and another couple. I was aware I had been on this trail before, but the others had not. We had been walking a long time; however, I was unable to recall anything before the moment we rounded the bend and discovered that the way to our destination through a pass was blocked by what appeared to be a huge landslide of gross looking, thick oozy garbage that seemed to be rotting waste from some wretched landfill. The landslide filled the passageway nearly to the top. It occurred to me that the rotting mess could have trapped us like quicksand, should we have attempted to move through it. For some reason, large green peas were floating on the top of the landslide of garbage. I became aware that the woman who was hiking with me was extremely upset because I had been at this same place before and, yet, I had taken them to this blocked passage anyway.

I reassured her there was another way to go to our destination, which was an ocean beach area where there was natural waterfront recreation, fresh air, and fine restaurants. I remembered the last time I came upon this same very thick garbage dump, I had backed off and had found another way around it. I reassured the woman I could take them the way I had found previously and led them to the alternate route, but the woman seemed even more disturbed with me. She was wearing *high heals* and neatly pressed pants that would get soiled if she proceeded. This woman complained she could not walk down the very rocky pathway, and then she began to verbally attack me for being so inconsiderate of her and the others. I explained that she could walk down the rocky path if she would take off her heels, but she became extremely upset with me and she began to shout. Her shouting stirred my sleeping self just enough for me to realize that I had been dreaming.

Though close to waking, I was still in that in-between state and soon easily re-entered the dream to begin lucid dreaming. In this aware state, I sensed the four of us were walking through an artery to my heart. I approached the garbage heap and saw it was thick sediment, perhaps plaque that had not yet fully hardened. However, the rocks in the other passageway appeared to be hardened deposits, not filling the passage but certainly making the journey difficult.

I could see the garbage was the kind of food I had eaten my whole life as comfort food. When I was not on a diet, I ate things like soft noodles, thick cream of chicken soup, and gravy covered potatoes. Peas were one of the very few vegetables I tolerated eating. But they sat on top, undigested because of the garbage beneath. I was aware the other woman in the dream was still irritated with me. Then I realized that this woman is a lab technician in waking life. Her angry shouting was literally a wake-up call that allowed me to wake enough to remember the dream I had not remembered in the past. This caused me to focus attention on the dream as something to do with the inner workings of my body. I kissed her cheek and told her that I was so grateful that she was willing to go with me, though she did not seem pleased to have had to be on this particular hike at all.

My lucid dreaming attention was drawn to her husband. I realized the man is a diabetic in waking life, one who eats differently than I have ever eaten. I decided my dream was telling me I needed to eat fruits and vegetables just as this man eats, to stay alive.

I turned to my ex-husband Jake and found he had taken charge. He was on his cell phone, placing calls to contractors to come look at the mess and figure out how to clean everything up to allow easy passage. I felt a little intimidated because I believed I should have been the one making the calls to bring in the "troops." After all, it was my body and my dream. Then I remembered he has more will power than any person I have ever known and can do just about anything he makes up his mind to do. This has been something I have always admired about him. I felt myself smiling through my tears as I kissed his cheek and thanked him for taking charge of this really bad situation.

I knew I would have to cooperate with this whole procedure in a way that was healthy and, yet, I found myself not willing to be so restricted. I hadn't easily connected with the will power to stay on this particular task like Jake had. Something in me didn't like to be trapped by following a single focused set of rules. Yet, I knew this was an important thing that needed my full attention.

A whole team of workmen arrived and Jake began giving orders about the work ahead. I kept getting the sense the garbage had to be flushed out with water but I was hesitant to let it happen. I preferred to have the workers find another way to get rid of the garbage. I sent a message that they should dissolve the garbage heap and take it out another way. I believe the two passageways, one with the garbage and the other with rocks, were arteries leading to my heart and I didn't want the garbage to be washed into my heart. When I allowed myself to watch what the workmen were doing, I stopped the work and sent the water backward, not permitting it to cleanse the passageway by moving forward. I was countering Jake's orders but was doing so because I believed he was not aware of the damage all the garbage would do to my heart should I have let it pass through.

I looked at the lab technician and was able to see her role in the dream. I saw her husband's role and Jake's role. Then I wondered what place I had in the clearing-out and cleaning-up process. I didn't want to be someone who was hindering the work. Then I realized I am the one who can see into things, see through things, and bring in help from other realms. I am the one who can see that a dreamtime-hiking trail could be a passage inside my body. I can see multiple realities in the same set of circumstances and know all of the multiple levels, meanings, and realities are real. I could see through the garbage in a passageway and see it as the plaque along the walls of arteries, as well as see this whole dream as my journey through life and how it has been blocked.

I moved to the outside of the arteries and found there were thin and weak places in the artery walls. There were cuts, cracks, and tears where the arteries connect to the heart. It appeared as if the plaque was being used as a cement compound to seal up places that might have leaked. Seeing all this, I called in healing angels to heal the cracks so when the workers finished cleaning up the garbage and rocks, the arteries would not leak. I seemed to move very closely to the outer walls of the arteries and saw some of the cracks were along the places where scar tissue met with regular tissue. I surmised that these were places where my heart had been broken and pierced in the past, and I would need to be able to do regression travel to bring healing to the times in my life or even in past lives when my heart had been so badly hurt.

While all this was going on, I got the message the workmen needed much more water to be able to flush out the garbage they were cleaning away. I knew this meant that when I woke, I needed to drink water.

Because all the systems of my body are connected, I realized I would have to get an overview of my whole body, something I had not done lucidly in my dreams or consciously in waking life for a long time. I told Jake I was ready to take him on a journey through my body beginning with my head and going to my feet. He let me know he was willing to go with me but he had a different agenda. He already had made a list of places he needed to go. I realized that pulling together important projects, such as this, has been his specialty and traveling to the places was mine. So I agreed to take him to wherever he needed to go.

I looked deeply into his eyes and thanked him for being willing to do this for me. He smiled and put his arms around me with the most comforting loving hug I had ever received from him, and he told me he was just doing his job. I had never felt more loved by a human being as in that moment. My whole body felt comforted.

I took his hand and surrendered to the journey he had planned, while he surrendered to my taking him as we began the trip through my body. I had no idea where we are going as we floated past living, moving tissue as if we were the size of molecules. It was like being on some strange planet with irregular landforms made of various shades of pink, white, yellow, and red. But then my attention was drawn to a dark colored form that looked like it didn't belong. It was an odd-shaped object with a smooth round top and seemed to be rooted in the pink tissue like a tooth rooted in the gums.

Workers appeared and began to pull at the object and it slid out, revealing a shape like ocean kelp with a large dark rounded nodule on the top and a long slimy root that had extended deep into the tissue before they pulled it out. I saw another object that was an almost diamond shaped stone that was of material I couldn't recognize. It was silvery colored and very sharp on the edges. The workmen covered it with some kind of gel-like fabric and slid it out of the place where it had been lodged.

I felt myself dropping into an even deeper place where I was no longer in a lucid dream. I lost awareness of what was happening, except for one tiny glimpse of a large field filled with many more knob-headed objects, and I had a feeling workmen were arriving to remove the dark, long-rooted kelp. I dropped into a very deep sleep and had no idea how long I was in that state. I woke feeling very thirsty and drank lots of water. I felt as if I was about to begin another significant journey weaving inner and outer experience that would take me into multiple realities.

From a Jungian perspective, all the people in dreams are parts of the dreamer, even though they may be people in waking life, as well. I interpreted this dream as an indication that my awareness needed to be drawn to an internal situation I had not paid attention to, in spite of the fact that it had been pointed out to me in the earlier dream and many times in waking life. Who would better cause me to take notice of a problem than a woman whose job in waking life is a lab technician who finds things that are wrong in people's bodies? A part of me knew my eating habits had been unhealthy and that part needed to let me know a drastic change had to be made. Who would be better able to let me know I had to eat fruits and vegetables and stop eating starchy foods than a man who in waking life has diabetes and has had to eat consciously or he would die?

There is a part of me that has will power and knows how to get things done. I have used that part regularly in my professional life, in my Ph.D. studies, and in my writing, as well as during the countless times I was on strict and painful diets. But I had not accessed that part for a long time in taking care of myself by drinking enough water, eating healthy foods, or exercising properly. So who better could point out my need to reconnect with that strong willed part of me than an image of my former husband, Jake who embodied such determined will power?

After recording the dream, I was convinced even more that it was about my heart and the plaque on the walls of my arteries. I felt the dream was a message from my body to change my eating habits and to heal my arteries and my heart. I began to do things differently. The morning I woke from the dream, I bought vegetables for salad and several kinds of fruit. I increased my intake of water, visualizing the fluids helping the inner-workmen clear out the garbage. Each time I checked with the dream image, the size of the garbage dump lessened. However, many of the rocks on the alternate path seemed to remain unchanged.

***

The night before the dream the weather in Florida seemed more oppressive than usual, likely because I was still feeling exhausted from the experience with my mother in Seattle. Normally, Florida summers were difficult for me, but that year, the weather had been exceedingly hot and dry, which seemed to touch extremely vulnerable places inside me. It helps to be able to have someone with whom you can express feelings of vulnerability, and one of the special people in my life is David from Oregon, who has remained a close friend for nearly 20 years, in spite of the fact that there were times when a year or more might pass without us actually seeing each other. Like the best of friendships, when we did see each other again, it was like no time had passed at all. David is tall, 6'2" or so, and is slender and strong. He is a tennis player, cross country skier, and avid fisherman, as well as a fellow psychologist. This dear person is one of those rustically handsome men, with graying hair, and clear blue eyes that can penetrate all the way into your soul. He is a spiritual shaman with access to other realms and uses them in healing himself and others.

When the heat had become so oppressive that I felt like I was on fire, I sent him an email message telling him about the hot and dry conditions. Nearly eight years later, as this writing of *The Mask* was coming to a close, I discovered this too was a puzzle piece that made sense only after I was able to see the larger picture. In late May of 2000, I wrote:

Dear David, It is still hot, with no rain. The air smells of smoke from the brush fires that have been exploding all over central Florida due to the heat and dry conditions; some of the fires are just a few miles away. This part of the state is dryer than the desert of Arizona having had less rain in the last 200 days than the desert usually has. It has been two full months without any rain at all, and then, two months ago it only rained about .33 inches. Florida is too hot a place for fireplace smells! For some reason this kind of heat really distresses me and I can barely stand the smell of the smoke and fire. Maybe there will be a break by the end of the week. Love, Sandy

As I reflect back on this message to David, even the dryness of Florida was a metaphor for the dryness in my body and the call for more water but it was about far more than that. I wasn't to learn the deeper meanings until I discovered much more, years later.

Another event that occurred the day before the hike dream had to do with my mother; she had been hospitalized again, three weeks after having had that massive heart attack. The only piece of information I received about her just before I went to bed was that the doctor was unable to locate the cause of her chest pain and couldn't say whether it was another heart attack or not, but they were going to keep her, at least overnight, for observation.

Earlier that same day and hours before the dream, I had gone to a body therapy appointment that dealt almost completely with constriction on the left side of my body. I hoped the session would help me relax enough to get the sleep I needed, and deeper sleep would let me rest enough to reconnect with my dissertation that had been neglected for too long. During much of the session, while my therapist worked with my tightly restricted muscles, I saw an image of a naked child curled up on a floor in some distant past, unable to protect herself from something that must have just happened to her in her time. I have come to know all these images that arise, especially during body therapy sessions, are important because they are connectors between whatever is happening—or, not happening—in the present with whatever occurred in the past. And what comes foreword provides an opportunity to bring healing to both past and present, but I didn't have the energy to work with the image; I just noticed it.

My intention in recording the context of the hike dream was to be able to work with what felt like its multi-leveled meanings in the days ahead without forgetting all that happened surrounding it. However, my exhaustion prevented me from digging into the dream to see more of what it was attempting to communicate to me.

On June 2, the day after the hike dream, I was able to see only two clients because I was simply too exhausted to see any more. Both people were struggling with having no sound financial base. Both came in feeling disempowered by their life-situations, but after intense work, both left with the awareness that they could choose empowerment regardless of the outer circumstances. Certainly the clients' expression of disempowerment in their lives seemed to match how I had been feeling physically, and I was feeling fairly fragile regarding my finances, as well.

I slept the rest of the day and nearly the whole weekend of June 3rd and June 4th of 2000. Just getting up to do some minimal task left me feeling completely drained. Brief times of being awake were followed by extended periods of deep sleep for several more hours. I was aware I had many dreams about Jake, but I was unable to remember them. Though I had slept with little interruption from Friday June 2nd to the evening of Sunday the 4th, I still felt exhausted.

On Sunday night, after that sleep-filled but exhausting weekend, an unexpected event caused me to feel as if I had been shaken to the core. Around 10:30 in the evening, my dog Jenny began to bark and wouldn't be stilled. The more I tried to quiet her down, the more incessant became her barking. She was almost frantic. Perhaps a minute or so into the barking frenzy I heard what sounded like a terrible domestic disturbance outside. People were yelling and screaming at the top of their lungs.

I looked outside, but instead of seeing a horrible fight going on as I expected, I saw thick billowing clouds of black smoke everywhere. The scorched smell assaulted my nostrils. I could see only shadowed forms through the sooty clouds and could hear the terror-filled screams of people running down the outer corridor that passes in front of all the apartments. My neighbor ran toward me screaming that her apartment was filled with smoke and she couldn't find her cat. It looked as if the whole building might be on fire.

My heart leapt with the intensity of all of this, and in a microsecond, I was in a state that automatically occurs within me in grave situations, which is a deep state of calm that allows decisive action and somehow knows how to override the feelings of racing panic. Red flashing lights along with the sounds and smells of exhaust coming from a dozen diesel engines filled the parking lot and mixed in with the smoke, the fire, and the screams of terrified residents. The turnaround parking area in front of my apartment building was filled with fire engines, aid cars, and police. Frightened neighbors in nightclothes were standing outside trying to shout above the sounds of the engines to find out if friends were OK and if they needed to vacate.

I suspect all of us had the current drought conditions and the danger it held on our minds. Just a few days before this event, another fire raced through two square blocks in Ybor City just across Tampa Bay from us, consuming an entire residential complex and a post office. The drought conditions had made everything tinder-dry and a single spark might set off a fire that could consume everything in its path. The shortage of water exacerbated the concern whenever fire broke out. The local news had been full of the dangers of fire in our area. All of this added to my concern for what was happening in my own apartment complex.

When I saw the amount of smoke that was pouring out of nearby units, I had no idea if the whole 120 apartments would go up in flames, or if it would stop at the laundry room that separated my apartment from the section that obviously was on fire. My focus was to get my dog and cat, as well as my friend Terry's cat out of danger from the smoke and fire. I had parked my car at the far end of the parking lot and believed I could take them there and drive us all out of harm's way.

I thought of my computer that held everything I had been working on for my dissertation, but realized I couldn't carry the three animals and my computer, so I left it for the moment expecting to return to retrieve it after getting Jenny, Rachael, and Fluff settled in my car. I looked around to see if there was anything I needed to take and was so surprised there was nothing else that seemed important. It was one of those moments when confronted with a real choice and I knew inside myself that nothing owned me. This awareness created such a free-ing feeling. I would be crushed should I lose my animals, and deeply disappointed if I lost the research on my computer, but all the other things didn't matter. It wasn't until I exited my place that I realized I had parked across from the apartment that had blown up and started the fire. There was no way I could get to my car and take my animals to safety. Carrying two pet carriers that held the cats, and holding on to my dog's leash, I walked as far away from danger as possible until the drama subsided.

Within an hour the fire was contained. By 2 in the morning the last of the fire engines pulled out of the drive. Nine apartment units were destroyed in the fire; everything outside was covered with a sheet of charcoal dust, and the smell of acrid smoke lingered in the air. While the two cats remained cloistered in their carriers the rest of the night, Jenny wouldn't leave my side and curled up very close to me when I finally collapsed on my bed sometime around 3 o'clock in the morning. I had to get whatever sleep was possible to prepare for a day of clients just a few hours later.

***

One of the clients scheduled for the day following the fire had begun therapy a few months earlier seeking help for his anger problem that he feared would sabotage him professionally. This client had been fired from his last job and was afraid he was about to be fired again. This time he had verbally attacked his supervisor as being inept and expressed anger that co-workers were getting promotions while he had been passed by. He saw himself as a much better employee than the others and more deserving of promotion. The client told me most people he has ever worked with were inept and all he ever wanted was to do his job and be left alone.

He said he was willing for me to reflect what I thought might be happening, but when I suggested that perhaps employers were looking for people who could work with them more than they needed someone who could do the job better than anyone else, he verbally lunged at me with vicious attacking words. He told me to *"shut up"* with rage in his eyes and a jaw so clenched I could feel pain in my chest, as my body recoiled from his obvious aggression.

I became aware of how much this man's anger reminded me of my mother's anger when anyone challenged her perception of things. Then he told me I was inept, incompetent, and incapable of helping him— and he continued with painfully attacking words for several minutes. In between his explosive moments, I offered reflective interventions by questioning or suggesting other ways to look at what he was saying, which led to additional attack. Finally, I told him I didn't know how to help him. Using the metaphor of the fire experience from the previous night, I told him I felt that perhaps he was right that I was inept and incompetent because I was unable to handle what felt like a wall of fire between us and I didn't know how to approach him without getting burned. He became quiet.

I said I had never had a client with whom I felt so disconnected as I did with him in that moment, which made me sad. I told him I believed there was a part of him who truly wanted help or he would not have come to therapy, but the angry part was so filled with fiery rage it was impossible for me to reach out to the frightened part that needed help.

My words seemed to go where they needed and he became quiet; then he looked directly into my eyes and he seemed to have made an opening to hear me. Based on the work we had done in earlier sessions, I told him I suspected his child-self had been betrayed by many people so many times he had learned to despise them. They had misjudged him and inflicted punishment for things he had not done. They didn't know how to love him for himself, and unless they were punishing him they didn't notice him. He had tried so hard to find a way to please them, but they couldn't be pleased. At first he tried to make them stop punishing him by being very good. He worked so hard to outshine everyone to prove he was worthy of being noticed; instead of being recognized, he became the target of their attacks. His peers turned on him for making them look bad and his teachers and employers turned on him for what they saw as his arrogance. Eventually this caused him to feel superior to all of those people who had judged him.

Because of the pain he had endured, he had come to despise not only the people in his life, but, also, God, whom he blamed for making him live with such horrible people. I suggested to him that his hatred for all of them might well have turned him into being like the very people he despised. He was punishing other people, pushing them away, judging them, and disregarding them, just as he had been treated his whole life. After finishing, I remained quiet to give him time to consider what I had just said. We both sat in silence, looking at each other, and then a single tear fell down his left cheek.

I asked him how he felt about my words. Tears filled the eyes of the man who had been raging only moments before. In a remorseful voice, he acknowledged that my speculation rang true. He asked me how he could solve his problem of anger. I recommended he go inside to find the parts of himself that felt so deeply angry that they had separated from not only the world, but from other parts of himself and then he needed to bring love and understanding to those angry parts by allowing the expression of the hurt from being so badly treated as a child, as well as in the years that followed, a hurt that was buried for too long underneath all the raging anger.

He was willing to do a relaxation regression to find the separated parts of him that held the hurt deep inside and for 20 minutes, this client let himself relax as a tear or two trickled through closed eyelids and down his cheeks. We had only just begun to make connection with the child-self when his appointment time was over, and he had to leave for another appointment. I asked him if he would be willing to reconnect with the inner child through dialogue or by journaling in the week ahead. He agreed. As he said good-bye, he apologized for having been so verbally attacking and told me he appreciated my help and followed that comment with a statement acknowledging it wasn't nice for people to try to kill the ones who are there for them. I reminded him I was not dead and we both laughed. But I was exhausted. It was a tough session.

***

The next hour was a supervision session. I began by telling my supervisor about the previous hour with the angry client, much of which he had already heard through the walls of his adjoining office because the client was yelling so loudly. When my supervisor asked how I felt about what had happened, I told him it felt like the client had punched me in the chest, and knocked me down. We worked with my response to the session, and how I might continue to work with the client in the future. After supervision, I had an hour before meeting another client.

I went back to my office, sat down in the over-stuffed chair, and began to do paperwork when a most devastating chest pain overcame me. It felt as if my breastbone had been crushed in and my ribs were broken. Pain radiated throughout my chest and down my arms. I couldn't move. Any movement made the pain worsen—so I sat still, barely breathing, but the pain increased anyway—and I waited. I did a relaxation-visualization and gave permission for my muscles to soften. I talked to my heart and asked the chambers to dance together just as I had asked of my mother's heart to do three weeks earlier. In a little while, the pain subsided, but I was left with a heavy feeling in my chest and pain in my arms. It was time for the next client's session.

By the end of the day, I had forgotten about the chest pain problem. However, I felt as if I had no energy left in my body. I went to bed early since I had gotten so little sleep the night before with the chaos of the fire. In the middle of the night, I woke with a "grandfather" of a chest pain much more intense than the one in the office earlier that day. I thought of calling 911 but decided I needed to wait until the morning because I had no health insurance and an ambulance and ER visit would be exceedingly expensive, so I planned to ask my nurse friend, Terry, to take me to a walk-in clinic the next morning.

I spent most of the rest of the night doing visualizations, sending healing energy to my heart and asking all the angels and higher selves of all my loving friends known and unknown, to send calming, healing energy to my heart, as well. Having seen the image of my mother's heart allowed me to visualize the dance in my own heart, as I had done in my office earlier, and I sent images of how my heart could heal, just as I had sent to my mother. About the time the sun rose, I fell into a deep sleep.

I woke a short time later feeling thick, tired, dizzy, unfocused, and had a heavy feeling in my chest that would not go away. Another wave of pain hit around 10 AM, and I called Terry to tell her I was not feeling well. She drove me to a clinic, but when I got there, they directed me to go to the ER immediately. Within a couple hours, I was on the telemetry unit of a local hospital beginning a battery of tests that would require a loan from the World Bank to pay off. A nitroglycerin patch eased the pressure on my chest but gave me a headache that came close to being as ugly as the chest pain.

***

Hospitals are seldom places where people get rest and my stay was no exception. After the first day of many tests that didn't reveal whatever was going on in my heart, I spent a night in a room right outside the nurses station—where everyone gathered to get orders, to admit new patients, and to do the nightly chores. Being strapped to monitors and hooked up to needles that were passage ways for medicine and nutrients to enter my body combined with the activity going on outside my door, resulted in my getting very little sleep and made the night seem exceedingly long. I did drop into a very deep sleep near morning, but woke with a heart-breaking dream.

In the dream, I was in what seemed to be a theater lobby standing with several people. A theater call was made and everyone who was seated began to stand and clap for the performance that was about to take place, somehow that was a signal that those of us in the lobby should go find our places, as well. Some people were seated but most were standing when we entered the theater. I began to walk down the theater aisle and saw Jake standing with a group of people to my left. Beside him was an empty seat. He seemed to be waiting for me and was trying to get my attention. I thought he might want me to sit next to him, so I turned my head to avoid eye contact; I didn't want to cause him to think I would sit next to him since I was with someone else. I went past him and continued to walk toward the front of the theater when I saw Jake again, but this time he was standing with several other men in a line in front of me and facing in my direction. He appeared to be so young. I looked at him as I walked toward him and a most devastating cry filled me. I felt such overwhelming grief that the intensity of the feelings wakened me. I could barely hold in the mournful howl sound, as tears streamed down my cheeks and onto the pillow.

The wires that were attached to my chest and the catheter in my hand reminded me that I was in the hospital. The day was filled with more tests, and after three echocardiograms, a heart stress test, a trip to nuclear medicine for lung and blood flow tests, and pain from a pincushion arm from blood tests, the determination was my heart and lungs were in excellent condition and apparently something other than a physical heart problem was responsible for these chest pains. To my surprise, their tests showed no evidence of a heart attack the previous day nor of the heart attack I had in 1997, though I knew both had happened. My mother, who had an extremely severe heart attack as indicated by the tests administered when she was admitted, left the hospital five days later showing no sign of major heart attack damage. I believe creating the thoughts of a healthy heart for both of us allowed healing changes to happen; something Western medicine may someday come to understand.

I was able to handle stress over graduate school, the worry about my economic situation, and seemed to be able to deal with the distress over my mother's heart attack and post hospital heart condition. I was able to handle concerns about where I needed to live and what I ought to do about my practice to make it more financially stable without losing any more time for my dissertation. I could handle it all until the experience of the fire the night before the heart pain began. Somehow stress from the inferno coupled with the fiery attack from my client seemed to have pushed me over the edge. I knew stress could lead to heart attacks and other physical problems, and how important it was to release the stress if I wanted my heart to heal completely. But this experience was adding to my indebtedness, as well as the stress over it;

but then, what was another ten thousand dollars, when I owed more than ten times that amount for my education! As I prepared to leave the hospital, a financial advisor and social worker came to my bedside to provide me with information about a program for people who had no insurance and had low income. The program took care of all the accrued expenses. After the paper work, I left the hospital with no financial obligations.

Chapter Six
HOLDING ON TO JAKE

If we are to embrace what is true, what is in our highest good, and what will lead us to experience authentic life, we must be willing to let go of our hold on what is not true—or perhaps even harder, to let go of what we keep wishing could come true—even when it feels like letting go will cause us to die.

In spite of the clean bill of health, the unshakable heavy feelings remained with me as I left the hospital. I continued to send relaxation messages to my heart and visualized healing taking place. Thoughts of the theater dream kept invading my consciousness as I continued to see the image of Jake standing expectantly in front of me. Each time the image appeared, tears filled my eyes and pain grew in my chest. In writing the dream, I decided the mournful sadness had to do with the loss of hopes and dreams I still held about Jake.

However, as I told the dream to a friend, an intuitive flash caused me to realize the dream had something to do with my wedding day. In that insight, I saw the theater was the church where we had been married. The people in the lobby waiting to enter the theater were those in my wedding party. The person I was with walking down the aisle was my father, though I didn't recognize him in the dream. The Jake I saw sitting on the left side, was the sensitive Jake who seldom came out to connect with me in all the years we were married, though I felt sure there were many times he wanted to. The men standing at the front of the theater were Jake and his ushers. The best man, who was standing next to Jake in the dream, as well as in waking life at our wedding so many years before, was the man who was diabetic and was in the hike dream a week before, the dream I had interpreted as warning me about my heart.

I believe as I was walking down the aisle when I was 21 years old, a part of me knew there were actually two Jakes, one who was heartbroken and hiding and the other who was demanding and controlling. Before I knew anything about masks, my young self knew that she was marrying a man who was living from the mask that needed to be in control but had a frightened part of him who was hiding behind the mask. I believe as I approached the altar to take Jake's hand in marriage, I had a premonition that I would not be staying with him. Somehow I knew in some future day he would be in my past and I would not be beside him any more, but would be with another man. I believe the theater dream was telling me I knew all of this on my wedding day, but the thought of it was so painful that I prevented my conscious self from knowing what I knew. Another level of the dream may have been telling me I was unable to stand beside Jake as a wife because I was still walking with the damage of my father's energy beside me. Still another level of meaning pointed out that my marriage was an act; it was a theater performance where we played roles instead of lived our lives in connection.

I thought the dream was given to let me know that holding on to beliefs that are not true as a way to avoid the pain of knowing what is true can be more excruciating and damaging than facing whatever pain may come from knowing the truth. And so many of us avoid knowing because we are so afraid of what will happen once the truth is acknowledged. I took on the role of bride and then spent too many years playing the role of wife living in agony. While attempting to create a wedding and later to make a marriage work, a part of me knew it was not right as I walked down the aisle. After the divorce, I spent years grieving the loss of the marriage. Apparently, the grieving was not yet finished. I knew I would have to face that pain I avoided so many years earlier on my wedding day when some part of me chose to not know what I knew.

***

The evening after I returned home from the hospital, I received a call from Bill, my colleague and dear friend who drove me to the airport the day my mother had a heart attack. We had been through training together to become certified in alchemical hypnotherapy a number of years before and had honed our skills over the years by doing exchanges. We co-facilitated healing workshops on a number of occasions and worked very well together.

Bill offered to help me find out whatever was going on with all that had happened and arranged for a phone session with me. Thursday evening, just one week after the "hike dream" and three days after being hospitalized for an illusive heart attack, I called Bill at 7:00 PM, as planned. For the next 3 hours and 45 minutes, we journeyed into the pain I held in my heart nearly all of my life, pain that I held behind my mask, though I didn't know it most of the time. I began the process by telling him about another dream I had wakened with early that morning, which somehow seemed related.

***

In the dream, I found myself in Jake's parents' house. I was there to pick up a few things I had left years before when I was married to Jake. It was painful for me to be there. I found some clothes and then discovered a bathing suit hanging over a towel rack in the bathroom as if it were drying from a recent use. It was obviously very small and I could no longer fit into it, but I wanted it back. I asked for it and Jake's mother looked at me in a way that indicated I would never fit in the swimsuit, but I wanted it anyway.

Just as I picked up the swimsuit, Jake walked in the front door. He had seen my car in the front drive and knew I was there. His mother seemed not to know how to handle both of us in the same room together and appeared to be upset because she was put in such a position. Jake acknowledged her and walked by me as if I weren't there. He went into his parents' bedroom, and I followed him. He turned around and passionately kissed me, but after the kiss, his face winced and he seemed to be really disturbed by my presence in his mother's house. He asked me, "*What do you want from me anyway?*"

I decided it was time to leave. I told his mother I would never come back to disturb her anymore. Somehow, it seemed important not to return to her house since it upset her so much. Instead of going out the front door, I went to the back door to leave when I saw Jake's father and two of his friends working on some project in the garage. I wanted to say good-bye to him, but I knew it would break his heart as the two of us had a very caring relationship. For so many years, he had been my daddy and I knew leaving Jake for good meant I would leave him, too.

My own heart was breaking because I didn't want to say good-bye to this beautiful old man who had been so important in my life. I walked along the sidewalk to the left of his house and Jake was walking behind me. He asked again what I wanted from him. I told him I was so angry with him and I dearly loved him, too. My heart felt as if it was being ripped in two by what was happening—and I began to sob, and the deep sobbing woke me.

I explained to Bill that this dream and the one in the theater-church would not leave me alone all day. I could not seem to shake the sadness or the heavy feeling in my heart. My friend asked me if I had not completed my grieving for the loss of my marriage and Jake. I began to cry again as I told him how badly I had felt that our marriage had failed and, in a voice that sounded more like a child than an adult, I said, "*I don't know why this hurts so bad. I want him, but he was so mean to me.*"

It had been 11 years since I divorced Jake, to take the "step into the darkness," and in those years I had created a completely new life and so did he. I knew there was no way I could go back, and even if I could, I would not be happy going back to the old life. But my heart was still broken from the experience.

I had worked on the issues surrounding my relationship with Jake extensively over the years and had come to a place where I recognized we had both created our marriage and we were both responsible for the pain we experienced. I knew the core of him was not cruel though he did cruel things at times, but I did things that hurt him, as well. I thought I had come to terms with that part of my life, but apparently I had missed something.

Bill waited quietly and then asked, *"What part of you married Jake? What part of you is missing him?"* I tried to talk but no words came out. The silence was followed by a series of incomplete sentences and half answers. I searched everywhere inside and could not find that part, and then I saw a flash image of Jake and me in high school. I told Bill I thought it might be the young romantic Sandy, the 16-year-old who talked with Jake while he and she stood next to the glass door in the high school science building before his 7:45 chemistry class. That morning the sun beamed through the glass, into the corridor, and into his beautiful blue eyes. In that moment of sunlight, I remember seeing the most radiant spirit in him, and deep within me I believed I would be with him forever.

Though I believed that romantic Sandy was involved in the decision to marry, somehow it seemed I was missing something significant. Then I heard the sound of a child wailing deep on the inside of my heart. The cry and the mournful feeling in my chest led me to an inner place where I found a little girl curled up on the floor. She had her arms wrapped around Jake's legs and wouldn't let go of him. She wanted him to be her daddy. Her own daddy had hurt her so much and she wanted this new one to make the pain go away. She was my 2-year-old child-self.

A most poignant memory came into my mind that has been etched on my soul since my second birthday when my parents gave me a beautiful baby doll. I named the birthday doll Trudy. She wore a pink and white dress that had a pink cap attached. I was so pleased with the doll with big blue eyes and a smile on her face. After allowing me to hold the doll for a moment, my father took Trudy away from me and spanked her several times saying, *"Bad girl"* over and over again, and then gave the doll back to me. I was in shock because the baby had done nothing wrong.

When I looked at the tiny doll-baby my daddy had placed back in my arms, I saw that her eyes were squeezed shut as if she were wincing from the pain of the undeserved spanking. Tears were running down her cheeks and she was frozen in a silent scream. Without noticing that the tears and the pained look were painted on her face, I broke out in a wailing cry that caused my mother and father to nearly fall apart in laughter.

While part of my child-self howled in agony, another part moved away from the pain and watched in wonder and confusion at what was happening. Nothing seemed to fit. The watching part wondered how they could laugh when their little girl was obviously in so much pain. With my parents laughter still echoing in my ears, my mother showed me the knob on the top of Trudy's head. By turning the knob, the doll's head turned, exposing one of three faces: one that had open eyes and a smile, a second had a sleeping face with eyes shut, and the third had the crying face.

I loved my Trudy doll, but was always afraid to touch her head for fear I would make the face turn and she would cry. Instead, my child-self chewed the knob down to almost nothing making it difficult to turn the head, and most of the time, Trudy was awake, not unlike my hyper alert child-self, who was positioned to observe everything. That memory has stayed with me for my whole life as seen from the vantage point of my observing self who stood outside the pain and watched the small child crying and the parents laughing.

As I completed telling all of this to Bill, my 2-year-old self seemed to shift to an older child. She was the 4-year-old who was first raped in the small forest that separated my parents' Alaskan home from the main street of the town where I was born. Over the years, I have worked with the memory and pain of this event releasing the many facets and levels of meanings attached to being so violently violated at that time and many times later. But apparently there was still something more to do; somehow the 4-year-old part remained attached to Jake, as well.

Both the 4 and the 2-year-olds wanted Jake to be their daddy and were very willing to let me marry him. I felt the tears of the 2-year-old, and in my mind I lifted her into my arms to give her comfort. She screamed a silent, yet, earth-shattering scream. She raged—and her face looked like one of the three faces of Trudy as tears of anger and hurt filled my heart. She did not want me to take her "daddy Jake" away from her, even if he was only a memory in my heart. The 4-year-old held tightly to an inner-image of Jake, unwilling to release her grip.

I held the little 2-year-old Sandy in my arms feeling her pain of resistance to separating from Jake and in the holding of my child-self, I remembered the basement struggle with Jake when I was 19, and how I, myself, dismissed it by dissociating from all of the pain around it, as if it never happened. I had forgotten; however, a week before my wedding day, I had one of those dreams that has remained with me in vivid detail all these years as if I had just dreamed it.

In the dream from so long ago, I was sitting in a courtyard at an outside table near the University of Washington student union building where, in waking life, Jake and I were both students. Jake came to join me to discuss our upcoming wedding and had brought with him some future set of plans that looked like blueprints for a huge building project. He began to criticize the plans I brought, when I turned my head and noticed there was another identical Jake standing behind a hedge looking at the two of us. The Jake behind the hedge had tears in his eyes. I was nearly frozen in shock. I began to look back and forth between the two of them and realized I was not sure which was the Jake I was supposed to marry, the controlling one with the plans or the silent one crying behind the hedge.

I continued looking back and forth to see if there was some way I could know which one was the real Jake. I got up and walked over to the hedge to get a better look at that Jake. He looked at me for a few moments with a pleading look in his eyes without saying anything to me, but I didn't know what to say to him. I looked back over at the Jake at the table who was busily working on the plans. The planning Jake called to me to get back over to where he was and pay attention to the planning. I felt torn. I looked back at the Jake behind the hedge and found that he had left. He was walking down a path with his back to me. I knew he was crying, and I didn't know what to do. The Jake at the table got up and walked into the student union building. I followed the planning Jake into the building, without looking back.

The dream distressed me, but when I was 21, I didn't know what to do with dreams. A day or so after the dream, my entire body broke out in a horrible burning rash. I had hot, red, irritated skin with tiny white bumps all over me that made me feel as if I were on fire. My skin was painful to the touch. I went into a panic, but a compassionate skin doctor told me it was just allergic reaction to something, or maybe a normal nervous reaction to my getting married. He gave me medication that quieted the outbreak.

The rash cleared a few days later, and on a warm summer afternoon in Seattle, I walked down the aisle and became Mrs. Jake Smith. I never told him the dream, and we didn't speak of the basement event for 25 years. After I divorced him, I asked Jake why he had attempted to force himself on me when I was 19. His explanation was that he was so angry because another man—the doctor—had seen me naked before he had seen me. He interpreted this whole thing as sexual and believed the doctor had stolen my virginity, something he saw as belonging to him. His belief saw the exam as a violation of his rights as my future husband and he felt he had the right to see me and to have me.

He didn't see my body, nor have me that night so many years before as he had intended. However, a few months after the basement incident, Jake told me because I would not have sex with him before we were married and would not marry him until I graduated from college, he would miss seeing me when I was at my very best, and that was a great disappointment to him. Going against all I had ever been taught by my mother, I allowed him to see me naked. I wanted to be released from the guilt I felt for hurting him when I went to see the doctor and needed to make up for the pain I believed I had caused him when he begged me not to tell his mother about what he had attempted to do in the basement.

Without knowing what was actually happening on the more subtle and unconscious levels within me, the guilt I felt about hurting Jake was fueled by the deeper guilt I felt years before when my daddy begged me not to tell my mother what he had done to me. There was, also, some unknown part of me that wanted Jake to see me before age would spoil me, even if the aging would take place between the three years from 19, to when we were to marry when I was a few months short of being 22.

I felt I had violated God's commandment to be pure and chaste when I allowed Jake to see me naked. Once I allowed him to see me, I had no excuse to deny Jake further viewing. Looking led to touching, and once I allowed him to touch me, I had no excuse to tell him to stop touching. His looks, his touches, his needs became dreaded requirements that left me feeling vacant, numb, and guilty.

I felt such heavy guilt that finally one day, I prayed to God for forgiveness and promised I would never let Jake see me or touch me again until we were married. If I did, I told God he could send me to hell. Almost as soon as I prayed the prayer, Jake came to see me, and wanted to touch me. I didn't know how to tell him I couldn't let him do that any more. I broke my promise to God and for many years, I believed I would never go to heaven; instead I would burn in hell. Part of the reason I felt I needed to marry Jake was because I believed I had ruined myself for being valuable to any other man, and perhaps, if I did marry him, maybe God might forgive me.

After graduation from college, I accepted a teaching position in a Christian high school. For years, I prayed with students, led devotions, and occasionally presented the service for the Wednesday chapel, all the time believing I needed to help the children find salvation, though I, myself, would never reach the "Promised Land."

On a Wednesday, some years after that diabolical promise, a chapel speaker read a passage from the Old Testament. In giving direction to the children of Abraham, the writer warned against making promises to God and then breaking them. The result would be judgment, as I well knew. But the speaker added something I had not heard before. He said in the day a father hears of the broken promise, if he forgives the child, the child would be forgiven in God's eyes. With those few words from the Old Testament, my heart exploded with hope for the first time since I was 19.

I told the school principal I was experiencing a spiritual crisis and needed the afternoon off. I rushed to my parent's home half-excited I was about to become free and half-terrified my father would not see the importance of his forgiveness and refuse my request. I believed the fate of my soul rested in the hands of a man who had seldom shown affection to me, a man who to my knowledge had never called me by my name, and once told me that he never wanted children.

I knocked on the front door and when my father answered, I told him I had something very important to ask of him. He came out and we sat down on the front porch. I explained about the passage from the Bible, and then told him I had broken a promise to God without telling him what I had promised. I begged my father's forgiveness. He seemed dismayed about my intensity and said he certainly would forgive me. I believe for the first time in my life, my father let me look into his eyes, though for only a moment. I cried—I hugged him—I thanked him—and I drove back home, praising God for showing me the way I could go to heaven. For the first time, it seemed something I desperately needed really mattered to my father. That was one of the very few memories in my entire life of feeling that my father cared for me.

Somehow, telling these things about Jake and my father to Bill allowed the little child parts of myself to see that daddy-Jake was not the safe protector that they had wanted him to be. While my dad had given me so little care, Jake gave me many more "knightly porch-like-moments" where I felt heard, loved, and cared for, but the times in between were so painful when he didn't express caring, or when he was explicitly cruel to me. The 2 and 4-year-old child parts were present during my conversation with Bill, and for the first time saw the whole truth. Jake was not the daddy they hoped he could be. They were ready to release the hold on Jake. However, the painful, emotional holding on to the image of Jake had provided a covering for the pain caused by my biological father. With the release of Jake, the father-related pain became more apparent.

Bill asked me if I would be willing to bring an image of my inner children's father to me. There, standing in front of me in my inner vision, I saw my child-self's father who was a very handsome, youthful man, tall, and slender, with dark brown eyes. I confronted this young man with how his cruelty and violent sexual abuse had affected his little girl's life.

Since my father died in 1996, I called on the aware part of him that had gone to the other side to let this young man see the after-effects of what he had done to his daughter. I directed him to watch an inner-screen on which the effects of his behavior on my life, on my marriage, on my health were projected. The young man saw the damage his violations had caused to my body, to my emotional system, to my responses to men, to my sexuality from childhood to adulthood, and to my life.

Something he had seen of little Sandy's pain touched something inside this young man that seemed similar to what he had experienced in his own childhood; he broke down in tears. For the first time, he realized he had done to me what had been done to him. He seemed filled with remorse for causing his own child to lose her trust in him and in all men. He could see how my body had become closed down and tense in a hyper alert state, constantly awake, much like the one face of Trudy-doll, and as a result, my stress levels were extremely high.

Bill asked me if there might be some kind of a symbol this young father could give to show his remorse. I watched him stoop down to be eye level with little Sandy and offer the 2-year-old child another baby doll. The little girl reached out and received the new doll, which had large, light-filled blue eyes that opened and closed. Little Sandy looked up at me and then back at her daddy…her eyes filled with tears, but this time they were tears of deep appreciation because the new doll's head had no knob on the top and only one face, not three; the doll was protectively wrapped in a soft, sky-blue blanket.

The child accepted both the gift and his apology. And for the first time in my life, I understood why I had fallen so much in love that night Jake brought me the gift of the soft-blue electric blanket many years before. Without my ever knowing it then, my high school self, standing on the porch on Christmas Eve was in connection with my future self who found the way to bring comfort and healing to a broken hearted little girl in our past…a little girl who was given another doll in a soft blue blanket, as an expression of a remorseful father's love. No wonder she attached herself to Jake when he brought the high school Sandy the soft blue electric blanket…and in that moment, though I didn't know it at the time, past/present/future were one.

I told the little girl's father he had a great deal to learn about being a father and asked the child if she was ready to release him to go wherever he needed to go in the universe to learn about fatherhood. She was willing to let go of both her daddy and daddy Jake as long as I promised to hold her and keep her safe. I promised.

Bill brought me back to the original question. He understood the child parts of me that had wanted to remain with Jake, but until the work we had just done, they did not know Jake had hurt adult Sandy; this fact had been dissociated information. Bill reminded me there was a part of me that knew Jake was not the one I should marry, as revealed in the *theater dream* in the hospital, as well as *the student union dream* a week before I married him, and, yet, she allowed the wedding to continue.

Bill asked: *Who is she? Who is the one adult part of you that married Jake in spite of knowing what she knew?* I could feel a narrow line of agitation that went between my stomach and my head, running along the left side of the center of me, the place in my body where I felt the energy of that part of me. As I became aware of this place in my body, I intuited this was the part of me that believed because I allowed Jake to see me naked, I had to marry him.

Before I had a chance to do anything with this part, I became aware of another part within me. I felt a piercing pain in my heart as I remembered a birthday card I had purchased for Jake when we were very young. This card was a significant symbol for me, and I worked with it many times in past therapy sessions. The picture on the front of the card is the view of the back of a very old gray-haired man walking along a path toward the sunset. The words under the picture read: *"Grow old with me, the best is yet to be."*

I had purchased the card shortly after Jake and I married with the intention of giving it to him on his next birthday, but on that day he was not in a place where I believed he would have appreciated it. So I decided to put it away and give it on another birthday when we were experiencing closeness and I felt he could value its meaning. Each year I would take the card out of my card box, look at it, read the words, and put it back hoping I could give it to him the next year. The "next year" never happened.

I believe the image in the card is the old man version of the young Jake from the pre-wedding dream who stood behind the hedge that walked away from me. My heart's wish was for the "hedge" Jake to have turned around, found a passageway through the hedge or invited me to come through to the other side where we could share why we had the boundary between us and what was making him cry. Then I hoped he and I could walk together on some new path as youth turned to middle age and middle age turned old. The hedge was the wall that remained the boundary between us all our lives together, and neither of us knew how to cross it.

My heart began to experience the heavy cutting pain again. I told Bill I had wanted a relationship to be the kind that would make old age a beautiful experience. I wanted to know if I died first, my partner would be there with me making my departure easier. He would assure me I would be safe when I let go, but if he died first, I would do the same thing for him. Then whoever went first would be there to greet the other on the other side when the time came.

I told Bill I had hoped Jake would be my connection between the worlds, my reminder of spirituality in the times I might forget. Somehow, when I saw the light shining through Jake's eyes that spring day in high school, I believed he would be that person. I saw *Godness* in him and I felt that spiritual presence very deeply. My heart broke when it didn't seem like he saw that spiritual connection in himself.

I explained to Bill that the work I had done in the past with issues around Jake had led to my uncovering many lifetimes Jake and I had been together. Jake seemed to be like a soul-twin, so closely together in some distant past that on some level we would always be connected. To abandon him felt as if I was abandoning a part of myself. I loved him so much; I couldn't bear to leave him behind. Just saying those words brought sobbing and tears.

Again, I felt the heart pain that let me know I was touching something so deeply wounded even my tears could not relieve it. After our divorce Jake told me we would always be married. For me to get married to someone else seemed to be a violation of our souls' relationship in spite of the fact that he had remarried. I had embraced the belief that it was acceptable to sacrifice my younger life for some possible future when we would be together in old age.

***

In work I had done earlier, I uncovered a lifetime in which Jake and I had been brothers. We were in treacherous territory, climbing through icy mountains when my brother in that lifetime had badly injured himself. He simply could not go on any further, but I knew if he did not get past his pain and move forward, he would freeze to death; if I stayed behind with him, I would be weakened and die, too. I opted to move on, with an intention of returning for him when I found help. My heart believed I abandoned my brother and knew he would die because of it. I died in that lifetime of a broken heart…and a part of my soul remained stuck there, suffering with the struggle that had not been resolved for many lifetimes between then and now.

In a much earlier lifetime, perhaps hundreds of years ago, I was a ruffian, who fought hard and drank heavily. I was in love with a bar maid I visited whenever I got the chance. She often danced for me and I thought one day we would become mates. On one drunken night, she danced in front of a huge fire, never looking so alluring, so beautiful as the shadows and lights of the fire seemed to dance with her. I reached for her to pull her to me when I stumbled and fell into her, which in turn caused her to fall into the red-hot flames. When she fell into the fire pit, she was filled with horror and profound anger towards me, and in moments, she burned to death as I stood in that drunken state frozen in fear, unable to save the woman of my dreams. As she burned in front of my eyes, my heart broke open and in the deepest wailing grief, I pleaded with her to forgive me, and swore I would never be caught by drink again. I lived out that lifetime in wrenching agony for what I had done that caused her to suffer, and my broken heart swore I would make it up to her, no matter what it took.

Lifetimes followed where I lived as a woman, bound in servitude to wicked masters who were reincarnations of that angry woman from the long and distant past. I spent numerous lives as black slave women, bound to cruel white masters or traders. In one life, I was chained together with many other Africans being illegally transported for sale in America, when a government ship approached the one we were on and the trader shoved us overboard, likely to avoid fines or imprisonment. Just as I was shoved off the deck and the waves covered my face, I looked up into the eyes of my executioner, and I felt my heart send him love. Though my conscious mind would have no way of knowing it, my heart must have known the trader in that life was the woman I had caused to burn to death in the distant past. And then the weight of the chain carried me to the bottom of the sea.

In one life, I spent my years as a maidservant to a demanding wealthy woman whose intention seemed to be to make me suffer. As these lifetimes spun into my consciousness, I was aware suffering was the common theme in all those lives. My belief that I deserved to suffer brought me lifetimes of suffering created by drawing to me people who knew how to treat me with the disregard I had exhibited in that drunken life, some were the reincarnation of that woman, and others were simply people who resonated with the same anger that she must have felt in that shocking moment when her body felt the flames consuming her.

A few years ago, when I finally came to a place where I could forgive myself for what I had done in that lifetime, I released the need to continue to punish myself by attracting people who would create their own versions of punishment. I found that all of my lifetimes with Jake were not tragic or filled with suffering. Some were beautiful and tender like the first months of our relationship in this lifetime and loving times existed in peppered moments during the difficult years that followed. I would imagine the combination of light and dark is what drew me to the man who was not only the love of my life, but also, the one who could break my heart more deeply than any one else.

The belief that kept me holding on to Jake was if I let him go I would never reconnect with him again, and if I lost connection, I could never be whole. I realized I had embraced a debilitating and painful belief that separation is possible. In this lifetime, holding on to Jake meant I had decided to make a spiritual sacrifice to hold myself back from becoming fully conscious of my wholeness in order to stay connected to him. In an instant, I was able to see I could not experience that spiritual connection with Jake, or with anyone, as long as I yearned for a connection that already exists, although in different form that I had thought. To yearn for connection is itself evidence of a belief in separation, which is impossible, because we are all connected. Only when I release my belief in separation is it possible to become conscious of connection and wholeness. As long as I sacrifice knowing wholeness in the hope of finding it in someone else, I remain unconscious of connection and, instead, experience what seems to be a lack of wholeness in myself.

I dropped into a moment of silence and felt myself move through time-space into a state of consciousness where I experienced the elation of unity and realized I have been connected to him and to everyone all along. In this "oneness" that exists within the universal flow in all of us, I understood that a belief in separation borne out of soul-piercing remorse and fear caused me to experience the lack of wholeness; I believed such a lack was the truth, and believed Jake would restore to me my wholeness.

As I reconnected to a greater truth, I was able to feel both connection and wholeness and felt myself fully connected to all that is in the universe. The fear of separation left me. Though I experienced myself as a substantial self, I knew I was more than this substance, this body, this name, or the composite of my personal history.

For a moment, I felt my body respond in subtle shock as I watched it diminish and become nothing and everything. And then there was peace. The part of me that had been holding on to Jake to be my connection between the worlds could finally see she has always been connected to the two worlds and the places and spaces between the worlds because I am connected to the Great I Am, to the mystery, to wholeness, and wholeness is in me, just as I am in wholeness.

Chapter Seven
THE BLACK SWIMSUIT

There is nothing more beautiful than the eternal light that is you shining throughout the temporal vessel into which you have incarnated, giving life, power, grace, and vitality to all that you are and all that you touch, as you move through the times and ways of your being.

Bill gently broke the silence when he asked if I could find the part of me that fit the swimsuit I retrieved from my former mother-in-law's house in the most recent dream. As I had been immersed in the depths of past lifetimes, I had completely forgotten about the swimsuit and about the dream. But as Bill was asking the question, I saw my 16-year-old self who was sitting in the summer sun on the edge of the Olympic-sized Coleman pool in West Seattle. From her perspective, the pool appeared to blend with the waters of Puget Sound as if there were no separation, and the sky blended with the water making all look like one beautiful panorama of multiple shades of blue.

The 16-year-old was wearing a one-piece black bathing suit. She looked so young, so slender, so firm, and so very shy as she splashed her feet in the sparkling water. Her longer than waist-length hair was wrapped up on the top of her head exposing the fine trim lines of her neck and shoulders. I had never realized that my body used to be so slender, so beautiful.

Jake was sitting beside her with one arm draped across her shoulder, obviously pleased to be so close. Another pain stabbed deeply into my chest. I realized that Jake was the only one who would be able to remember me when I was at my very best. Tears filled my eyes as I heard the words to an old 1967 Ed Ames song, *"My Cup Runneth Over with Love."* It is about a man who looks at the women he loves, he lies beside her and watches her sleep, he memorizes the small things she does, and he wants to remember everything about her. The song continues with the understanding that in only a moment they both would be old, and that they wouldn't even notice that the world had turned cold. The singer, speaking to his Love, says that in these moments of sunlight above, his cup runs over with love. I felt my heart mourn for the loss of such a love that could embrace the young girl in the old woman. I felt a shift occur and in that moment, my heart seemed to discover a truth hidden in the lie I had believed all my life.

***

I told Jake who sat on the edge of the pool with his arm around my 16 year-old-self that he didn't own the young and "beautiful" Sandy. I told him that I was taking back my teen age self's youth and her beauty. But as I said these words, sadness filled my heart, once again. When I entered the sadness, I discovered a belief that Jake was the only one who knew what I looked like when I was young. I thought because he was the only one on the planet who had seen the body of the girl in her fullness, before she turned into a woman, changed shape, gained weight, and was no longer a teenager, he would be the only one able to remember my beauty when we are old. Anyone else I might have someday as a mate would only remember a woman without her youthful beauty. If I took the 16-year-old away from Jake, I believed I would loose the knowledge of my youth; no one in the world would ever again be able to reflect her to me. I began to cry. As if to stop the overwhelming sense of loss, I took in a deep breath and held on to it to ease the sharp pain that filled my chest.

In the moment of stillness between breaths, I felt myself enter a spiral and spin into another journey. I was taken to a place where I could see people of all ages, some of them I knew, some I don't believe I had ever met. I watched them for what seemed like hours. I learned when people are fully living in a present moment, not blocking or yearning for the past and not anxious about or longing for the future, a time when they are open and experiencing the moment in its fullness, they possess all ages at the same time.

An old man, who is playing cards and enjoying the bliss of a victory with his arms lifted high in pleasure, has light flowing from his eyes. In that light moment he is his teenage-self embracing the joy of a touchdown with his arms raised high holding the football. He is at the same moment his child-self jumping into the swimming hole with arms raised in the joy of freedom, the day school gets out for the summer, and the infant splashing with delight in his bath.

An old woman holding her great-grand child in her arms feels her heart delight as she embraces the light of her soul connecting with the shining from within the eyes of this infant. In that moment, she is also, a grandmother enthralled with the experience of holding her child's child in her arms. And within the great-grandmother, is the young mother in awe of the being she has just delivered, and she is the infinite, innocent, infant looking into the eyes of her mother, her grandmother, and her great-grandmother. When my heart opens to see the old woman, I see her as innocent and wise, as young and old, as infinite and finite in the same moment. The same is true when I look into the eyes of a child who holds within her, the infant-self that she used to be, the adult-self that is growing within her and her self as an old person. It is all there if I allow my eyes to see. I released the holding of my breath and I knew.

The belief that Jake held the only image of my youthful beauty, something no one else could ever know, is a lie. I, like Jake, had accepted the cultural belief I could be fully beautiful but one time in my life, when I was still young, firm, and tender, a virgin teenager—an *American Beauty*. I was mistaken about beauty. Jake, the adolescent culture from which we emerged, and I had such a limited view of what it means to be beautiful. I believed, as did Jake that I would go down hill after 16, and for Jake, certainly after 19, and I would continue to decline through maturity and old age, becoming more and more a disappointment to all who saw me. I could see how that belief could make it happen.

Instead of seeing beauty in character lines, in the rounding belly of middle age, in the depth of ancient eyes, and in the sheen of gray hair, we only allow ourselves to see surface beauty in youth. Instead of seeing the innocence in wisdom and wisdom in innocence, we blind ourselves to the wholeness that we are. Shame, sadness, and a belief in loss, drain the beauty that is inherent in all our ways and all our times of being. I hold my own sense of my beautiful self, and I create this energy any time I am fully in the present, accepting all of who I am. I can allow beauty to be present and be seen no matter how old I grow. And, I can look again at that photograph that my sister took of me at my Masters graduation and see the light shining from the inside of me as it has from the beginning of time and will continue until the end of time, and instead of a "stupid grin," that I first saw, I was able to see a radiant smile that contains all the smiles I have ever had and all the ones I will have in all my future times.

I invited the 16-year-old from the pool, to return to me and as she did, I embraced my youthful beauty and my innocence. As she came into me, she started to choke, and in an almost joking manner, told me she was drowning in all the extra fluid and fat I was carrying around. She told me she would help me let go of it. Excitement filled me—and then I felt a wave of fear surge through me that caused the excited energy to freeze and then withdraw inward. This feeling was followed by the thought that if I allowed myself to become slender and attractive, I would attract men to me who would be dangerous. This thought was coming from my child-self who believed what her daddy had told her, which was that he did the things to her because she was pretty.

My child-self gave me flash pictures of one of my sisters, who had been a stunning and beautiful, well-developed teenager. She always seemed to attract the "bad boys" at school. My child-self concluded that if she kept herself from being pretty, the bad things wouldn't happen from bad boys. She felt it was safer not to let me attract any "daddy" at all because they all end up making her heart and her body hurt like daddy did and like Jake did.

Bill asked me to look at my sister's energy. She had always been sure of herself, strong willed, and had a very active rebel-self that challenged injustice and inequity. She attracted rebels and seemed to enjoy the challenge of being able to handle them, where I would have been less able to do so. When Bill asked me to compare my energy with my sister's, I noticed I hadn't lived from the fiery rebel and wouldn't attract the same type of men as my sister. This thought seemed to create a sense of calm.

Bill reminded the little girl that her daddy had admitted he was responsible for his own actions, and it was not her prettiness that made him do what he did. It was his own anger, pain, and emptiness; it was his own thoughts and feelings that caused him to draw conclusions about him and me and that led to his behavior, which had nothing to do with her. Bill asked her to notice that adult Sandy is strong and capable of making decisions, which would help her be both pretty and safe.

My child-self had believed that if she could only find the way to fix her daddy, he wouldn't do the hurtful things. Bill reminded her that since her daddy admitted that he was responsible for what he did wrong, it was his job to fix himself, and not hers, and Adult Sandy could protect her, even if her daddy didn't fix himself. Bill asked her if she would be willing to play with her doll and let her daddy leave so he could find the way to fix himself, should he decide to do so. She seemed relieved and agreed. Then Bill asked her if she would be willing to let Jake go so that he could fix himself, too. She nodded her head and began to play with the doll wrapped in the beautiful blue blanket.

***

Bill asked me to check inside to see if there were any other parts of me that still held on to Jake. There was a whole energy shift inside me. I felt my body stiffen, and my head lifted in an almost arrogant, defensive stance. The part of me that lived in the middle of me, slightly to the left of center, a place that existed from my stomach to my head, seemed present again. I sensed it was not so much holding on to Jake that was important as it was holding on to the idea of being married.

Though I had violated the religious precepts of my upbringing by becoming involved with a man who was not my husband and by getting a divorce, this part of me felt I could maintain a sense of righteousness by not getting married again. Somehow this part had held on to Jake's words that we would always be married as proof that I had not really "sinned" in divorcing him. As long as I stayed single, I could still feel socially and religiously upright. I had felt this before in some nebulous way but I had never before allowed these feelings to be formed into thoughts and then into words. If I stayed fat, the likelihood would be that I would not get into a relationship that could lead to marriage.

Deep on the inside of my heart, I felt painful sadness. For all my life I wanted to have a spiritual bond with a man. Because I had failed to find that with Jake, I believed I could never have it with anyone. My heart believed that only the first love could be spiritual because it is the one that is innocent. Jake was the only one who could fill this role. I had always believed that the union of spirits would allow two individuals to flow in and through each other's energy, to be filled by, and to fill each other with overflowing love. Such a union would be joyful, supportive, nurturing, challenging, revealing, and healing. Difficulties worked through would draw the two even closer together while honoring the uniqueness of both. Difference would be cherished as deeply as likeness.

I wanted my mate to be my partner, my friend, and my lover, someone with whom it would be safe to share the inner sanctums of my being and who would feel safe in sharing the deepest aspects of himself with me. He would be someone with whom I could trust my life and my soul, and someone who would trust me with his, as well. Though it might be possible for there to be disturbance and turmoil at times, neither of us would wish the other harm. I believed in my heart that marriage occurs when there is this heart-to-heart connection. To me, this is a description of true union; this is a real marriage when two are brought together in this love, it cannot be broken because it chooses not to be "torn asunder." My heart knew that the union of two is a reflection of the sacred union of each of us to the All…to Spirit, to God.

As I felt all of this, a realization filled me, which was that *Jake and I had never really been married* in the sense of heart-to-heart flow. As in the dream I had before we were married, Jake had been split into the planner and the one hiding behind a boundary-hedge, not knowing how to come over to share himself with me, and neither part of him seemed to be capable or willing to be a partner in connected love. The same split revealed itself in the theater dream where there were two Jake's, as well, one waiting on the side and one waiting in front. I had been a dartboard, split between obedience and detached empathy, as well as separated and segmented into too many damaged parts. As much as I had wanted it, I was too afraid to experience such deeply intimate connection with anyone, and I suspect, the same was true for Jake.

Both our early histories equated connection with hurt. As much as the two of us wanted a marriage, a union of two hearts, we resisted it in our own painful ways. I had not lost this kind of heart-to-heart union when Jake and I divorced because I had not had it to begin with. For the first time, my heart understood that the union I wanted had not yet occurred. Perhaps Alanza and the man on the bus from so very long ago were right. I was never really married!

Chapter Eight
ENDING A CONTRACT TO LOVE

Love is not an obligation. It is the gift that exists in wholeness. The most loving gift you can give to yourself and to another is to embrace wholeness in yourself and release both yourself and the other from an obligation to love.

Even though I did spend much of my married life as Jake's "dartboard," I had come to understand how we both created the drama in which we lived out our lives and our roles, and I, also, knew I would always love him. From the many hours of working together over the years, and what we were uncovering in this phone session, Bill wondered if lifetimes of experiencing a soul-mate relationship with Jake might be tied into some heart-contract. He asked me if I would be willing to take whatever contract may still exist between Jake and me and sign a cancellation to be filed in the Akashic records for all time. Though I wanted to do this, I felt a restriction in my heart at the mention of it.

The heart pain came with an aching cry that I needed to be loyal to the end. Somehow, I believed loyalty, which is expressed by never giving up on someone—even if it means self-sacrifice—seemed to hold integrity. Images of people making sacrifices for others flooded my mind. I watched scenes of battlefield sacrifices through all time, people willing to risk their lives to save someone they might not even know, all beautiful, yet, sad. I saw parents not giving up on wayward children, siblings supporting each other to the end, strangers running into burning buildings and jumping into frozen lakes...all to save someone. A world without people who are willing to help one another even at the risk of their own lives would be too cold, too uncaring. I couldn't imagine wanting to be in such a world. Then, I heard my mother's voice in my head telling me that she stood by my father and I should have stood by Jake, no matter what!

When I told Bill that I was feeling a hesitation and explained to him what seemed to be underlying it, he asked me to go to a higher authority than my mother's truth. Almost before he finished speaking, I saw an image of wheat being thrown into the air and heard a Biblical directive to *"separate the wheat from the chaff."* This made no sense to me in relationship to Bill's question. For a few moments I struggled with the meaning of the image and the words. Then I heard, *"Do not be unequally yoked,"* another Bible verse I had memorized in my childhood. I had never liked the image of yoked oxen, as a metaphor for marriage. I always hated to see animals forced to work for humans and felt as if that verse made marriage seem to be some barbarian entrapment. But as I watched the movement of the oxen, I realized that they were a team, a partnering of two equals. I knew that the message was not about forced labor and entrapped yoking, which is the chaff of the story; it is about two joining forces to accomplish something of significance. This was the wheat of the metaphor.

***

In alchemical work, when the deepest levels of our being are plumbed for transformation, it is not enough to release external patterns or relationships that don't work; it is necessary to embrace new ways of being that do work. One of the assumptions is that whether we are aware of it or not, we are all whole individuals. As a whole individual, I, like all people, hold within myself, all the ways of being human. Therefore, in my wholeness, I carry every other human being just as every other human being carries me. I can become aware of aspects of myself by recognizing these same aspects in others that I bring into my life experience. In practice, this would mean that I could discover more of myself by looking inside to see how what I experience in Jake is, also, in me.

Another assumption from this viewpoint is that external relationships are reflections of internal relationships between and among aspects of the self. To the degree that I am conscious of connection with all aspects of myself, I can experience connection with others. If I judge, reject, or attack someone or even if I put another on a pedestal, this is evidence that the self I am experiencing as me, is disconnected from some part of myself with whom I don't identify, or that I judge, reject, attack, or admire, and even in the admiration I feel separate.

From the alchemical perspective, unintegrated trauma causes a loss of experiencing internal connection, which impacts external relationships. If I lose my sense of connection with an aspect of myself, I feel as if there is an internal void. It is not uncommon to seek someone in the external world to fill what feels like the void rather than working through the trauma that created the experience of disconnection to find that lost part of self.

Any relationship created to fill a void, by its very nature, will be unsuccessful. The relationship will be based on needing the other person to fill an empty space and the other person is experienced as a "void-filler," valued, not for the whole person that he or she is, but on whether or not the void is adequately filled. The other person is seen as an object, not a person that is loved, though at the beginning it might feel like love when the partner seems so grateful, so appreciative of the other's filling them. However, if the void-filling person does something or fails to do something that prevents the filling of the void, the partner can turn on the other with anger and hate, so opposite of the love that was first expressed. The only way the void can really be filled is to re-integrate what has been internally experienced as separate, not by covering up what feels empty by filling it with something or someone external. Once wholeness is experienced, it is possible to relate to other people in their wholeness, to love them for the person that they are, not for how well they serve us in fulfilling our needs or filling our emptiness.

In my own life, when my father betrayed me, I lost a sense of connection with my inner masculine aspects, the inner father, and the inner mate. The inner father is the part of my wholeness that knows how to protect my vulnerability, my innocence, and the feminine aspects of my child-self. This internal father knows how to make decisions that are in my best interest and knows how to provide for my needs. The inner mate is the part of me who romantically connects with my adult feminine aspect. My inner mate rejoices in my sensuality, my sexuality, my beauty, and my femininity and draws to me someone of like energy in the outer world.

My biological father betrayed fatherhood when he became an abuser instead of a protector. He created confusion within me between the aspects of father and mate, and made both roles seem dangerous. My response was to distrust and dissociate from my own inner masculine aspects, which produced a sense of emptiness, and then, I attempted to fill the void with Jake who I believed could be both daddy and mate. But in requiring him to fill both roles, my wounded child-self would see Jake as just another man, like my daddy, who confused me, used me, and abused me.

Another more subtle disconnection that happened from my father's betrayal was my sense of separation from my inner feminine. There were parts of me that blamed my feminine self for causing her daddy to do what he did. And if she was guilty, the feminine deserved to be punished. Certainly, one way to punish her was to take away her femininity and make her feel unattractive and unworthy of being loved by a man. Later, I was to deal with this aspect of my wounding and healing.

***

I could see that my mother sacrificed herself for 55 years, while married to my father. She, also, had sacrificed the health and safety of her children; however, her sacrifice was not for my father, but was for herself. I believe that she remained loyal to him in hopes that he would turn into someone capable of loving her and saving her from her misery. This was not sacrifice for other; it was manipulative sacrifice that didn't notice the damage it was inflicting on others. What I was doing with Jake was no different. In remaining emotionally attached to him long after our divorce, I failed to fill the void with my inner masculine, my inner mate, and as a result, I was incapable of drawing to me a whole man. I had cut myself off from opening to another relationship that might give me deeply enriching and joyous heart-connection, with a man I could create a true partnership rather than someone to be a void-filler.

I could finally see that the sacrifice of not allowing myself to have a loving relationship was for me, not for Jake. It was still holding on to my deeply buried hope that if I did not remarry, Jake would remain connected to me and the boy who knew me would someday return to grow old with me and my heart's dream would finally come true, which was to feel myself as whole. I could see that as long as I continued to "sacrifice myself for Jake" by not setting myself free of our contract, I would not experience myself in my wholeness. It was as if a veil had been lifted from my eyes. I was ready to complete a ceremony of release.

Finally, I understood that heart-to-heart connections are not formed by contracts. True connection spontaneously forms out of love that only exists in wholeness. I took what I visualized as the contract that had bound my soul to Jake's soul for what seemed like millennia and burned the document. Then, with thoughtful intention, I signed the Akashic divorce decree. To my amazement, as soon as I signed the decree, Jake's signature unexpectedly appeared beside mine. It seemed as if something deeply powerful had just happened, and that it might take time for the deeper meanings of the ending of the contract to unfold.

Chapter Nine
JON-LUKE

We hold within us all of what we seek in the external world; however, we will never find satisfaction if we hold onto the hope of finding completion outside of ourselves. Deep disappointment from loss of whatever was our external focus can offer a profoundly valuable gift when we allow it to lead us to what exists within ourselves.

Bill directed our work toward the internal aspects of myself, from whom I had felt disconnected for too long, by asking if I had been in contact with my inner mate recently. In a microsecond, I was no longer an adult in the present, but instead felt as if I were a child standing in the middle of a ballroom peering through a crowd of dancing people, and I knew I was experiencing myself as a small child because I stood just a bit above knee level in relation to all the people on the dance floor. I was feeling a bit intimidated by the atmosphere of music, swaying bodies, and the sparkling lights reflecting off the mirrored aspects of a large rotating glass ball reminiscent of a high school prom. While the child felt out of place, I became aware that I, also, experienced myself as a woman searching for some inner mate with whom I had not made heart connection. In my woman-self, I felt that I was both slender, as well as the mature large-figured adult, both present with the child, simultaneously. So three of us were present, together at the ballroom dance, the child, fat Sandy, and slender Sandy.

Through the crowd, I saw a man dancing on a slightly raised platform. He had become the center of everyone's attention as he moved his body in amazing ways flowing with the rhythm of the music. He looked like a professional dancer, charismatic, handsome, and spontaneous in his enjoyment of the moment. Then I noticed another man seated in a chair along the wall, looking a bit out of place at the ballroom dance. While my split-adult self was interested in the dancer, my child-self was immediately drawn to the man in the chair.

I asked Bill if he thought it might be possible for my inner-mate to be split and as soon as I spoke the words, I heard an inner voice tell me that these were simply two aspects of the masculine that I had come to meet. When Bill asked what the man's name is, I heard the name Jon and then Luke. I realized one was Jon, one was Luke, and somehow they were both Jon-Luke. It seemed to fit.

The child weaved her way through the crowd to get to the man seated near the wall, and without any encouragement, she climbed into his lap. She introduced her doll to the man and asked him to read her a story. The two of them were no longer at the ballroom dance but in the living room of some comfortable home. His clothing changed from an awkward looking suit to a comfortable soft shirt and warm smooth wool pants held up by suspenders. Even his physical appearance, his build, and his color seemed to shift, but I knew he was the same man I had met years before, when I first began to do Alchemical healing work. This man had come to me as my inner father, but after that first meeting so long ago, I had not really felt connected to him.

Bill has always had an uncanny way of knowing exactly what requires focus in the work he does. He asked me if I could see the book the father was reading to the child. I hadn't thought of doing that, but after his suggestion, it seemed like it might be important. I moved behind the man. Peering over his shoulder, I saw that the book had big print with pictures to coincide with the story. As I looked closer, I discovered that the book title was my favorite book as a child, *Boxcar Children* written by Gertrude Chandler Warner. I was surprised, since I expected it to be a book for younger children like Dr. Seuss or Winnie the Pooh. The story was about a family of four children whose parents had died. The children were terrified that they would have to live with a mean, old grandfather so they ran away into the forest and found a broken down, abandoned railroad boxcar, which they turned into a home.

Each child had age appropriate responsibilities to create comfort and safety. They furnished the boxcar so all children had a place to sleep and the oldest girl found boxes to act as cupboards, chairs, and a table, while another salvaged utensils and dishes from a near-by garbage dump. They found ways to get food and found a goat to supply them with milk. The children had created a home and made it safe from all outside threats until one day their secret was discovered.

Near the end of the story the grandfather found them, took them to his home, and all of them supposedly lived happily ever after. As a child, I loved the story, but I hated the ending. When I first read the book, I believed that the children could only be safe if they were left alone in the forest without the painful interference from adults. I tried to make up another ending in my mind that would allow the children to remain in the forest.

While watching this fatherly gentleman reading my favorite book to my child-self, an awareness came to me with a surprise that brought me to tears. The inner father was reading to my child-self the sequel to *Boxcar Children*. It was the rest of the story of how the children grew to love their grandfather. They were truly safe, and could grow beyond boxcar survival to become the most amazing children, young adults, and adults. He was reading to her the story of connection and love. I discovered that he *is* the rest of the story.

Tears flowed down my cheeks as I felt myself surrender to the embrace of the daddy I had yearned for all of my life. I had sought him in Jake and in Jake's daddy. My heart had broken when I left Jake and in so doing disconnected from both Jake and his father. With a single decision I lost the two people I had believed might fill the void that had been there from the time my father abandoned his role by violating it so profoundly. Finally, after all these years, I knew the little girl was safe.

***

My awareness turned from the child and the inner father, to the ballroom. I walked closer to the man who was dancing on the platform and noticed that he appeared to be searching the crowd for someone when his eyes met mine. It was like a billion stars exploded between us in that moment, as if all of my energy-centers opened simultaneously. I felt excited and sensuous to the core of my being.

His gaze drew me closer to the platform. As I approached him, he held out his hand and invited me to join him. I had never seen a more radiant man. His hair was Irish dark and his eyes were the most beautiful sky blue, the kind of eyes that draw you in and make it safe to melt into them. Love filled me and I never felt so connected to the feelings in my body. I could have been 16 again. But as I moved closer to him, I lost the beautiful feelings as I became aware of my weight. I didn't want to join this man who seemed far more vibrant and exceedingly more attractive than I, and I felt so ashamed. He seemed not the least bit concerned and beckoned me to come to him in spite of my reluctance.

I asked him why he wanted me to be with him when I was obviously overweight and not the beautiful young woman I used to be. It seemed as if he had no idea that he could feel anything for me but love. I couldn't understand why he wouldn't be ashamed to be seen with me, especially in front of all of these people.

Again he beckoned me to come toward him. His eyes penetrated my soul as he told me that he loved me. I felt my heart melt as I extended my hand to him and accepted the embrace of the man who knew me when I was young, who recognized me now in spite of my size, and who would grow old with me because the best is yet to be. The two of us danced as I have never danced before. I surrendered to him as he surrendered to the flow of the music and I felt the weight of my body melt as easily as my heart melted just moments earlier. The two of us seemed to float above the dance floor; yet, I felt more grounded and supported than ever before.

***

Three hours and 45 minutes had passed since I had begun doing this process with Bill. It seemed as if the hospital and theater dream were light-years away and the pressure that had been in my chest for so long was gone. I felt light, joyful, and extremely tired. Bill wished me a good night and suggested that I might want to invite Jon-Luke to spend the night with me. I laughed, and I do believe a shy giggle might have slipped out. My heart felt warm.

I understood what I needed to do, not just to allow the weight to melt, as Alanza said it would, but to let me know that I was deeply connected to everyone in the world. I needed to connect with my inner-mate, the stunningly handsome young man whose heart was eternally connected to mine...my masculine self who, when he looked at me saw me as my beautiful feminine, whether I appeared to others—or more importantly to me—to be fat or slender.

My inner feminine had long been separated from my inner masculine, and as long as there was this basic separation in me, I would be at war within myself, and as long as I was at war inside myself, my body would be in constant fear of destruction since the inner war would be reflected by outer conflict. Without the masculine-feminine connection within, I would remain in a hyper alert state, highly stressed and inflamed, experiencing all of the illnesses related to that inner war, including obesity.

What was happening within me would be reflected in my outer world, as well, and I would experience separation and conflict out there. The answer to my internal separation and my world that was filled with separation and war, would be to find the way to heal the split between my masculine and feminine, to create inner peace, which would result in both inner and outer harmony. I needed to find a way to experience this peace in my body. That would mean I'd taken back what belonged to me: my childhood, my life, and my joy.

Chapter Ten
BEGIN HERE

There is no better place to begin any endeavor in our lives than from the open heart.

Beginning in early 2000, I had begun going to weekly body therapy sessions again, after a few years of cutting back because of graduate school. I chose a particular type of deep-tissue process to help in the release of what my body had held onto on the deepest levels for far too long. When I first began to work with this therapist, he told me that my muscles were like solid mahogany and my tendons were like rods of steel in spite of the years of work I had done in the past. Over the months, the outer muscles and tendons had softened to the point that the therapist was able to access the deeper layers of what he identified as rock hard muscles.

On the 14th day of June 2000, two weeks after the hike dream, a week after my stay in the hospital, and just a few days following that marathon session with Bill, I had an appointment with my body therapist. He began the work on my right side and noticed how constricted it had become. The psoas muscle near my right hip became the center of the work. That place was connected to a muscle pattern deep inside me he described as a boa constrictor wrapped around my core. This matched what I was feeling inside. As he applied pressure, lightening-bolts of pain tore through my abdomen.

I knew immediately that I was finally accessing the muscle tension that contained the deeply buried raping incidents from my childhood that split my energy in two ever-tightening and opposing systems. The memories had long since been accessed, but the muscles had not learned how to let go. While in excruciating pain from the bodywork, I called on Jon-Luke, and asked him to help me release what had been held tightly for so long. It felt as if my right arm extended to connect with my inner masculine energy and I felt myself breathing into the pain. That was the first time in the 14 years since I began working with body therapists that I asked for help from my inner masculine energy. I could hear Jon-Luke whispering to me giving words of encouragement as the sharp pain turned to intense burning that finally gave way to the persistent interventions of the therapist.

In all of the earlier sessions, resistance was an integral part of my response. This time, I was not feeling resistance. The question I felt coming from my muscles didn't ask if they should let go, but how to let go. The answer was to simply surrender. I had to stop resisting feeling the pain and simply had to allow myself to feel what I had been fighting for my entire life. I stopped holding myself away from the pain and fell into it by letting it move through my body. Something shifted. The therapist told me that he sensed a huge amount of "junk" was being released by the "shovels-full." The boa constrictor had finally released his hold on my core energy.

As the session came to a close, the therapist squeezed my hand as he assured me that we had gotten most of it and then he added: *"There are just a few rocks left on the path."* I was too stunned to speak. I had the dream of the two paths, one that was filled with oozing garbage that had been mostly cleaned out in the days since the June 1ˢᵗ hike dream and the other path was filled with rocks that had not changed each time I had visualized the paths. I had not seen the therapist since I had the hike dream and had not told him about the dream, the paths, or the rocks.

***

After the body therapy session, I went back to read the hike dream and the context notes I had written. I noticed the therapy work I had done on Wednesday, May 31, the day before the dream was left sided, the side of the heart, and the side of the feminine. I had forgotten that the image that remained with me in that session was an unprotected naked child curled up in a fetal position on the floor. I went back to the image to see if the little girl needed help. I discovered that she was the child sitting in Daddy Jon-Luke's lap. She was now wearing a soft pink cotton nightgown with ivory colored silk ribbons at the neck. In her arms she cradled a baby doll wrapped in a blue blanket. Her daddy was reading to her from her favorite book before she went to bed. I felt a hot tear run down my cheek and a smile opened my heart.

The child shifted her gaze from her daddy Jon-Luke's eyes just long enough to look into mine, and somehow I knew she had been with him all along. It was I who had been disconnected from his love; it was I who had to awaken from the dream I had been in without knowing it, a dream in which I experienced my life disconnected from my inner masculine, and, therefore, disconnected from an external mate.

Feeling overwhelmed with all that had happened in the previous 30 days, which included heart attacks, fires, hospitals, and dreams with all the anxiety surrounding those incidents, and the exhausting work with Bill, I scheduled an appointment for an acupuncture session. I filled my therapist in on the month's events. Still unsure of whether I had actually experienced a heart attack or just a major anxiety attack, I asked her to administer a kinesthiology test to ask my body if I had a heart attack, or if something else had been going on.

Kinesthiology is a muscle strength and weakness testing procedure that allows direct communication with the muscles to gain information about the body. I wanted to know if I was still at risk since no cause of my distress had been determined by the hospital tests, and my dream showed two paths, one had cleared, but the other still had rocks. The result of the muscle test was that I had a heart attack and had healed most of it even before the tests began at the hospital, and the only thing that was still distressed was my pericardium, which is the sac that supports the heart. I would not have been aware of this on the conscious level, because I was unaware that there was such a thing in my body. The acupuncturist placed the needles to assist in healing those tissues.

***

The evening after the acupuncture appointment, my eldest sister called to tell me the pain that sent my mother back to the hospital on May 31st, the day before the hike dream, was a distressed pericardium, the same thing that was distressing me. I told my sister I believed I was able to heal my heart because I had seen the images of my mother's heart on the screen and could visualize muscles interacting and I could talk with them, as I had talked to my mother's heart muscles. However, I had not seen an image of my mother's pericardial sac on the echo-cardiogram monitor. To my knowledge, I had never seen an image of one and had not been conscious of it to send any healing to the membrane. Now that I knew it existed, I told my sister I would send healing thoughts to my mother's pericardial sac, and to mine, as well.

A few days later, I received a package from my sister. It was a magnificent book by Frank H. Netter, M.D. entitled *Atlas of Human Anatomy.* She had placed a note card as a marker for page 200, the beginning of the section on the heart. On the card was a simple directive: *Begin here.* I suppose there could be no better advice in the entire universe, than to begin with the heart, advise that connected not just with Alanza's prediction of a teddy-bear man who would be a heart connection, someone I wouldn't be able to meet until I let go of my hold on Jake and reconnected with my inner mate, but, also, with my weight melting away, though it took more work for these connections to be made. And at the time, I had no idea that my sister's lovely gift had roots into the past, as well as connection to the future.

Chapter Eleven
SYNCHRONICITIES

There is a mystical and magical rhythm that pulses in the universe that, also, exists in the oceans, in all of nature, as well as in our bodies and in our lives. That rhythmic pulse becomes increasingly more visible to us in flawlessly timed synchronous events when we release the need to resist or force the rhythm and allow ourselves to surrender to the gifts within the pulse.

The roots of the synchronous gift from my sister went back to an experience three years earlier. While working on my Master's degree in 1997, I had come across a book, *A Brain is Born,* by Dr. John Upledger and had noticed the author was from Florida, five hours from where I lived. Upledger is the D.O. who identified the CranioSacral system in the early 1970s and has since then incorporated a number of body/ mind therapy processes in healing as the foundation for his internationally known institute in Palm Gardens, Florida. His work is based on the theory that all that happens to a person is somehow recorded in the body and reflected in the dura matter of the CranioSacral system and the connective tissue that holds the body together.

After reading his book, I called the institute just in case I could make a connection with this surgeon who seemed to know so much about body memory. As I look back, I am not sure what I wanted to get from making contact with this man, but I felt his work might interact with my own work on cell consciousness and healing. To my pleasant surprise, I was able to talk directly to him. He explained to me about some of the work he was doing and I talked with him about my work. The doctor told me about a special project with Vietnam vets, and in passing, I mentioned that I would be interested in working with him during one of his two-week intensive therapy sessions with these trau-matized people. He suggested that I send him a resume, which I did. But I didn't hear back from him. In the years since that first contact, I had forgotten all about the conversation and the resume I had sent.

On June 23, 2000, I received the Netter book from my sister in the morning mail, and in the afternoon I received a voicemail from Dr. Upledger, three years after my original conversation with him. The message he left began with a comment regarding the amount of time it took for him to get back to me and that he imagined I likely had con-cluded I would never hear from him. Despite the delay, he expressed an interest in my work. He wanted to see if there might be a way for some type of connection to be formed between us and invited me to his institute for an interview.

On June 30, 2000, I drove to Palm Gardens to meet Dr. Upledger. After visiting with him for an entire day to discuss our mutual per-spectives, he invited me to select and attend one among many 4-day introductory training courses in his healing method, which is offered throughout the country. He wanted me to become more familiar with his work before discussing the nature of a possible affiliation.

I registered for the course in Seattle for September, made plane res-ervations, and arranged to be in the Northwest for 11 days instead of the necessary four days for the training. At the time I made the arrangements, this extended time seemed exactly right, but shortly after making the reservations, I could not imagine why I made the trip so long at a time when I needed every dollar I could earn from my practice to keep myself financially above water. Not only had I made the "away time" longer than seemed necessary, I had given myself four days before the training and three days after. In retrospect, it seemed that putting all the free days together, either before or after the train-ing would have allowed me to make better use of the time. When I attempted to inquire within myself about the bizarre arrangements, I received an inner message that this would be *a time of letting go*. I had no idea what that answer meant, but I have learned to trust what I hear from inside, when I ask.

A couple of weeks after registering for the course, I received the reading list for the class I was to take; one of the two required texts was Netter's very large and very expensive 1997 *Atlas of Human Anatomy,* the exact book my sister had given me as a gift. Though my life has been filled with synchronicities such as this from the day I decided to make that 1980s nightmarish dream a reality by leaving my husband and stepping into the unknown darkness, I remain in awe of how everything seems to fit together exactly right. So I decided to accept the strange travel booking and prepared myself for something totally unexpected to happen in the days before and after the training, and my expectations were fulfilled.

***

In one of the few days between the work I did with Bill and the call from Dr. Upledger, I decided to rent a movie I had seen years before when it was in the theaters. It is unusual for me to want to see a movie twice, but for some reason I selected the 1990 film, "Awakenings," with Robin Williams as lead actor and Robert De Niro in a supporting role. When something happens like this, I have learned to accept the fact that there is a message I need to hear. The film was based on the true story of a physician working with catatonic patients who had been frozen in single positions for years, some for decades. The young doctor was assigned to a ward with these statue-like people. He treated the patients as human beings, talking with them, attempting to interact in whatever limited way was possible.

The Doctor believed that within the "statues" there were people who were there, but who were simply sleeping most of the time. The medical director and staff, however, saw the patients as *vacant... with nobody home* and medicated the bodies. Experts who had specialized in catatonic patients had concluded that the brains of these motionless people were non-functional and the persons were essentially *gone*. However, the doctor, who had no specialized training, noticed something different. He was able to see what the other doctors and the nurses had been trained to not see. He believed that catatonic illness was connected to palsy similar to Parkinson's disease, but in these people, the palsy might have become so extensive that many of their systems simultaneously were involved in the tremor pattern. He proposed that eventually their bodies froze in one position when all the movements crashed up against each other into one blocked movement.

The doctor pressed the hospital authorities until they finally allowed him to test the use of dopamine, a drug that was just being introduced for Parkinson's disease at that time, to see if it could stimulate brain activity to counter the non-movement in his catatonic patients. It worked! For one summer, in 1969, a whole ward of people began to move for the first time in many years. They became aware of the years they had been still and were now aware of moving. They discovered that many years or even decades of their lives had passed while they had been frozen in non-movement and discovered that their bodies had grown old. On some level, I am sure I identified with what was in the film because there were parts of me who were frozen in non-movement, just like the people in the story.

The patient, Leonard, played by De Niro, was introduced in the story at the onset of his disease in 1944 when he was a 10-year-old child. The story then shifted to early 1969 when Leonard was in the mental hospital. There is no way to know how accurate the film was in portraying the child and the adult Leonard, or his mother in 1944 or 1969, but in the film, the child was shown as an obedient boy who excelled in everything until he became ill. The mother, portrayed as an overprotective woman, did not allow any conflicts or disturbances in her son's life or in her relationship with him as a child or a man, whether there was actual conflict or not.

Leonard had not recovered from viral meningitis that struck him down when he was about 10, and he had been hospitalized from that time until the time depicted in the film, which was 25 years later. Leonard became the test patient who first received the dopamine and to the dismay of the staff and physicians, he woke up. As a test case, he was monitored constantly as he began to deal with being 10 years old in one moment and then 35 years old in the next. After this first success, the drug was given to all the other ward patients and all of them woke up, as well.

Leonard embraced his newfound adult life and in time wanted to experience the freedom of going for a walk outside without hospital staff around him at every moment. He petitioned the hospital board for a day of independence. When he began to sense their reluctance, tremor-like behaviors re-appeared. The hospital administration denied him permission to have a period of independence, and he became angry. In the middle of his anger at feeling overpowered by the hospital authorities, Leonard led a patient "revolt." Other patients began to demand freedom, as well. But they were all denied.

The effects of the dopamine began to wane. As a result, Leonard began to regress. Without the dopamine working in his body as it did in the beginning, Leonard began to experience tremors that turned into increasingly longer periods of non-movement, as before. And then in a most bittersweet scene, when Leonard was on the edge of returning to his previous catatonic state, he insisted that the doctor not give up. Leonard said, *"We've got to remind them how it is to live."* In time, Leonard and the others went back into their catatonic poses and never came out again. I felt like he was not just talking about the patients, but about all of us who spend most of our lives in a metaphoric deadened state, frozen in some form of non-movement, whether of body or mind.

The film presented an interpretation of Leonard's childhood as one that was confined, cut off from friends, and from his own feelings. One sequence of lines attributed to his mother near the end of the film was spoken in angry protest to what the Dr. had done to her son by waking him up. Mother said: *What have you done to him. You've turned Leonard into something he's not. My Leonard was sweet and kind, obedient...I don't know who that man is; he is not my Leonard. He is angry.* I speculate he had an overly controlling mother who did not allow her son to express anger as a child and did not recognize the angry adult who protested being controlled by an ignorant system, something he could finally express. I believe this was actually redirected anger that he felt towards his mother that was not allowed to be expressed when he was a child.

It seemed to me that the film revealed something about a body process that stops movement to prevent the expression of some feeling, especially if the expression is seen as dangerous, and for many of us, anger may well have been dangerous to express. One part of the self wants to explode in anger and the other is terrified of what would happen if the anger came out. So the two parts of the self struggle with each other, frustrating the energy and causing emotional depression or physical limitation...or both. But when the struggle is intensely focused, as it seemed to be with these people with catatonic disorder, perhaps with all parts of themselves involved on one side or the other, non-movement of the whole body resulted. The two sides locked in the fight with neither winning and both losing.

I understand that not knowing what decision to make in life, or knowing what that decision needs to be but holding great fear about making it, can cause depression and depression can inhibit body movement. Years ago, when I was struggling with the most difficult aspects of remembering childhood trauma, there were times in my worst depressive state when I felt catatonic. Many days I sat motionless in a Papasan chair from sunrise to sunset. The only thing that brought me out of the stillness was the tap of my puppy's paw on my leg letting me know she was hungry; she had puppy-training pads, eliminating the need for me to take her out on a regular basis. Until her intervention, I had no idea that the day had passed. Apparently full-blown catatonia does stillness so well that a paw would not create any incentive to move. It was clear that I had lived in a form of emotional catatonia.

I suspect that most human beings are living in some kind of emotional catatonic state, pretending that all is well when it is not well...a catatonia that we call the waking life. And we need to find the way to awaken from the catatonic dream. The problem is that awakening can be a painful process, and many choose to return to *waking sleep* rather than to heal the pain that allows true waking to be the natural state.

***

Just a day after seeing the film *Awakening*, one of my clients, who was considering divorce, called and left a message that concerned me. Her husband threatened that he had connections that could take care of her and indicated that he would take care of the therapist whom he blamed for her decision to divorce him, and she was afraid that he would come after me.

Based on my work with her, I understood that he and his family had a history of violence. Her husband's brother called me to tell me that he didn't like me "messing with family business" and though his actual words were not *legally* threatening, his tone of voice caused me deep concern. I knew my address was public record, and anyone who wanted it, could get it. I tried to dismiss the veiled threats, and go about my business, without focusing on negative thoughts.

I guess I was more distraught than I thought. One evening after seeing this client, I felt extremely stressed and decided to go to movie, and after the film, I went shopping, something I had never done before. I knew I was intentionally avoiding going home. I hadn't felt safe there since I had received that call. When it was obvious I couldn't avoid the inevitable, I finally returned home. But, I felt surges of fear as I got out of my car and looked up at the front door of my second floor apartment. I wondered if my fear was a premonition of some horrible event that was about to happen.

***

Though nothing terrible had happened, my body remained on edge and sleep was not a restful experience. Early the next morning, following my movie-going avoidance behavior, I woke with a dream, I called, *"A Dream of a Dream in a Dream."* As this dream began, I was with my two older sisters in a hotel room. We had been traveling for some time and found this hotel to stop for a rest. In the dream, I fell asleep and had a dream. After waking from the dream in the dream, but still in the main dream, I wanted to tell my sisters about it, but they didn't want to listen.

We walked outside and looked at the view. My eldest sister pointed out two mountains in the distance, but I couldn't see through the fog to discern what she was seeing. However, I did see two hills and when I looked closely, I saw they were very narrow and steep and had roads that circled around the hill several times to get to houses that were precariously placed on the top of the very tall, thin hills. We went to the back of the hotel and sat on a plateau area to talk, and, again, I wanted to tell my dream that had to do with our whole family. I told my sisters that they were in the dream and maybe the rest of our family was in it as well—but neither was interested. I was frustrated because I thought it was important.

In the dream I was not able to tell them, my family and I were in a rowboat, and my father was rowing us someplace. There were torpedoes being shot under the water and were passing beneath us, but no one seemed to be aware of the danger, but me. I decided to get out of the boat and into the water that was waste deep and tried to make it to shore on my own. The others must have decided to remain in the boat with my father. I became aware of the danger of the torpedoes and I could see how close they were coming to the boat and to me as they whizzed past me. I began to walk. I was no longer aware of the boat, or my family. I was able to see for a great distance under the water and could see that there were many torpedoes. I was in the path of a war and I was now fully aware of it.

I thought that maybe I could tell my sisters the dream later, but didn't understand why they wouldn't take the time to listen. My two elder sisters decided to check out of the hotel and still neither wanted to hear the dream. We walked outside and to the sidewalk, turned to the right, and walked a long way. The hotel was in a dangerous part of town where there seemed to be a lot of poverty and crime. We made another right turn and went down a hill past lots of very old looking buildings with open windows. Clothing and frayed curtains were hanging out the windows; everything looked war-torn. It looked like a third-world country that has been at war for a very long time.

We made another right turn down what seemed to be an extremely rocky alley and arrived at my oldest sister's car. But then we realized we hadn't checked out of the hotel and had left all our belongings in the hotel room. I was not sure I wanted to go back for our things. My eldest sister got into the car and I turned to get in, but she drove off before I could do so. She drove away from my other sister and me. My other sister began to run. She is older than I, and was able to run much better. I tried to catch up but I simply couldn't run as fast. I watched the backs of her legs as she ran and noticed how strong she was. However, her legs seemed more like those of a child, though when we were walking together before, she was an adult.

As I ran, I was too easily winded. I became aware of my heavy weight. I was out of condition and couldn't keep up. I decided I needed to get into shape so I could run as fast as she could run. She disappeared around the corner, and I continued to follow behind, but more slowly, as I retraced our steps along the rocky path.

I made it to the corner and looked up the steep hill. No longer distracted by trying to follow my sisters, I more clearly saw the place where we had been walking. It was in a foreign country. There were a number of workmen using old-fashioned tools to repair major war damage. A man who was filling in cracks in the sidewalk was using hand mixed cement and an old shovel. His skin was black and was covered with a layer of dust from the repair work. He spoke to me but I didn't know his language. I responded to him and hoped he might realize from the tone of my voice that I was friendly. I kept walking up the steep hill and saw that I was in an extremely poverty stricken ghetto. I didn't seem to be afraid; I was just focused on getting back to the hotel. I noticed that the buildings all had signs with Arabic words, though I don't know how I knew that.

A woman came out of what seemed like an apartment building. She appeared to be very familiar though I had never seen her before. She told me she was willing to show me a short cut. She took my hand and led me into a building through the side entrance to the hotel my sister's and I had slept in the night before. There were many Arab people in the building. She was Arab as well; though she spoke English. Then I noticed that we seemed to be in another hotel. I didn't think it was the same one from the night before, because I didn't recall it being Arabic, but I remembered it from another time (perhaps a previous dream or another lifetime).

She took me down a hall and in that moment, I realized I was trapped. There were many people milling around in the hall looking at us and I became aware of two men who seemed to have cornered us at the end of a hall. She told me everything would be OK. She explained that she had discovered that if she didn't fight, it wouldn't hurt and that it could actually feel good. I realized she was telling me that we would have to accept being owned by these men who were about to use us sexually in whatever way they wanted. We had no say and no rights. I was able to see into her mind and I saw her being raped but not fighting it. She was owned and totally under the control of the men. Her life did not belong to her. She could die if they didn't like her. I didn't want any part of this. I wanted to go back to find my sisters and get out of that place.

I turned around and saw that the two men were now behind us. They were handsome and dressed in clothing styles that seemed decades old. They seemed to be aroused. I believed they were deciding which of us they would take. I felt extremely threatened. I attempted to escape by making a quick turn and darting past them, but I got caught. One of them dragged me by the hair to a car, threw me in, and drove for some time. I have no idea how long we were in the car but it seemed like we had traveled very far.

I escaped from the car and began to run as fast as I could. I eluded them and discovered that I was in a place that seemed to be Israeli. I ran as if I were in the place where I was before the Arab woman came out and took me on the short cut. I believed that all I needed to do was to get to the top of the hill, turn left, and run down the street to the hotel and I'd be OK. But then, I realized I had no idea where to find the hotel where my sisters had gone. I was in a completely different country and the hotel was not just around the corner anymore. I was fully terrified. I didn't know how to find my two siblings. I realized that a great amount of time had passed since I had been gone. Even if I could have found my way back to the Arabic hotel, it would not have been the hotel we stayed in because I had entered it through a side door that seemed not to be the same place. My sisters would likely not even be at the original hotel any more. Everything I owned was in that hotel and I had no money to call home. I didn't even know how to call home from the foreign country—and I didn't know if I would be kidnapped again.

The dream turned into lucid dreaming, and I became aware that I had been dreaming of a lost part of myself running somewhere inside me in what only seemed like a foreign land to her. The inner territory seemed to be involved in wars that had inflicted terrible damage on many organs inside me. I called out to the one that had been frantically running without knowing where to go, so she could hear my voice and follow it back to me.

I woke with a sense that this was an important dream. Certainly it reflected the conflicts that had gone on in my childhood—not too much of a stretch to figure out the dangerous torpedoes that were flying everywhere—and it seemed to represent the anxiety I was experiencing at the time. Apparently a part of me was still traumatized, feeling very separated and alone, and she had not found a way to connect with me for decades. She was still terrified of surrender, believing surrendering meant loss of self and most likely destruction.

I intuitively knew I had contacted my wounded inner feminine in this dream, the one who had been so terrified by raping men who treated her as if they owned her, and she has been running in terror for decades if not lifetimes. I needed to help her find safety by ending the war and reconnecting to wholeness…but I really wasn't sure how I would do that.

Chapter Twelve
THE STILL POINT

Be still, for in the stillness you can find the path to the light within you that brings authentic life and healing.

Shortly after having had that war dream, I was back in my office with an hour between clients and began reading a book from the office library; one I hadn't noticed before. The book was a dictionary on feelings. Out of curiosity, I looked up the definition and explanation of anxiety since my life and my dreams were filled with this debilitating feeling. There was really nothing new in the information, but the way the explanation of anxiety was written impacted me. Using the metaphor of an automobile to explain how our bodies use energy, the author suggested that the body produces electrical currents in times of stress in anticipation of needing to fight or run away from something that may not, yet, be manifested. The author compared electrical overload of bodies to overload in an automobile's electrical system—both systems experience arching in times of too much energy that disturbs the system if the energy is not used. The arching disturbance in the body is interpreted as danger, but without an identifiable cause. This creates more energy input to permit fight or flight; however, the danger is now within—the overload— instead of some real threat from the outside.

Anxiety is simply energy that was intended to be used for something external, but is given no outlet, so it overloads the system, and the overload becomes the new problem. Anticipation of the overload can cause additional anxiety. While I was reading about anxiety, I was experiencing a great amount of it in my life and its effects were visible.

In the center of all the turmoil, I decided to shift my focus from all the anxiety-creating thoughts and move it to the preparation for the CranioSacral class that I was to take in a few weeks. I read Upledger's

1997 book, *Your Inner Physician, and You,* and then began to study the anatomy and physiology oriented text, *CranioSacral Therapy,* also, written by Upledger.

Upledger's work, which is related to the premise held by quantum physicists—and understood by many others—is that the universe is made of energy. Like everything else that is in the universe, matter, which is the densest form of energy, is in constant flowing motion that moves first in one direction and then back with a still point between the movements. He proposes that the energy regulation center of the body is the CranioSacral system, which operates as a hydraulic system. The spinal sac, which holds the system in place, encases the brain and spine providing the container for motion of body fluids within its own system and within the body.

Upledger explained that the body pulses with a nearly undetectable rotation movement, which shifts between an external rotation and internal rotation. If the rotation were to be exaggerated, it would appear that a body, if laying face up on a field of grass, would rotate outward and inward, outward and inward in an ebb-an-flow-like motion.

When it rotates outward, as if opening to take in the sun, it is involved in the flexion-expansion movement. The top of the head would tilt back toward the ground, and the chin would tip upward. The shoulders would roll outward toward the ground and the arms roll to a palms-up position. The legs would be rotating outward with the feet rotating outward, too, and away from the body, and the thighs would open outward, tipping away from each other. Of course while the front of the body is moving outward, the back of the body would be pulling inward, toward the spine. This external rotation is the time for widening and filling of the CranioSacral system with spinal fluid, and expansion of everything in the body, like a bellows taking in air.

The contraction-extension part of the cycle is the period during which there is emptying of the CranioSacral fluid, the time of letting go. The body lying on the grass in the open field rotates inward the head rolls forward with the chin coming closer to the chest, the shoulders roll in, and the legs rotate inward with toes pointing toward each other. Every part of the body participates in the subtle widening and narrowing pulse; even the cranial bones subtly extend and flex with sutures allowing for expansion and filling, and contraction and emptying. Though most of us could live our entire lives never being aware of this subtle motion inside us, if you let yourself become very calm, and quiet, it is possible to detect this pulse inside your body, sort of like becoming aware of your body breathing.

The functioning of the CranioSacral system with ongoing pulsing regulates the autonomic nervous system and responds to the needs of the body for movement. When healthy and calm, it works with a 5-10 second pulse cycle in the Cerebrospinal Fluid that fluctuates from extended and full to flexed and empty with a still point afterward, just like a breath in, breath out, still point, breath in, breath out, still point.

In the autonomic nervous system, the sympathetic system takes charge of the external roll, the outward movement, like the breath in, like stepping on the gas when driving a car. Then it releases being in charge of the filling movement to the parasympathetic part of the autonomic system, like the breath out, that allows for a letting go, an emptying of the Cerebrospinal Fluid, not unlike putting on the brake in a car to slow down. The still point between the pulses allows a shift to rest, sleep, digestion, and elimination, which shifts again to the sympathetic system to filling, activation, and extension of the sympathetic system. That quiet moment when neither brake nor accelerator is engaged is the still point.

In each complete cycle there is a continuous flow between the two systems like a dance of lead and surrender, lead and surrender, with both parts of the autonomic system taking the lead and then surrendering to the other system. This same pattern of lead-surrender-lead-surrender occurs in every body system, every body part, every body organ, every body cell, and every body process. The wake-sleep cycle and the conscious state and hypnotic state cycle have the pattern, as well. All movements were reminiscent of the heart-chamber dance I watched on the echocardiogram monitor that imaged my mother's heart when she was in the hospital. When all is well in our lives, the dance is peaceful and both sides gently take the lead and release the lead, not unlike the ebb and flow of ocean waves on a calm and quiet day.

When there is an extraordinary circumstance—an attack, an earthquake, a threat, a tornado, an examination, to which the autonomic nervous system must respond, the sympathetic system becomes highly stimulated and the parasympathetic system is put on hold for the duration of the event. The sympathetic system is activated to run or fight with no rest until the need or the danger is over. If run—then run until safety happens or until the goal is reached and then fall down and surrender to rest. If fight, then fight until winning or losing happens, then fall down and rest to let go and allow the parasympathetic system to take over or to let go and die if the fight was too much for the body to handle. If living is possible, in the rest after the extraordinary event is ended, there may be a complete letting go into a long still point that allows the parasympathetic system to reorganize itself to take over, which allows deep rest. This returns the CranioSacral system and the remainder of the body to the normal pulse of activate out, activate in, rest, activate out, activate in, rest, activate out, activate in, rest…with rest allowing a letting go into sleep, digestion, and elimination between each activation cycle.

If you have ever pushed yourself hard in a sports activity or in some physical project and then come to a halt where you let go of the push just to take a breath and then let out a long extended breath, you are aware of what it feels like to shift from a long period of extreme flexion-expansion with short contraction-extension periods to the long breath that goes the other way to a moment of long contraction-extension with only minor flexion-expansions. This resets your nervous system, your body, and your breathing back to normal. If you didn't restore yourself to balance, you would burn yourself out with too much pushing, or wind yourself down with not enough movement.

When there has been unreleased energy related to an extraordinary event because the still point was not complete enough for rest, sleep, digestion, and elimination to occur, the body becomes out of balance. It becomes stuck someplace in the extension-contraction cycle or stuck in the flexion-expansion cycle. The fullness of each cycle is not met and stillness is never completely found. The rotation rhythm is out of balance and total relaxation does not happen.

That unreleased energy may become energy cysts that accumulate in the tissue or perhaps as agitated free-floating anxiety with no identifiable cause. In my case, after hearing what felt like thinly veiled threats made by relatives of my client, I became anxious because I was not able to release the flight-fight energy, but at the same time, I was unable to stop the source of the discomfort. I had to dissipate pressure of the energy by going to a movie, going shopping and finally studying, but the underlying anxious energy remained, and my anticipation of what might happen created an energy overload inside me that was the new, real threat to my system. And that extra energy was causing arching inside me, which became a problem in itself. In the cases of the catatonic patients in the film *Awakening*, the patients were not at rest as it might have appeared; instead, I speculate that the energy became frozen in conflicted movement, perhaps caught in an inner war between fight and flight.

When there is unrelenting trauma that does not stop or if there are potential captors that maintain the chase, resting means increasing the chance of being caught and hurt, while sleeping is tentative, requiring at least a part of the self to remain awake and alert. Sleeping can, also, mean dreaming about torpedoes and forever running. In these kinds of situations, the sympathetic system is activated and re-activated while the parasympathetic system is not allowed to take the lead. Not only is rest stressful, but the idea of rest is stressful, as well, because to rest means the possibility of being vulnerable to attack, which reactivates the already activated sympathetic system.

When attempts to rest create activation of the sympathetic system and sleep is only partial because the system needs to remain alert, the body does not rest. Healing that naturally occurs during the moments of complete rest and deep sleep cannot occur, and the body cannot effectively eliminate toxins in the system. Movement toward elimination is a part of the parasympathetic system that shuts down when the sympathetic system is activated. Someone running from threat or staying to fight threat cannot be stopped by the need to eliminate, either on the cell level or on the whole system level. Activation without any hope for still point will cause a build up of toxins that are not released; it will deplete the energy system, prevent healing, and create burn out. To survive, still point rest must be found.

If rest is not restful and sleep is not releasing, it occurred to me that sending messages to the mind/body to eat particular kinds of food might become the parasympathetic system's only remaining solution to the problem of no rest, no sleep, and no elimination. Certain types of foods, the kinds that were reflected in the hike dream avalanche, induce lethargy and sleep. The pressure of more food may eventually overwhelm the gastrointestinal system forcing peristalses. Elimination may occur simply because there is no more room to hold all that is being held inside. Unhealthy eating may be the only way left to slow down the racing sympathetic system that becomes stimulated to increase action by the very thought of rest. These sleep-inducing foods can temporarily slow down the excited sympathetic system's energy by drawing the blood away from the extremities and toward digestion. The rest that happens with eating in this way is a false rest because there is not a total letting go—but it feels better than no rest at all, and requires additional eating of lethargy inducing foods to maintain the feeling of rest. So watching the film called *Awakening* woke up something in me that helped me to understand more clearly what I needed to release the weight I had been carrying for so long…and for so many other reasons, as well.

Another consideration that occurred to me is that when there is no rest, cell level toxins cannot be properly eliminated. Like garbage piling up on the streets during a garbage collectors strike, the toxins pile up in the body. Since fat cells absorb toxins and store them, it is possible that the body produces more fat cells during stressful times to store what would kill the body if toxins were allowed to remain uncontained. Healing all of this would require the discovery of a way to truly rest inside, despite possible outer wars that are raging. This would not just be a call for a truce to the inner wars but a surrender that creates inner peace…and rest.

It made sense to me that obesity, for some of us, may not originate in an eating disorder. Instead, it is possible that some forms of eating disorder may originate with the body's need to stop the sympathetic nervous system from burning out the body and to prevent unreleased toxins from poisoning the body. But this solution, being a false solution, creates more anxiety since being obese is physically debilitating, which is an anxiety causing condition, itself. Obesity is, also, socially unacceptable, which creates ostracism and a sense of being socially unsafe, thus the pattern goes on in a vicious cycle. Overweight bodies and eating disorders may be a biological response to bring movement and inhibition of movement into balance the best way the body knows how, when a sympathetic system has become so overly stimulated in social systems marinated in fear and stress, and personal lives so filled with threat that the bodies in that system have lost the ability to surrender to rest, and to peaceful sleep. When we live in fear, we go into hiding behind masks, sometimes attempting to pretend even to ourselves that we are fine when we do not feel fine or we may enter myriad patterns used to cover what is going on inside. Fear keeps us from reaching the still point where we are connected to out authentic self that knows it is eternally safe.

Alanza's comment that my weight would be melting away when tied together with this information about the still point, suggested to me that I would finally be able to discover living life without the oppression of overabundant stress and the inner wars that had been so much a part of my life for far too many years. I was soon to learn more about how to do that.

Chapter Thirteen
LETTING GO OF WANTING TO DIE

Too many of us have unconsciously chosen to disconnect from life by going to sleep while seeming to be awake. We close down our knowing, we numb our feelings, and silence our thoughts, and if something stirs us into wakefulness, we find ways to put ourselves back to sleep. When we face what caused us to withdraw from life and go to sleep, we can awaken and discover the life we came to live, maybe for the first time.

After finalizing my plans to go to Seattle for the CranioSacral training, I decided to schedule an appointment with a CranioSacral therapist to get a sense of the work I would be learning. I felt I would get more out of the training if I could experience the process before attending the long weekend workshop. CranioSacral therapy is a very gentle process in which the therapist works with the natural rhythms of the body to discover the location of the blockages that prevent the natural rhythmic flow of movement that I described in the previous chapter. The therapist I selected used perhaps the gentlest touch I had ever experienced in body therapy. She found an area of blockage in my spine at about the level of the thoracic diaphragm, which is made up of the muscle sheet across the bottom of the ribcage that controls breathing. She worked with a number of points connected to that blockage. The process led to a major shift in body energy.

While the shift was happening, my awareness drifted to a time and place in my childhood. I found myself unconscious, laying on the side of the road of the Alaskan Highway when I was just about eight years old. This was a memory I had worked with many times in the past over a period of years, but something must have not been resolved for it to come back to me during the therapy session. After a devastatingly pain-ful rape by my father, my child self concluded that the horrible events that had been ongoing since I was 4 years old would never end. My child-self decided to use gas fumes that leaked into the family car from a hole in the side panel to help her "go to sleep and never wake up."

We "back-seat children" had been warned about breathing in the fumes that came into the car through what had been a cigarette ashtray on the left side panel of the back seat. As a precaution, we rode with the windows down and used an old wool army blanket to put over our legs to keep us warm on cold Alaskan car trips. On this particular day, I crawled under the blanket and breathed in the promise of forever sleep.

Sometime after the trip had begun, my mother turned to offer the four of us girls something to eat when she saw the family cat fall out from under the blanket. The fumes had asphyxiated our little pet. Then she noticed that I was under the blanket. Somehow, while the car was still in motion, my mother managed to pull me, as well as the blanket, out of the car through the open back seat window and laid me down on the side of the road. I lay unconscious on the old blanket for some time, and then in a heaving release, I vomited a very long stool and was conscious again.

Though I had worked with many aspects of this event in both psy-chotherapy and body therapy, apparently there was something more I needed to discover. While on the therapist's table, waves of painful choking energy exploded out of my lungs in the form of thick mucus as surges of pain raced through my body that left me limp. After all of that, I dropped into an unexplainable grief and deep sobbing filled me as some aspect of the sleeping child's body finally wakened. I embraced the child and let her know I finally understood how desperate she had been to choose to die and told her how grateful I was that she didn't. I told her I would stay with her and help her make it through the rest of her life. Something in her let go of needing to fight life, and she surren-dered to it as she surrendered to me. In the release, I felt myself breathe more deeply than I ever remember breathing before. I experienced a vibration in my liver that I described to the therapist who told me this indicated life was pulsing into places that seemed lifeless before.

I felt wonderful after discovering how deeply I could breathe. I decided that afternoon to begin bringing more life and breath into my whole body by swimming, something I hadn't done for a very long time, in spite of the fact that my apartment complex had three pools and I lived just fifteen minutes from the Gulf of Mexico. Finally, I went swimming!

The morning after the swim, my entire body felt as if it had gone into extreme muscular contraction and withdrawal. I assumed it was just a reaction to more rigorous exercise than I had been used to, but a disturbing pain in my right knee began to worry me. For several days I was unable to walk. As the pain increased, I feared that my exuberance in the pool might have resulted in some type of knee damage, perhaps a torn meniscus.

Not long after this difficulty, I noticed what seemed like a nerve irritation deep inside my body that felt as if all my tissues were having an allergic reaction to something. The irritation became overwhelming. I couldn't stand feeling the pressure of any thing against my skin. Standing and feeling my feet touch the floor sent me into reactionary internal irritation, but so did sitting or lying down. I hated my fatness; I hated my inability to walk, and I hated being in a body that was making it unbearable to be living in it. I didn't seem to fit anywhere and nothing fit with me. Exercise, the one thing I needed more than anything to lose weight, put me in touch with being in my body, a feeling that was intolerable.

***

For the first time since selecting the dissertation topic that had to do with researching overcoming obesity, I lost hope in being able to find the solution to this problem that appeared to be killing me. My intention was to use the experience of being in my own obese body to discover how to release obesity. But I didn't know how I could present a research method that only promised pain and failure. I no longer could see myself walking across the stage at graduation to receive my Ph.D. All I could see was a morbidly obese Sandy too ashamed to show up for any ceremony, assuming of course, that I would complete my dissertation and earn my degree, which seemed impossible, now.

I had to deal with the possibility that my research would lead to no solution and that I would someday, and maybe soon, die as fat Sandy. For several days I was very depressed. All the years of my dedication to heuristic self-search inquiry seemed to be a waste. I could not see proposing a method to others that I, myself, had failed to successfully implement.

While still in the throes of depression, before going to sleep one night, I asked for another way to view all of this. I woke with a picture that let me know if I fail to solve the obesity problem, I could teach others about the effects of childhood abuse from all that I have learned from my use of the self-search method. Maybe future parents would learn to see beyond their own angers and appetites and treat their children with care. I, also, felt an acceptance of the possibility that maybe only a very few people would be able hear the message about not inflicting damage on their children's bodies and their lives. Perhaps, I would be the only one who would hear the message as a result of my inner search—and deep inside me, something let me know even that would be enough to make my learning worthwhile.

For the first time in my conscious awareness, I felt as if I had finally set the world free from having to be saved from itself in order for me to be willing to be here, and in doing this, I set myself free from having to save the world. I concluded that any who would choose to remain cold and distant, unwilling to notice the spark within themselves or in the hearts of those around them, and hold on to being unloving, even to the day they die, would have a great gift to bring back and share with us all when they return to the Universal One. Perhaps what they learn about living a life in such conflict, isolation, cruelty, and pain could provide enough information so those who choose another path won't have to discover this lesson for themselves should we reincarnate in another lifetime.

***

The sense of extreme irritation from being in my own skin and the worsening of my knee were enough for me to make an appointment with my acupuncturist. She recorded my symptoms and administered another kinesthiology test. The results showed that I was experiencing allergy but it was not to anything external, I had become allergic to my own blood. The previous two months had so depleted my immune system that my very own blood was irritating my tissues.

The doctor checked my adrenals and found them nearly shut down, and my kidneys were close to being shut down, as well. Kidney and adrenal acupuncture points were directly on the spots that were painful in my knee. I suspect that had I not gone in for the acupuncture work, the stress from the blocked energy points may have compromised my kidneys, as well as the strength of my knee muscles, perhaps leading to cartilage or joint damage.

I was allowed to stay for an extended time to let the needles have more time to open the flow of my energy. I spent the time talking to my blood, welcoming it and the life force that it carries into every one of my cells. A sense of peace filled me and I knew I wanted to be alive. Somehow I knew that the bodywork was related to the dream filled with torpedoes and wars, of running and escaping, of control and being controlled, of struggle and being lost, all of which had not stopped for my entire life. Finally my body was learning to be free to let go and surrender into the still point.

I began hearing the words I spoke to a client only a few days before who was dealing with the issue of "not wanting to be here" because she found the world too "mean" a place to live. The answer in discovering how to be here in a world that is ugly and beautiful, hateful and loving, mean and kind, is to release the need for everyone to be beautiful, loving, and kind in order to want to stay. Two hours after my acupuncture session, I was walking fine and feeling wonderful. Being in my skin was a good thing.

The first therapy session that led to working with the plan to escape the pain of being alive by going to sleep forever, and second session that worked with allergy to my own life force led the way to the work that was done in a third session. The deep tissue therapy work took me to the child who concluded that continuing to live was not acceptable. Again, this was a memory that I had dealt with in previous therapy sessions, but not on the tissue level of the memory.

One dreadful day when I was almost 8, before I had made the decision to use the sleep inducing exhaust fumes to free me from a life too painful to live, my father had been drinking and was very angry when he came to the schoolyard looking for my eldest sister and me. We had been playing on the merry-go-round when he approached us and ordered my sister to go home. Then he began to push the bars, spinning me faster and faster, as he cursed me for disobeying him. I started to get dizzy and begged him to stop, but he kept pushing until I was completely disoriented. He pulled me off and dragged me into a wooded area and sodomized me with a viciousness that engraved itself in my bones. The pain was so fierce that I literally tried to separate from the pain by attempting to wrench my upper body from my lower body. If I could have ripped myself in half and remained in my upper body, I wouldn't have to feel the horror of what was happening below. It was then that I decided that I didn't want to be in the world anymore. It seemed as if the brutality would never stop.

Having wakened this sleeping part of me in the earlier session, I was able to reconnect with the part of me that tried to cut herself off from her lower body in that horrible rape. Though she was unable to sever herself physically from the lower part of her body, she did cut herself off from feeling and from knowing what had happened to her. When my body began to re-experience the trauma, I could feel the energetic pull that seemed to be an attempt to withdraw life force from my lower spine by drawing it upward. Though the therapist tried to help me release this experience, the excess energy overwhelmed the upper portion of my CranioSacral system as the fluids filled the membrane that covered my brain until it felt like my head was about to explode. I left the session feeling dizzy and disconnected, with an excruciating headache that lasted into the following day and beyond.

Two days later, my brain was in a really strange place: It felt as if I had meningitis like I had in China a decade earlier. When I put my head down, everything spun out of control and my head pounded like there wasn't enough room inside for my brain. Everything felt swollen to the touch. Ice helped some. But the only way I could find any hope for sleep was to sit up on the couch to ease the pressure against my brain. I was afraid that this time I might have done irreparable damage to myself in my attempts to find healing.

After waking several times during the night, each time feeling like my head was getting worse, I began to fear that whatever was happening to me could cause brain damage. I felt betrayed by the healing process I had believed in for over a decade. I felt betrayed by angels and God who seemed to have directed me to walk on a path that was leading me deeper into pain and hell. I felt myself give up. I didn't want to do any more body therapy. It seemed that when I got through one thing and felt good for just a short time, the next uncovering would put me in a spin that was even more unbearable.

I thought that maybe all this belief in healing was a cruel hoax, one that proclaimed no matter how much I cleared out of me, there would be new levels that would take their place, worse than the previous ones. I felt like God was putting me through some wicked test and that maybe this existence is really hell and we are all trapped here. Some souls don't seek healing and just keep coming back, one lifetime after another doing the same mean actions or having the same cruelties done to them. Others try to heal but the healing never stops because the wounding is eternal. And this hell on Earth continues forever.

I don't recall ever having felt quite that hopeless. I tried to soothe myself by holding a pillow and rocking, something that worked in the past when I was struggling with emotional pain, but nothing helped release the overwhelming physical pain. I wanted more than anything for everything to end so that I could just go to sleep forever. I entered the center of the blackest despair; and, in what seemed like a moment of absolute clarity, I realized that the feeling in my head and the desperate thoughts at this moment of my adult life were exactly what my child-self experienced just before she tried to go to sleep and not wake up.

It occurred to me that though I worked through the memory, a long time before, I never worked though the feelings of utter hopelessness. I guess I had to go into utter hopelessness to find the part of me who felt it. For some reason, I remembered my path of healing chart that showed that the only way out of hurt is to allow the expression of feelings. This is not just expressing angry thoughts, though doing that could be necessary. The process requires feelings to be felt and then communicated to the one who caused the pain or to someone else to allow the energy of those feelings to be released. For a time, I became the child to feel her hopelessness, which, finally, allowed me to express it, in order to release it and discover hope again.

Tears rolled down my cheeks as I allowed my child-self to tell her daddy how much he had hurt her. As I spoke to that man of the distant past, I realized how terrified I was that what had happened to me in the hurting and in the work to heal the hurt had irreversibly damaged my brain. A sense of panic filled me as I contemplated that I would not be able to finish my studies, that I would not get my Ph.D., and that all these years of work had been wasted. I would not be able to make anything positive out of my life. From the perspective of the inner child, I could hear her speak.

"Daddy, I am so afraid that in trying to heal what you did to me, I have hurt my brain. I tried to get away from you and went into my head and now my head hurts so bad. I can't sleep. It feels like my head is going to explode. What am I to do if I loose my brain? My brain is the best thing about me and it is my only chance that I can change all the painful things you did to me, but if I have hurt it by trying too hard, I would rather die.

Oh Daddy, I don't want to die. I just want all of this to stop hurting so bad."

A wailing sound come out of my body and filled the room. I told my father that I didn't want to die without ever knowing what it was like to feel love, to die without feeling happy about waking up in the morning. I told him I wanted to feel what it would be like being in my body without everything hurting. I wanted so much to have a day that felt joyful. In my heart, I believed it was possible to feel love, but I had never experienced it. Words cannot express the intensity of the feelings that poured out of me as I rocked, and cried my heart out to a daddy from so long ago, telling him how broken I felt.

When I allowed myself to feel and express this agony that had been buried for so, so long, the tears washed the pain out of my head and finally, I fell into a deep sleep. On reflection, I was able to see that the three body therapy sessions let me access the hopelessness of the child that had been locked in the past, whose energy patterns were embedded in my tissues. I have learned for myself that I have to feel what I am feeling in the moment, let it take me to anything that is buried, experience it, own it, bring truth to my whole self, especially the part of me that experienced the trauma, and speak that truth.

***

Maybe you never experienced being raped, or brutally treated, but every one of us have experienced some kind of shattering. It might have been emotional rape that shattered you, or being overpowered by someone who was bigger or in a place of power that left you feeling vulnerable and helpless. You may have experienced a deeply humiliating embarrassment or heard a sound in the night that made you feel as if something in the closet or under the bed was coming to get you, and no one paid attention to your fear, making you feel so abandoned or alone. You might have wanted something and your wanting was made out to be stupid or unacceptable. There are a billion stories that could be told of shattering experiences, and it doesn't matter if the shattering that was done to you was wickedly intentional, if it was caused by someone's ignorance, or was an accident; shattering caused by anything is still shattering, and most of us do all we can to avoid re-experiencing or remembering it. But whatever we avoid becomes a blockage that prevents the full pulse of the CranioSacral system from happening. When energy is blocked anyplace inside you, the blockage becomes a place of weakness, and eventually leads to illness. To find healing, we need to find what was buried, experience it, own it, and bring truth to the part of us that was shattered…and, we all need to speak that truth.

It sounds so easy to simply speak the truth, but from the time we first learn to speak, we learn to disconnect from our feelings and from what our bodies know. Words can become swords that cut us off from being embodied as we choose to say what is socially acceptable or family approved instead of what is true for us. When we disconnect from our truth, we get to a place where we no longer know our feelings, we no longer know our truth, and we feel so separated that we can no longer act in integrity with ourselves, our bodies, or with others. This discon- nection causes us to put on the mask and in doing so, we are trying to make a part of ourselves go to sleep, and never wake up. It is time to wake up.

Chapter Fourteen
LEARNING FROM AN UNEXPECTED FUNERAL

It has been said that you can't go home again. But you can if you allow yourself to be conscious of the fact that you and the place that used to be your home, as well as the people who used to be a part of that home, have changed; then in going home, you can know something of yourself and of home for the very first time.

After arriving in Seattle, for the CranioSacral training, I contacted my ex-husband Jake, who had provided space in his warehouse for my storage cabinets for the previous 11 years. Since I had a few days before the training, I wanted to get a few personal items from storage, and I hoped to make arrangements to visit his mother, who was in a nursing home. When I called, he told me that his mother had died just that very morning. I was stunned— but then, I remembered the dream from three months earlier in which I promised I would not see her again because seeing her son and me together when we were no longer together had distressed her so. If she had lived even a day longer, my visit would have been the first time since I divorced her son that I would have seen the woman who had been like a mother to me for 28 years. I know we know more than we think we know, and I believe on some level she knew I was coming. I have often wondered if sometimes people make decisions about when they leave this Earth to make it easier on them, or on us. Perhaps there is far greater choice than we want to believe. I am very sure that people choose holidays or birthdays as a way to be remembered by people they love or a way to spoil the special day if they held anger toward family members. Other times they seem to wait until something happens, such as when a particular loved one arrives, or until the moment that people who have been hovering over them for days finally take a break for a few minutes and leave.

Later that afternoon, my former husband called to invite me to join him in checking on a couple of his job sites that were close to where I was staying. He needed to verify on-site measurements, something that we did together nearly every day in our work when we were married. I thought he might want to talk about his mother and agreed to go with him. We spent two hours together talking about our lives and he commented, as he had done on other occasions that though we were divorced, we would always be married. For the first time, I told him that I believed that I would always love him, but that he was married to someone else, not me. I, also, shared with him some of the feelings I had been working with over painful times in our marriage. It felt empowering to be able to express my feelings about those painful years without needing to judge or attack him; I simply wanted to express what I had felt.

The next day I visited Anne, a dear friend from Seattle, a gifted psychic who for years has helped me sort through my inner conflicts to come to understandings about my spirit's journey. Anne is a petite woman, with soft looking blond hair and gentle blue eyes, whose nature reminds me of a mystical Earth Mother. She communes with spirit guides, the powers of the universe, and the ferries and little people that tend the magnificent land that embraces her country-like home. Entering her space is like going back in time. It is filled with the aromas of incense and sage and is decorated with images of wolves and Indian artifacts. When people come to her with a concern, she invites them to sit in silence as she studies their energy fields to begin her work in guiding and enlightening. Her energy protects the space inside her home, as well as the streams, the waterfall and flowering plants that grow abundantly around it. She and her husband turned one small plot of land in an urbanized suburb of Seattle into a Garden of Eden. So tiny, herself, and so wise, she reflects back to those of us who come to her, what we already know, but are too embroiled or entangled to know what we know or remember that we know it. I used to visit her in her home often, but once I left Seattle, except for occasional visits, we worked with each other by telephone.

She began our time together by saying I had spent my life believing existence is about avoiding pain and I am in the process of releasing the belief in struggling with pain and opening to the truth of living with the peacefulness of love. She reminded me that the plane of "pain avoidance and pleasure seeking" is one that can never be satisfied. To avoid pain, one's focus must be on pain; therefore, a person who is trying to avoid pain is never free from it. Even in times of pleasure, there is an underlying fear that pain will return, which means that awareness of the prospect of pain is ever present. Seeking pleasure is based on a belief that pleasure is not present and must be found, and can never be fully experienced because pain is an ever-present threat. The belief in which a pleasure seeking person can become entangled is that more and more pleasure seeking can erase the pain, and this becomes the motivation for addictions that can never be fully satisfying and no matter what addiction is chosen, they always end in pain.

Anne indicated that I was moving to a place where I was becoming conscious of my embrace of love, from which joy and pleasure are natural emanations. As she studied my energy field, she told me I was at the threshold of immediate manifestation, in which I would be more conscious of my creation. She said I was making visible all those things I hold in my mind to notice what is true and not true. My interpretation of this whole concept of manifestation is that human beings always manifest their beliefs, but, for the most part, are unconscious of those beliefs, as well as their manifestations. More likely than not, people blame or praise others or God for creating what they, themselves, have created. God does not create what happens in our lives; but Spirit did give us the ability to create. She reflected that I felt more centered and confident that everything I was experiencing was exactly as I needed it to be.

Based on what I had experienced as a child, the Sandy at age 19 believed that all men were rapists; I believed that I was trapped and helpless to stop raping men from trapping and assaulting me. At the same time, I held on to a deep hope that the raping would stop, but had no idea how to end it. In that basement experience with Jake, I could have looked into the eyes of my high school sweetheart and said to him something like, *"I am feeling like you are trying to force me to do something I don't want to do; can you tell me what is going on? I want you to know that I am not going to let you do it."* Or, I could have been much more assertive and said, *"Stop it, Jake! What has gotten into you?"* Instead, I ran to the door in terror, and I cried when I found it was locked. My belief in the trap reconnected me with the trapped child, and from this place, I was prevented from standing in strength and speaking, and I was unable to see the bolt that needed a simple turn to be unlocked. I believed in being trapped and created a trap and I played out the role of being powerless, subject to someone else's power; I created an experience where I felt as if I was the helpless one who cried, with unconscious hope that my tears would cause him to not hurt me.

Jake's belief, I presume, in not being able to have what he wanted because someone else got what should have been his, was verified by his interpretation of my visit to the doctor and fulfilled by the event in his basement. So my running to the door playing out my drama fit perfectly into his drama and together we manifested what we both believed was true. But at the time, neither of us knew that we were just playing roles in dramas we had both written, with ourselves as the main actors in our dramas and the other in a supporting role.

This understanding is not one that blames my 19-year-old self, as causing what happened. I was not responsible for what Jake did; but what I have become aware of is my responsibility to transform my perception of the world that caused me to respond to what he did the way I did…and knowing this in the present can lead me to change what I believe, which can, then, change what I create.

A few hours after my visit with Anne, I met Jake at his warehouse. An employee was still working in the front office while Jake and I went to the storage area to open the two cabinets that contained all that was left of what I owned from our marriage. He seemed distant and formal with me as he pulled out the storage cabinets and helped me open them. It was as if he had no idea of how to respond to the person who the day before had told him we would always be friends but that we were not married.

The items I wanted were easily accessible, so what might have been a time-consuming task was finished in a few minutes. Jake helped me carry the items from the warehouse, through the showroom, and to my car. As we were leaving, he offered to show his secretary and me the most recent photos of the home he was building. It is a gigantic Northwestern mansion made of cedar and nestled in a forest. The entry leads to rooms with 30 foot cathedral ceilings with windows that provide a floor-to-ceiling view of Puget sound and Seattle. It was clear that the furnishings were magnificent in style and design, and I suspect that the dining furniture, alone, cost more than the entire household of furniture that I shared with Jake when we were married. As elegant as it was, I felt a sigh of relief emanating from the heart of my heart. In spite of its opulence, I was so glad I was not living there.

It wasn't that something was wrong with the magnificent house or with the beautiful furnishing; deep inside me, I knew if I had decided to stay so many years before, instead of following the nightmarish dream and walking into the utter darkness, I would likely have continued to hold on to my old patterned beliefs. I would have created more situations where I felt trapped and wouldn't have been able to be me. Likely, I would have accepted being a fixture in his life, a dartboard for the rest of my life rather than having a life of my own. The only way I could have defended myself would have been to continue to numb myself and disconnect from my feelings. In essence, the only way to live would have been to die. It felt really good to experience knowing deep inside me that I had made the right choice for me, the choice to live.

Looking at his beautiful home in 2000 caused me to remember an incident sometime after I finalized the divorce in late 1989. Like in the dream I had before our marriage officially ended, where I discovered that there was no place for me in the new offices, Jake actually did remodel the office space. One afternoon, just before I left for China, my former husband invited me to see his newly remodeled showroom in the business that was still legally half mine, and one of the first things I noticed was that it was filled with plants, trees, and flowers. At first I thought they were real but when I looked closer, I saw they were very expensive silk replicas. I expressed surprise that they were not real because they looked so much like the real thing, and in a matter of fact response he said, *"They have to be artificial. Around here we would kill anything that was alive."* I knew he was referring to plants, but on a metaphoric level, I interpreted his comment as a verification that for me to have remained I would have had to be artificial or I would have been killed. Realizing all of this felt healing.

While getting ready to leave the warehouse with the few items I had come to collect, Jake mentioned that he would let me know about his mother's funeral and suggested that it might be nice for us to get together for lunch following my training class. With a promise to talk again, we parted. He drove to his beautiful home on the Olympic Peninsula and I went to my mother's home to stay while I attended the CranioSacral training.

***

When I arrived at my destination, I was told my younger sister had prepared a place for me to sleep. In anticipation of my arrival, she had cleaned out the basement bedroom where my father spent his last years before his death in 1996. She had prepared his bed with new sheets, blankets, and pillows. It was in that bed where he suffered an eruption of his abdominal aorta before he died in the operating room a few hours later.

My immediate felt-response was that I did not want to sleep in the bed of the man who first raped me when I was only four years old and continued to abuse me throughout my childhood. I knew I had a number of options. I could tell my mother and sister that I didn't want to sleep there, perhaps defending myself with reasons these two women—who deny that anything bad ever happened—wouldn't understand. I could have decided to get a motel room someplace, or return to my eldest sister's home where I had stayed the first four days of my visit, but I was still a student in graduate school and didn't have money for a motel or rental car, and I didn't have the time it would take each day and night to catch a bus between Seattle and my sister's home outside the city.

For many years it was difficult for me to even enter my parents' home, and the thought of staying over night—in my father's bed—seemed impossible. I did consider the fact that when I returned to Seattle in 1996 to be with my family after his death, I became ill while staying there, and went to a nearby city to recover. But I had, also, experienced significant spiritual and emotional growth since then.

I looked at the room and remembered that before the basement became the underground habitat for my father to live out his life, the space belonged to the girls in our family. It had been our bedroom for a few years prior to our father taking over the basement for his office and bedroom. The girls moved to the third floor when I entered high school, where we stayed until each of us left home. I decided that I could consider my sister's cleaning as being a removal of my father's energy and a replacement with her energy. I could then reclaim my right to be in the space that used to belong to my sisters and me, but my underlying fear was that somehow my father's spirit might still be in the room. I stayed there for four nights and no ghosts appeared.

However, the first night, I was aware of a smell that was overpowering—like the smell of death—that gave me a terrible headache. I sent healing energy into the space and for the next three nights, though the smell remained, it didn't bother me nearly as much. Months later, I found out that the horrible odor came from the aftereffects of a toilet backup and overflow that apparently had happened on numerous occasions long before my father's death but had never been cleaned up. The sewage had saturated the carpet under the bed and had long since dried. The toilet debris had decayed the carpet backing and pad, leaving a horrible crusted mess and nasty smell. What a vile metaphor for my father's life and death. After I left, my brother found the source of the problem, tore out the last remains of my father's mess, painted over the stains, and moved into the basement, himself.

***

In the 4-day CranioSacral course, I learned basic anatomy and was introduced to the fascia tissue that, according to Upledger, has no beginning or ending in the body. I learned that the fascia is a single membrane that forms the protective shields around all muscles, all organs, all nerves, and all cells. Upledger stated that *abnormal tension patterns in the fascia might be transmitted from one part of the body to another in what may appear to be most bizarre ways unless one appreciates the 'oneness' of the fascial system.* The instructor pointed out that this fascia not only forms the membranes that support the organs and muscles, but somehow it transforms itself at exactly the right place and forms the organs, the muscles, the tissues, the bones…it is everything and at the same time is connected to everything in us. For the first time in my life, I realized that my body; though it looks like many separate parts, is one. What appeared to be separate parts was the result of directives given by the mind, fulfilling patterns stored in the DNA. So, anything that happens in one part of the body, influences every part.

In the past, I had always identified myself with mind, and had dismissed my body. Somehow, it finally sank in that my body is not separate from my mind; they are two aspects of the same force, the same pulse that moves inside me. As the days continued, I became more aware of my own CranioSacral rhythm and felt the oneness within me. I could feel the subtle shifts of energy in one place in my body and trace the complicated flow into other places I would previously not have known were connected. Each day opened to more and more empowerment brought on by my sense of myself connected to my body. I learned how to identify the subtle movements within myself and within others and left the class after four days feeling I knew myself more deeply than I had ever known before.

With all the walking to get to and from the training course in downtown Seattle to the bus that took me to my mother's house, my feet were in agony. Instead of dismissing the pain and pushing myself forward in spite of it, as was my usual pattern, I asked all of my body to be aware of how much work the "feet" were doing, and asked the feet what they needed from me to feel better. They told me they needed to be able to rest and to be massaged. I asked all the other parts of me to work together as a unit to alleviate the cause of the hurt by supporting my feet as they supported everything else. And I asked my body to help me deal with the major cause of the pain, which was the extra weight I was carrying. I asked my whole body to work together to find a way to let me know what I needed to do to support it in the letting go process, and I put my feet up when I got home and massaged them. Talking *with* my body was so different from my previous pattern of talking *to* my body.

An understanding came to me, something that was more a feeling than a thought, regarding an even grander sense of the connection that I had discovered within my body. I saw the relationship within all parts of my body as a part of a connected string, and when I moved into shamanic vision, I could see the energetic-pattern that formed a string connection between human beings and humans connected to the Earth and the Earth connected to the Universe.

Then I began to see the more subtle energy connections between man and woman, which seemed to be a metaphor, or perhaps an outer expression of the relationship between the inner masculine and feminine. All of this reflected the relationship between mind and body, between mind-body and soul, and between spiritual and physical. Just as I could sense the oneness of my body, I saw the oneness of all that is in the Universe. For so long there has been a sense of domination of one aspect over the other—man over woman, mind over matter, human over earth— and the result has been disastrous for us, individually, nationally, culturally, racially, and globally. Any system based on one aspect dominating another is doomed to failure. That kind of a system is out of balance and *will* collapse.

I recognized that any system based on domination creates a subsystem of codependence. The dominator is actually dependent on the submissive one to be submissive, and the submissive one is dependent on the dominator to take charge. Both have created a reality where neither takes the responsibility for taking charge of him or her self, but wants the other to do it for them. Images of the codependent triangle flashed in my mind and I knew on a feeling level not only the truth of how this system is formed, but also, how prevalent it is in every aspect of human interaction.

What I felt was a feeling-awareness that if I am to find healing, I must shift from a vision of domination and submission to mutual cooperation in relationship, from mind over matter, to mind respecting matter and matter respecting mind. It had something to do with the surrender of both sympathetic and parasympathetic systems to each other for health in the body to be maintained, as the heart must do if it is to provide the pulse of life in us. It all made sense to me.

The night after the last CranioSacral training was finished, I returned to my sisters' home to spend the night. After discussing what I had learned, I gave her a hug before going to bed. I told her that I loved her and was surprised at what happened next. For the first time in my life, I *felt* the hug *in* my body. I had never *felt* a hug before; but I didn't know I had never felt a hug before. I broke down in tears—happy tears—from feeling hugged for the first time. I pressed my cheek against her cheek and I felt her skin. I didn't understand how I had never felt this before. It was such a profound moment to actually be in my body feeling love flowing in from my sister. I asked her if I seemed any different to her, and she responded, that I felt more alive to her, and somehow, I felt softer. This caused me to wonder how many people think they love, or think they feel something, but have no way to know that they really don't. I guess you don't know what you don't know until something directs your attention to it, and then for the first time, you know what you didn't know before, and now you do.

***

Earlier in the week, before there were any plans for the funeral, Jake had asked me if I wanted to go to lunch with him when I was finished with my coursework. The best day for him would have been Monday, so I told him I would let him know. I had planned to go to Oregon to visit my dear friend David, but I was feeling torn about wanting to see him, but also, feeling ashamed about having put on so much weight since the last time we had been together.

By Saturday night, pure exhaustion from the intensive coursework seemed to make up my mind for me that I didn't feel strong enough to take the 3-hour trip south, but I was still unsure. By Sunday, I was convinced that I couldn't drive to Portland after the class, and had pretty much decided to cancel the visit with David.

When I called to tell him I wouldn't be coming, David asked me to think about coming on Monday morning after getting a good night's sleep instead of Sunday night. He followed the request with a statement that he really was looking forward to my visit and hoped I'd reconsider.

I noticed I had created for myself an interesting choice, and an important one. After allowing myself to connect with my inner feelings, I made the decision to let go of the past and not meet my former husband for lunch. I decided to drive to Portland to spend a day or two with the friend I had been so afraid would reject me because of my obesity. I had heard the tenderness in his voice when he invited me to come and reminded me that he cared for all parts of me, including the part that was ashamed for her size. His response touched my heart; I said yes. Decisions to let go of something really do mean so much more when there is a choice.

***

Monday evening, after a really fine day together, David, and I were standing in the front entry of his home, as he shared with me the sadness he felt for his dog who had been quite sick. Our arms were around each other's waists as we stood talking, side-by-side. I was telling him how much I cared for him and wished that he didn't have to feel sad over all that was happening in his life. I knew I was unable to help him relieve the pain around the possible loss of his furry friend, and I kissed his cheek. My entire body responded with a feeling I had never before experienced; for the first time in my life my lips felt a kiss. I had never known that I hadn't felt the feeling of a kiss before, not until that moment.

I was so deeply moved by the feeling of closeness that came from standing next to David, feeling arms touching and skin touching. Like with my sister, I truly felt the presence of another human being, something I had never known before. His hand gently rubbed my back as he commented about how important our relationship had been to him and I could feel the truthfulness of his words in his hand. It was as if my back was feeling a human hand on it for the very first time in my life. I could feel the warmth going deep into my muscles and all the way into my heart. I had never let anyone's energy enter me that deeply before. What a gift I received in allowing that moment of closeness!

***

Late that night, I received a message that the funeral for my former mother-in-law would be the next day. Somehow, it felt very important to allow myself to experience this letting go of a person who had been in my life for so many years. After spending less than 24 hours at David's home, I drove back to Seattle the next morning. On the way, I began to feel anxiety about returning to the people who had been my family for half of my life. I had not seen Jake's relatives for 14 years, and I had no idea how they would respond to my return. I assumed that Jake's wife would be there and I couldn't imagine how she would feel about my presence, or for that matter, how I would feel. It became apparent that the speculations were causing my body to go into stress and that felt unacceptable. I decided to let the fearful thoughts go, since a positive reception was as possible as a negative one, and my body calmed down. I figured I would know what to do to protect myself if their reception was cold.

I parked behind the church where I had been baptized as a young adult, where I taught Sunday school and worked with the youth group, and where I had attended many mother-daughter banquets with the woman whose life was to be honored that morning. My heart was beating fast in both excitement and fear. One by one, I saw people who had been my relatives as they approached the church. Only my ex-husband knew I would be there, so they were so surprised to see me. Every one of them embraced me with love as if I was someone who had been gone on a very long journey and was presumed dead but was found to be alive. I felt their love in their embraces. No one seemed to care that my body was much, much larger than it was the last time they had seen me. Some cried and kissed my cheek; some squealed with authentic delight; some touched my face so very softly and no one seemed angry with me for leaving.

An aunt, who had always made it seem as if Jake was her favorite nephew, embraced me as she looked into my eyes and asked me if I was happy. I said, *yes*. I told her that making the decision to leave was one of the hardest things I had ever done in my entire life, but I would have died had I remained. I found out that she left a 50-year marriage a few years before for the same reason, and later married a man she dearly loved. She told me she was glad that we both had chosen to live.

The reception table had photographs of the woman who had been my mother-in-law for 23 years. There, among the other photos, was a picture of Jake and me at 21 years of age on our wedding day. It felt good not to have been erased by the family. What felt so wonderful was that I could feel all of these people's love for me, as Sandy. I had never felt their love for me in that way before because I always believed they accepted me as wife to Jake, which made their love feel conditional. The day of my mother-in-law's funeral, I allowed myself to be received for myself.

Jake's wife saved a seat for me beside her at the reception. She said she wanted to meet me for so long, and hoped we could talk. I never could have imagined how comfortable I would feel in such a situation. She invited me to come to Jake's home, but I declined since I would be returning to Florida the next day, but noticed she identified it as Jake's home, not as theirs. I watched the interaction between the two of them and felt relieved I was not still living out those familiar patterns he and I had played for so long.

I believe it felt so good to have returned home because I had released both the former home and my former image of myself, and I was just Sandy, loving just them. In the loving, I had no wish, no longing to go back to how things used to be. I can't imagine the trip to Seattle without experiencing the funeral. Maybe I kept the promise I made to Jake's mother in the dream that I would not return to make her distressed from having to see her son and me together when we were not together.

Those Seattle days let me see how seldom I had felt myself in my body. It must have been difficult for Jake to experience that something was missing in me without having a clue as to what it was; it must have been a great frustration for him to live with a wife who was not really there. This might account for the subtle passive aggressive behaviors and, at times, not so subtle aggressions that eroded our relationship, but at the time there were no words to explain what was happening.

For the very first time, I discovered how *breath-givingly* beautiful it is to be alive and how the Universe is flowing with an abundance of blissful love that it wants to give freely, but our fear, our doubt, and our disbelief create blocks to receiving it. I blocked love because it was connected to pleasure, which, for me, was connected to pain—so my body became numb and when someone held me or kissed me, all I experienced was the thought of being held or kissed and all the while, unconsciously I was controlled by the fear of closeness. All the years of my life, up to the transformational trip to Seattle, I thought the *thought of closeness* was closeness, but the connection I made with my sister, with David, and my former family, taught me that closeness is something I experience in my body because I accept being in my body. I knew that something important had happened inside me, and when I returned to Florida, I was ready to resume the work on my proposal and dissertation. But I didn't know it would take another two months to fully come to terms with the actual subject of my research question.

Somebody once said—*you can't go home again*—I think what I found out is that you can if you allow yourself to be conscious of the fact that both you and the place that used to be your home have changed, and that change is something that can be very good. I think part of the power of what happened from September 9 to 20, 2000 was that I became far more aware of how much I had really changed and how much I had let go.

I remembered that before I left for my trip to Seattle, I asked why I had needed to make the trip for 11 days and why I scheduled the time as I did. The answer was that this would be a time of letting go, but I had no idea how much letting go was to take place or what it was that letting go would entail. Although I have been receiving inner directives all of my life, I became more consciously aware of them since I made that decision on Christmas Eve of 1986 to leave my husband and create a new life for myself. Most of the time, I follow what Joseph Campbell called "*the thing that is moving me*" without even knowing that I am following it, like I did when I scheduled my trip to Seattle. But, there are times when I make conscious decisions to listen. I remain in awe of the mystery that directs my life...the Sandy under the mask, who seems to know far more than I, what she is doing and where we are going. I am so glad that I have learned to trust her...at least, most of the time.

Chapter Fifteen
THE DARK SIDE

We all have both light and dark within us. This is not a flaw in us or in the universe; darkness allows us the contrast that offers us the opportunity to choose. What causes the dark side to become negative and damaging is the denial of the darkness.

Alanza's prediction about my weight falling off continued to lead me to stories of my past that seemed to be disconnected from what was happening in the session with her and appeared to randomly move from one to the next like highways and byways in my mind that often didn't look like they were going in the right direction. But, in fact, each one was taking me exactly where I was supposed to go.

The path that took me to the funeral shifted and I recalled another event, soon thereafter. During Thanksgiving week of 2000, I had an experience that allowed me to connect with the dark side in a way I had never done before, something that contained a vital puzzle piece that would lead to understanding the mask I had worn my entire life. The experience was so very important, though I had no idea why it would be key to what was unfolding in my life at the time, nor did I know it would be an important key to the story I am telling you, now, when recollections of it came to me in that eternal moment between predictions during the session with Alanza. The experience felt so important at the time it happened, that I wanted to share it with my Oregon friend, David. I explained that the experience caused a great amount of inner searching and struggle and that I'd been unable to articulate it before, but after much effort, the words came to me.

Dear David, Last Monday I had a client, an exotic dancer, who asked me how parents are able to pass on cruel energy to their children. When my client was a small child, she and mother were vacationing with her mother's father, a man mom hated since she, herself, was a child. The three of them were in a fishing boat on a lake near the old man's home, when he clutched his chest and fell to the bottom of the boat. He cried out to his daughter to get his heart medication in his backpack. But my client's mother remained seated and watched while the little girl's grandfather died of a heart attack. The mother refused to get his heart medication and her only words were, "Die, you bastard," which he did after much agony. While all of this was unfolding the little girl was terrified and wanted to get out of the boat, swim to shore and run away, but mother held her child's arm tightly and made her stay in the middle of the horror as she watched her grandpa die. Apparently grandpa had sexually abused both his daughter and granddaughter and mother considered this his payback. The client has been running ever since.

I decided to provide the answer to her question about cruelty by demon-strating energy as I have with others who asked similar questions regarding the transfer of feelings. I asked her to be aware of the flow of energy that was going on between us as we were in rapport. Then I told her that I was going to withdraw my energy and cut off the connection. What this does is allows the client to become aware of the experience of energy flow by feeling its presence and then feeling the stopping of it. This allows them to discern the quality of the energy that flows from others and from themselves to others, to discover intentions of energy, and to observe what is attached to it. This process can work not only with individuals, but with large groups, as well.

If the question they ask is about fear, I attach fearful thoughts to the energy I send; if anger, I attach angry thoughts so they can discern the feelings embedded in the flowing energy, something that is always in relationships but most of the time without any conscious awareness. It is a powerful exercise that came to me a few years earlier when I was working with another client whose mother had been an unavailable martyr. In that case, my mind visualized the withdrawal, and then attached an intention to make the withdrawal felt. The client felt it without my saying a word; she connected what happened in therapy with what her mother had done, and then saw that she had done the same thing to her own children by adopting the family pattern of being an unavailable martyr. After she consciously experienced energy and the withdrawal, the session became a time that held lots of pain, expanded awareness, grieving, and asking for and giving forgiveness.

The idea I hoped to get across is that energy is real, it is powerful and can be felt, even if only subconsciously. When someone withdraws it, even if the other is not conscious of the withdrawal, the body registers it and responds. When cruelty is connected to the withdrawal of energy, that, too, is registered. A child can experience cruelty in a parent and attempt to overcome it by matching it or trying to get bigger than what is coming—or not coming—from the parent. Or, the child can withdraw and attempt to run away but in the running, will carry the cruel energy, usually turning it inside and inflicting the energy on him or herself or on something less powerful. This pattern of cruel energy can turn into self-sabotage or into destructiveness to others on the outside.

After drawing attention to the caring and loving flow of energy between us, I withdrew my connective energy with the client by drawing an energy curtain in front of my internal eyes, so the client could no longer look in. She sat there with a quizzical look on her face. In the past few times I have done this demonstration, I asked the clients what they experienced and we would then talk about energy and how we use it to connect with people, to disconnect from them, or to control them and how other people do that to us.

However, this time I felt something happen that had never happened before. It was as if a gearshift took place automatically within me and for a microsecond the withdrawal of my connective energy moved to a place where I opened to an intense surge of what felt like raging, almost killing energy that flowed out of my eyes and touched the client's eyes. And in the moment that happened, the client tipped her head to the right; a questioning smile came over her face and she said, "Whoa, you're good."

I immediately let go of that shocking inner place and shifted to rapport. I asked her what she felt, and without taking time to construct an answer, she said…"my mother." We spent the rest of the hour working on her energetic response to her mother and how that influenced her life, including the client giving up her own daughter, just like her mother had given my client up when she was small to be raised by grandmother; and generational patterns were lived out again and again. Now my client's daughter, who is living with her grandmother, is pregnant without a husband like mother and grandma, and is too young to take on motherhood responsibilities living out multi generations of a life-pattern.

For the next five days I struggled with what I had felt in my own body during that session. It was not the client's mother's cruelty projected onto me that I was feeling. It was my own dark side, a microsecond experience of what I sensed was a huge arena of dark energy. It felt as if that experience held just a tiny puff of energy that escaped before a crack in the door could be closed again. The energy behind the look that I sent to my client was the energy that my own mother had sent to me…and somehow, I had taken it and it was in me, as well. I no longer wondered if I had children, would I have sent the same cruel energy into my children, and without even a doubt, and as much as I would have preferred to say no, the answer was, yes. Even if I had tried to push it down or cover it over with sweet, caring energy, the dark would be there, and on occasion, I know it would have leaked out.

At first, I was very sad that this energy was in me, and then I went into a depressed state. I could not believe that after all the work I had done for all those years, I had failed to bring light into that particular dark place. The thought of having this dark energy in me made me believe that I might have to come back another ten thousand lifetimes to get to all of this hidden stuff and release it.

The struggle I was experiencing was about my own beliefs in not being good enough that caused me to have failed to do healing right. I felt embarrassed that not so long before I believed that I was nearly completed with my healing process and on my way to some other way of being that would free me from coming back in future lifetimes.

By the day before Thanksgiving of 2000, I was exhausted from the inner struggle with knowing I had a huge dark side that I had never addressed. I had no energy left to deal with facades of my own making or in others. I think I was still too afraid that if I could see that dark side in me, others might be able to see it too, and I was too ashamed...and unable to defend against it. I didn't have the energy to put up walls to hide the darkness. As a result, I turned down three Thanksgiving invitations and decided to spend the day by myself.

A call from Bill, my Atlanta friend, telling me that he would be in Clearwater later on meant that I would be spending Wednesday evening with him and I decided that would be my Thanksgiving. I have almost no shields up with him, so it would not be a struggle. When we get together we talk about all the things we don't get a chance to talk about to other people, and this was no exception.

In the course of our conversation over a Boston Market Turkey dinner, Bill asked me what I think of men. I insisted that all of my life, I have always found it much easier to be friends with men than with women. But when he pressed me about what I think of men when it comes to sexual intimacy, I avoided the question by telling him that I wanted a relationship with a spiritual being, a kind, nurturing, loving soul who respected and honored me for who I am. He would be a being who is experiencing himself as a man who respects and honors himself, as well. In that kind of a relationship, it would be beautiful to express love, to touch, to feel sensual and sexual.

I told Bill I was not interested in the general run of men. He kept pushing for an answer. In exasperation, I finally told him something that I had never said to anyone, not even to myself. I told him I think that most men are hard, slimy, leaking penises looking for a vagina in which to ejaculate. They manipulate women in any way they can to get it...and I wasn't will-ing to be a just any vagina for some man to use and discard. I could feel the seething anger as I spoke these words. I added to this general attack of half of humanity, an attack of the other half. I told Bill that I believe that most women are ungrounded, insecure manipulators even if they are well educated with high earnings, looking for someone to take care of them and make them feel safe. They look at the men as status symbols, and they value the men based on their possessions and positions. Men's cars and suits are seen as indicators of the potential for being husband material. Both sexes see the other as fulfilling their needs, as filling a role in their life-plays, a role that can be awarded to a better actor should the one filling it not perform up to expectations and neither feels safe enough to surrender to the other. Relationships end up being about status, acting, and roles, not about people loving each other.

With all the work I have done, I am painfully aware that what I say about other people is true about myself, which made me feel even more ashamed about the very dark side within me that became exposed.

Bill and I talked about love and surrender, safety and trust, connection and freedom and about choice. He agreed with my comments about our species and then added that for most men, the only time they ever get to surrender is for a brief moment during sex. He suggested that perhaps sex was the only time they could ever feel body and spirit connected, though most might not say it that way.

For the first time it made sense to me that many men desperately seek some-one, anyone to help them feel what they don't know how to feel otherwise. But too often, when a man enters a relationship with a woman as a way to feel more of that surrender, she requires security on the physical, emotional, and perhaps spiritual planes before she provides the space for his surrender. Because she won't surrender to him until she feels safe, he cannot surrender to her and he has lost what he believed was his only hope to feel connected with spirit. She feels hurt that the one who was supposed to protect her and let her feel safe enough to surrender no longer makes her feel safe. So they struggle...and struggle...to make the other perform the role better... Even though I was very sad about what I knew was still in me, I was thankful to Bill for getting me to articulate it, which gave me the chance to begin working with what had come into my consciousness.

On Thanksgiving Day, I decided to make myself a turkey dinner and while the bird was cooking—a surge of grief washed through me. I had purchased all the things I like for the holiday meal. I envisioned myself enjoying the spaciousness of my own place, having candles lighted, incense burning, and music playing. I found safety and comfort, as well as some kind of warm spiritual connection in eating my favorite meal in this pleasant atmosphere of my own creation, a connection I had not learned to make with people. But it struck me that I was so very alone. I had a late evening dinner and went to bed directly afterward.

Two weeks before all this happened, I had made an appointment with a CranioSacral body therapist for the Saturday after Thanksgiving. So when Saturday morning arrived, I drove to her office. She found my body to be extremely congested with little flow, which was not a surprise because I was feeling shut down from my struggle with the darkness inside me. As she worked, she noticed that my right arm and my left leg were extremely congested... almost completely shut down, while my left arm and right leg were much less blocked.

When I took this information inside to let my body understand, it was like a light bulb turned on. My upper body (spiritual chakras or energy centers) and my lower body (physical chakras or energy centers) were split and my right masculine and left feminine sides were split, as well. My heart, the central place where the upper and lower and the left and right come together, was experiencing a major double split, not to mention the walling off of my dark side from my light, and the split between my thinking and my feeling selves. No wonder I had been experiencing heart problems!

My right arm (spiritual masculine) has been terrified to reach out to connect with the spiritual world, to trust Spirit with my life, while my left arm (spiritual feminine) has been much more open to receive spiritual connection. This so completely describes the split in my spiritual experience. My right leg (physical masculine) has been willing to move out and explore the world to travel and to teach, but my left leg (physical feminine) has been terrified to receive the world into me, including men or one special man in the world. I can be in the world when I am in charge, and I can be in a relationship with a man when it is a friendship that does not require physical intimacy. But I do not trust the world or the physical to surrender to it...or to a man who is a part of the world.

The split between the dark and light was so present in all of this. I allowed myself to be in the light, and in spirit, but resisted being in my body, in what felt like the underground of existence—the dark side—because I had labeled it as bad. When I was in the CranioSacral course in Seattle I had that amazing experience of "being in my body" for the first time. I discovered feeling skin on skin, feeling a hug, a touch, and a kiss from within my body and not as a thought about feeling. I opened to experiencing my body, and that seemed so good. But knowing I had a dark side could lead to experiencing darkness from the inside, feeling it not just thinking about it. Really knowing it through visceral experience was something I had always feared.

Intellectually, I understood that we all have a dark side, but I thought the idea was that we needed to bring healing and light into the dark side to make it light. This is probably a reflection of the mind over matter idea, the idea that the mental needs to dominate the physical. This seems to have a built-in assumption that physical matter and the physical world are dark and, therefore, inferior to the intellect and the intellectual world. Because of the years of training from my mother and the church, which taught me to believe the world, the physical, and the body were dark and evil, I believed the dark side had to be healed, not embraced. To have awareness that half of me is still the dark side was so shocking since I had truly believed that in all of the years of working on myself I had healed the majority of my dark side and turned it into light.

Later, I allowed myself to go back to the crack in the door and the feeling I had while working with the client. It was terrifying. I stayed in that energy long enough to be able to separate out the meanings attached to the energy and simply feel the vibration of the dark side energy without trying to interpret its meaning. What I felt was an impulse, a surging of vibrant energy. The energy that I had called "angry" or "raging" was an impulse to change what is not wanted into something that is more wanted...or something that is not satisfying into something that is satisfying...boring into exciting, uncomfortable into comfortable...and on and on. I had always connected dark energy with evil, but when I let myself stay with it without judging it, I saw that my previous interpretation was not true. I discovered that the impulse to change, when carried out with disrespect for the self and of the choice of another, is destructive and with respect for the self and for choice it is constructive.

For most of my life, I have considered sexual energy to be a part of the dark side that I believed was evil even though I had tried to make it acceptable for me if it could be experienced with a highly evolved spiritual man. I am sure I felt that way because my first experience with sexual energy was so violently entangled with violation of my choice to connect and surrender. My mind has been racing with reorganization of meanings, melting of walls, and opening myself to new insights. This has been a most fantastic experience—the dark side is not bad—it is beautiful when used with love. The light side is fantastic and beautiful when used with love—and both light and dark can be used without love and can be damaging. I feel as if there is a deep level transformation happening inside that I am not control-ling—it is just happening—and now and then it is revealing itself to me.

In retrospect, I can now see I put clothing on the dark side and labeled it as unacceptable, ugly, dirty, cruel, wicked, destructive and more, when all it is, is energy that can be used in those ways, but can be used in healthy ways, as well. I am sure I will discover much more about the nuances of the dark side as I open and explore this whole half of me that I have avoided all my life. I think I am in for surprises—and not surprisingly—I feel I am in for surprises. What a gift from the universe by the way of an exotic dancer who saw my dark side but labeled it as her mother. The Universe has a wonderful sense of humor.
Love, Sandy

My dear friend, David, responded:

Sandy, I have always embraced the darkest parts of you that you are most uncomfortable about, sometimes wondering when you would join me. And little Sandy might notice if she looks around that I've been sitting there all along accepting her even while she is looking outside terrified that they might find out or would reject her. I, her helpful dragon, was already there having seen it and fit it into the beautiful picture that is her wholeness.

I always knew that when you accepted that we are a mix of dark and light, which is different from good and bad, that many important valuable and healing things would happen. You have heard me talk about this a lot, but you never liked it too much. It was not the time yet. Someone who has been so hurt in childhood from misused darkness can have great difficulty embracing his or her own dark side without condemning it. Also, abusers use the knowledge of coexisting light and dark against us. "See, if you look inside you will see things just like me there. So you can't really condemn me." That is a manipulation and distortion but rings somewhat true because we are afraid to look at the bigger picture where the Godly is a mix of lightness and darkness. So we live in fear and denial of the dark door, believing it is a flaw to be erased. But if we can embrace the whole of the light, bright and dark, then great things can happen.

Obviously, you are now ready to embrace all of yourself. How nice that you will stop attacking those parts of Sandy that scared you so. They can join the team of healing and love at the highest level. They do have a role with the highest values when included. Their "danger" is when they become discon-nected and denied and not included. "Darkness" is not evil when part of the whole.   Love, David

***

I really didn't understand all of what Oregon David had reflected to me, at that time. It took several more years for his message to become something I could embrace, without fearing it. Probably, most of us fear our dark side and, like I did, try very hard to make ourselves believe that we are basically good, light, and love, or something similar. We justify what we do and resist looking deeper into the multiple layered motivations behind our actions, most of them either out of mind, or unconscious. We want to see ourselves in the best light, which, too often, means seeing the other in the worst light. The value of holding judgments against other people is that when we become more conscious, we can begin to see the places inside us that are being reflected by what we see outside. A statement, *"I can't stand people who are prejudiced"* is a prejudiced statement. This one is so simple to see, but when we begin looking more deeply into any judgment we hold, the search will eventually lead to the place inside us that contains what we judge out there. And, it exists within us because we absorbed a similar judgment about us, usually when we were very young, and vulnerable.

If, as a young child, I experience a significant adult person in my life judge, ridicule, reject, or act afraid of some person based on a characteristic identified with that person, my fear is that if I ever exhibit a similar characteristic, I will be equally treated as the one that person rejected. I grow up trying to prove that I am "not that." As soon as I separate myself from others in fear or with judgment, I have embodied that fear or judgment response. As my consciousness expands, I might learn that such judgment is unacceptable and do all I can to show the opposite position, but until I reenter the original formation of my embodied beliefs, I will be covering up the destructive dark with the light, and the light as a cover up is inauthentic.

If I was rejected for expressing my authentic being in a particular way, I learn to reject that expression in myself by hiding it behind my mask and reject that expression in others. Their behavior reminds me, even if only unconsciously, of being rejected, as well as my own self-rejection, which feels too painful to re-experience. Instead, I reject them as a way to keep myself from feeling the pain. This projection of my hidden unacceptability onto another is a far too common condition in the human experience. The wonder of any judgment we hold or rejection we make is that it reflects back to us what was wounded or shattered in ourselves, and if we have the courage to face it, we can bring the highest truth, acceptance, and healing to what had been hurt when we were so vulnerable, and we can transform our experience, which will change ourselves.

When we live in a world that we experience as containing so much destructive darkness, we need to know that dark destruction comes from us…it couldn't be any other way. If we are willing, one-by-one, to face the pain of what we have hidden behind our masks, we can heal the destructive darkness in each of our worlds and when our numbers reach the critical mass…what our world reflects back to the whole of us will change.

***

At the time of the anger incident with my client that seemed to have awakened a very significant place inside me, I had no idea that I had just begun to discover another enormous arena behind my mask. In the many years of inner work, I uncovered so many buried and hidden parts of myself that had been deeply wounded, but I had not looked at the parts of me that had taken on the beliefs of my abusers. I had projected the dark side outward onto the wicked people and didn't see both the good and bad aspects of the dark in myself. Up to that time I had no idea that the amazing wholeness of who we truly are includes the dark side, so simply expressed by Oregon David.

Chapter Sixteen
DIGGING DOWN INTO THE GARBAGE

Every darkly negative word we hear, every negative thought we think, every painful experience we have is composed of heavily dense vibrations that when taken in and stored inside us acts like rancid garbage that blocks our path and buries our sense of wholeness. We must be willing to dig down into the garbage to find the part of ourselves buried beneath, to bring the highest truth of who we are, which, then, allows us to live from our wholeness in a higher and lighter vibration.

Most of the significant transformative work that happened while I was at Saybrook, working on my Masters and Ph.D. began with dreams that intertwined with coursework as the coursework intertwined with my life, but this particular unfinished piece began as a waking life experience rather than a dream. By mid-February, 2001, I was ready to undertake a final proof of the chapters in my dissertation, and finish writing a summary of my research on obesity and all that came from it, when a client called to arrange a phone session later in the afternoon.

After scheduling the session, I checked messages and found one from a friend telling me she would be stopping by if I was going to be home. However, my apartment was a mess from being neglected while I was so intently completing my dissertation. I scurried around cleaning up the carryout and delivery cartons that had held the only meals I had time to eat because I didn't want to be distracted from my work by cooking. A week's worth of mail and papers, along with a week's worth of kitty-litter sacks that I had been putting in the garbage but not into the outside dumpster were added to everything that had piled up over the days I had been intensely focusing on writing.

Cleaning took longer than I had anticipated, and it was nearly time for the client to call; so I loaded up the garbage in a wheeled basket and rolled it out to the trash chute only to find the chute was clogged by other people's garbage. I didn't have time to unclog it so I could get rid of my garbage, so I left the cart in the alcove by the laundry with an intention of getting back to it after the call. The call took over an hour, and in the meantime my friend left another message telling me that she couldn't come after all; I got back to writing, completely forgetting about the garbage I had left outside.

By evening, I took my dog out for her walk and remembered that I had forgotten to empty the trash, so after the walk, I went to the alcove in front of the laundry room to get the basket filled with garbage bags to take it to the main floor to empty it. When I got there, I noticed that one of the garbage sacks was open and some of the kitty litter had fallen to the floor. Because the chute was still clogged, I took the garbage down to the main floor and threw it in the large Dumpster, and when I turned to go back to the elevator, I saw something posted on the community bulletin board. My name was printed in big bold black letters on a large envelope and under the envelope was a poster-sized paper with words written on it, as well.

Apparently somebody had seen the garbage in the basket on the second floor and returned to the first floor with a nasty note in hand condemning someone for leaving the basket full of garbage and posted it on the community bulletin board. Then that person, or maybe someone else, returned to the basket, dug through my garbage and found a large envelope addressed to me. Then my attacker wrote my name on the envelope and pinned that to the bulletin board above the other larger sign.

Big block letters written on the envelope spelled out my name, **SANDY SMITH** and beneath that envelope was what appeared to be the first note because it didn't identify me as the culprit. It, also, was written with very bold magic-marker ink, which read:

WHOEVER LEFT THEIR TRASH IN THE GROCERY CART ON THE 2ND FLOOR NEXT TO THE LAUNDRY—NEXT TIME, WALK YOUR <u>LAZY ASS DOWN</u> TO THE DUMPSTER. HAVE SOME RESPECT FOR THE REST OF THE RESIDENTS.

And the "Lazy Ass Down" was heavily underlined. A surge of adrenaline rushed through me that felt as if it burned the skin off of my chest, neck, and face. I walked over to the sign and the envelope and removed both of them as I looked over my shoulder to see if anyone was looking—feeling so shamefully humiliated, so totally assaulted. I felt publicly disgraced and so worthless and returned to my apartment in shock. There was something that stung deeply about being identified like that, so degrading about seeing my name connected to such condemning words. I didn't know how to "save face" from being publicly shamed.

I wrote a letter of apology to the residents basically telling them about my forgetting and that it wasn't intentional that I left my garbage out. I posted it where the note had been pinned and returned to the laundry alcove with a broom and dustpan to clean up the scattered litter. I was too filled with shame to notice that the person who condemned me for the garbage, created more garbage by spilling what had been neatly tied up in garbage bags, and did the very thing he or she accused me of doing, something that seems always present in accusations. But, at the time, I didn't know what to do with the shame, and found it difficult to sleep that night. I woke several times feeling sick. The whole next day I didn't want to go out, but I had to walk Jenny. Normally, when I walked my little dog, people would talk with me, or wave when passing by in their cars. But that day all I could hear was my own "mental noise" convincing me that the people were disgusted with me, yet, all the time knowing that it was in my own head. It was amazing how everything changed.

As aware as I was that the incident was really quite an insignificant event in other people's lives, that most of the residents had likely not even seen the sign, and few people would care about it, much less remember it in a day or two, I could not control the feelings of shame and ostracism. I noticed I was watching to see if people were reacting to me differently and was trying to figure out if they were avoiding me or not seeing me. It was an amazing experience to know what was happening was in my own head and, yet, to feel totally unable to control the huge shame I was carrying.

My mind became preoccupied with trying to figure out which person may have written the note, who might know, and who didn't know. When people walked past my apartment, I could hear their footsteps, their talk—and I couldn't concentrate on my writing. The metaphors were jumping out all over the place, and though I could see so many embedded meanings in what happened, I couldn't shake the feelings. I was aware that I had chosen to not get into any inner work with it. I had a couple of opportunities but decided that I would work it through on my own, later.

I put the bold lettered sign on my kitchen counter so I could look at it and desensitize myself to it. Each time I went into the kitchen, I could hear the words "Lazy Ass" shouting at me from the page. I could feel the angry words coming out of the mouth of the writer, and then I could see the writer as a child hearing those same words. So, it is easy to imagine how humiliations get passed on and on again.

The metaphor of having my garbage being made public—something I had feared my whole life—seemed so obvious. I know that as a child I was terrified that people would find out about what was happening in my family, what was happening to me, and what that meant about who I was. All my life I had kept myself isolated, almost petrified that this horrible family filth would be made public and everyone would be disgusted with me because of what was happening behind our front door. I was just touching the tip of the iceberg here—I knew that the shame went so deep. It was hard for me to stay with it.

I held in the tears and pushed away doing anything with this situation for the whole week and I became miserably sick. My lungs filled with fluid; my throat became raw and my sinuses were full and overflowing. There was something all encompassing about this shame. It was a shame I had felt my entire life every time I did anything public. When I turned in a paper to a professor, I wondered if he or she would find out what might have been hidden in it that I didn't see. I believe that everything we create has all that we are in it, and I knew it was possible that the very astute reader would find it—and most of the time, I, myself, was not sure what I was afraid they would find. If they found out, it would be because I had not been careful enough to hide what should never be known, not even by me.

***

All of this became compressed inside as I tried to figure out what to do with the shameful pain that exploded with just the idea of telling what was happening inside me to any of my friends. When I finally recounted the incident to Oregon David in an email message, almost a week after it happened, I still was feeling deeply wounded. My reactions were far more than the current situation deserved, which made it clear that they were about something much more deeply wounding in the past that I had not faced. Feeling what was happening in my body was devastating, and feeling the words as I wrote them to David was crushing. After telling him the whole story, the pain of the present opened to that deeper pain from my childhood, and I added:

Oh my, as I write this, my throat is nearly choking itself off...so tightly closed. Such a horror of being outcast, of knowing that people know...Oh my, oh my...of knowing that my mother knows what my father is doing. So much garbage...so much...so much! There is a little Sandy who feels painfully ashamed that something so ugly might become known and she feels—oh my—she feels it is her fault...that somehow she is complicit. She has to be sure that she leaves no evidence; she needs to hide it all, to cover the garbage.

I am feeling ashamed to write this to you. I am thinking of all the reasons that I should not write this to you. I don't want to—I don't want to take this any further right now but I know there is more work to do with it. This is starting to get into "my garbage" and I think I will try to get a hold on what this is before I take it any further. I want to be sensitive to our friendship since you didn't ask for me to open this up to you.

Shame is a powerful thing. I don't know how to handle this right now... no matter what I do, it feels wrong...erase what I have written, don't send what I have written, send...finish, don't finish. Wow...such powerful control over how to be in all this. The witnessing part of me watches; the thinking part of me is confused at what is happening, and the feeling part of me is so ashamed that she is ashamed, that somehow she is not doing this shame thing right, either. She is screwing up again. Oh my.... I will get through this! Give me a moment. SSS

My dear friend wrote a very loving, supporting message back to me. He reminded me that we all have parts of ourselves that we are sure belong on the bulletin board, and hope don't get seen. But we need to bring them back inside and embrace them. He encouraged me with a reminder that I am getting closer to dark sides of myself, and embracing them into the fold, not just transforming them before they enter. In so doing, I would be healing the deep shame that goes with every house of abuse. He tenderly reminded me that out of that place of "darkness" came the light that is who I am. What he said next was so powerful. But I was in so much pain I couldn't hear his words at that time. He said:

Sandy, If you had dreamed the dream of the garbage and the sign on the wall, you would be more quickly grateful for the guidance it gave you about the little girl's need to deal with the shame and guilt when she allows the helpers to see all that went on there.

I had tried to contain the feelings, but they would not be contained. No matter what I did to distract myself from feeling, my body ached with shameful pain. I wrote again to David:

Tears flowing, heart aching...and broken...Shame, not shame, shame...can I say and still look into eyes and not feel their inability to hear, their not so hidden revulsion of one who is covered in garbage. I remember the very first time I told a group of women. I had been invited to participate in a woman's consciousness group. The subject for the daylong activity was embracing your sexuality. I really wanted to go to the group to embrace my sexuality and it took all I could do to go. I felt somewhat isolated from these women who seemed to know how to talk amongst themselves, something I had avoided all my life—I never was a part of any group of women, or of girls. I never belonged to junior high school or senior high school cliques that girls are famous for, so I never learned to just have girlfriends.

The day started and then a "surprise" guest was introduced, a belly dancer, who performed a dance depicting the unfolding of girl child to adolescent, and into a woman. Likely I wouldn't have gone had I known she would be there. I could not watch her movements; I felt such embarrassment.

Every now and then I lifted my eyes to look at other women who were enjoying the performance and couldn't understand how they could do that. At the conclusion of the dance we were each to talk of our response to what we had seen. When it was my turn, I said I couldn't talk about it. The facilitator wasn't willing to accept my response and asked why I couldn't talk; I could no longer hold back the words.

It was if a dam burst. I told them that to watch a woman so free with her body was to know my lack of freedom. To watch a woman who was express-ing the pleasure of sexual awakening in the body of the adolescent was to realize that mine was not allowed to awaken. My sexuality was ripped out of a deep childhood slumber and was torn awake with pain until I learned how to anesthetize it. There was no excited anticipation of my "first time" because for me it was unexpected and terror filled—and it destroyed my later first time on my wedding night. I was in agony as I spoke. I was angry at what had been stolen. I couldn't stop the words or the tears once they began to come out. And everyone was silent.

Instead of being embraced by these women, the fear I held all my life of what would happen if I spoke became reality when my words had made them uncomfortable. No one spoke for a moment, and then the facilitator asked the remaining women for their responses, as if I had not spoken. At the lunch break three of the dozen or so women acknowledged my courage for what I had said and the rest avoided looking in my direction. In the lunch line they collected in twos and threes and talked with each other about shopping, and recipes, all facing each other, which meant that their backs were turned to whoever was not in their circle...and I was not in any circle. No one sat next to me or talked with me during lunch and I was more alone than before I spoke. I left the workshop, and swore I would never speak publicly about my childhood experience again. I kept that self-promise for a dozen years. And though I acknowledged the general facts, I did not express the feelings again—the ripping, painful feelings, not only of body, but also, of soul.

So I held in the tears and got pneumonia, and the flu, and sinus congestion —all uncried tears that filled me with undrained fluid...and I felt shame that I have this rancid undrained fluid in my body. I have hated to sweat because it smells so horrible. It is so disgusting. It is so toxin-filled, so like the liquid decay that spills out of garbage when it sits in the heat of the sun.

My body fluids feel filled with the smell of men's saliva from 50 years ago, rancid with the smell of their cigarette butts and liquor, with the stink of sloppy salty sweat and unwashed urine made thick with semen spilling on to my body and being absorbed into my skin. It is a stink that I am afraid others will smell no matter how many years have gone by, no matter how many days of three baths a day in burning-hot water that could not remove it...and I feel so ashamed for what is in me.

My thinking self knows that this is not literally in me, but I cannot stand the smell of my own perspiration because on some level, every time my body becomes wet, I smell what I have not been able to wash away. I need to find a way to wash away the filthy slime of rancid garbage. I have worked with so many levels of this...and still it remains. Why...why in the hell would I hold on to this?

Thank you my dear friend. Your loving care in all of this means so very much to me. I love you, Helpful Dragon, the one who has seen me and loves me still. Namaste, Sandy

***

In spite of all the agony that I had been feeling, I finally pulled together everything for the dissertation without including the shameful incident, believing that my work had finished when I discovered that my research question was not about overcoming obesity, but instead was about embodiment, which required significant rewriting of chapters. My work felt finished. I concluded that this last difficult situation was just incidental and not connected to my dissertation. It didn't make sense to keep adding and adding as my life and healing unfolded. I decided it was time to end it and move on.

And then something happened that was totally unexpected. I was ready to do a final editing of my dissertation, something I had been anticipating for over a year, when I felt as if I were going to die. In spite of being so close to manifesting the dream of earning my Ph.D., a dream I had held since I received my BA at 21, I was overwhelmed with a sense of hopelessness that seemed to have no cause. Again, I wrote to Oregon David:

Something happened...can't figure out what...can't seem to find a way out... can't shake the feeling of being in a really dark place. Feels like I am afraid to move. Keeping very still. Sitting right on the edge of terror. Feeling very alone. Only darkness ahead! What have I gotten myself into? This feels really awful. I know it is just a place...maybe because I wrote about that original place of fear some part of me decided to send me there. It feels so very real...so very trapped...so very isolating. But while this is going on... inner screams...inner silencing of the screams...my thoughts are quite clear like my witnessing self is taking notes. I am OK...just in a very strange place. Needed to write this to somebody so I wouldn't be hanging out all alone with this. It is such a really strange place. SSS

The oppressive feeling remained with me, but I decided to move on with my dissertation anyway. Everything was finished except for the final review of the data. I wanted to be sure that I had not left anything of significance out when I looked again at the hike dream that began this whole process. With shocked amazement, I read what I had written regarding the dream I had almost nine months to the day before I was

183

preparing to submit my dissertation. I had completely forgotten that I had written this foretelling statement as an introduction to recording the hike dream in my narration, and all that followed.

A digression within a narrative that has just begun may seem to be confusing and appear to be a departure from the direction that a story is going, and yet, what seems like a diversion may well be the main path that leads to the journey's end. What happened next was such a departure. What began on June 1, 2000 with a dream, and continued through the summer months as the dream played out in my life, turned out to be the main path.

When I wrote that paragraph, I believed the hike dream was a digression from my narrative on overcoming obesity. I had interpreted the dream itself to be about my heart and the difficulties that sent me to the hospital less than a week later. I believed the digression from obesity was what led to all the emotional heart work I did in freeing myself from personal myths that had kept me attached to an ex-husband, and to old beliefs about the loss of beauty, about unspiritual spirituality, about unloving love. I believed it led to discoveries about body functioning and the need for rest and what happens when rest is not possible, all covered in the data in detail. I believed the dream led to my finally understanding that I was the one who resisted being embraced, which then led to allowing myself to be embraced. It did lead to all of these places but it did not stop there, though I had decided that it did.

In the dream from nine months before, the hike led to a pile of garbage that I needed to clean out in order to continue a journey to a delightful playground by an ocean. I did not recognize the garbage as having anything directly to do with me, except to point out my bad eating habits and to foretell a heart attack. Yet, the garbage was something that needed attention. I had dealt with the people in the dream, obvious symbols for parts of myself, but I had not dealt with the symbol of the garbage; so I drew to me an experience with garbage in the physical world. When I decided to leave out the humiliating garbage incident in my waking life experience, and not work with it as a part of the dissertation, a part of me went into terror believing that I was going to move on without ever having found her. Hope of being freed from the shame that this part of me carried for decades seemed to be dashed by my decision to move on without handling what I had experienced.

***

It took nine months of struggle with unresolved issues revealed in the hike dream on the inner path, woven together with the struggle with the focus and question of my dissertation to prepare me to face the shame from which I had dissociated when I was a child. It took the horrible waking-state incident with its shaming sign attaching my name to garbage, to lead me to the child who hid in the inner garbage for nearly five decades because she believed she was garbage. With my decision to move on, without working with the garbage, that part of me believed I was abandoning her forever. She was devastated. She had been there all this time wondering if anyone would ever believe that she was worth it for someone to dig down into all that repulsive filth to find her. She believed my answer was, "No."

When I saw the introduction to the dream saying that a digression may be the main path that leads to the end, I realized that the garbage incident in real life was the same place where the hike dream had led me months before. I knew I had to go back to find the child. I had to dig through the garbage of shame, and tell her that I was not ashamed of her. I had to tell her that I knew it was she who fell into the deepest dark place when she believed I would complete the dissertation without finding her. For the first time I finally got it. The over-the-top pain I feel in some current incident is the pain that a part of me, who is stuck in some former time, trapped in an unresolved incident, is feeling all the time, as if that past event is her eternal present. And...I truly believe this is the same for all of us.

I went back, and I found her. I dug down into the garbage and brought her out of the darkness and into my arms. She shared with me what she had been buried in for all those years and I *knew* that what happened to her, had happened to me.

When the incident occurred that caused me to separate this child-part from myself, I was about six years old. An abuser was drunk and physically filthy. Before the rape actually began, I had already dissociated from the experience as I had learned to do from earlier incidents. But when his cold sweat dripped on me, the splashing shock on my skin brought my awareness back into my body and into the experience. With each drop, I became aware of what was happening in interrupted flashes. Each snapshot event was experienced as a whole, globally sensed, but disconnected event. The vile smells, the feel of body fluids, the sight of the raping man's unshaven face, the excruciating pain, the sounds, the terror, and the feel of the cold splash that vibrated throughout my entire body were all one sensation.

Each whole, interlaced single event was experienced as being "me" because I felt it on me and experienced it in me. I was the smell of filth. I was the repulsive being; I was the garbage, and I had to cover it up so no one would know, not even myself. I lived in terror that someone would find out that at my very core, I was rancid stinking garbage, but my unaware self had no idea what I was so afraid of and terrified that someone might find out. When the person from my apartment building attached my name to garbage and posted it for all to see, it felt as if what I had been hiding from myself for 50 years finally became known. The sign was only the catalyst to connect the inner fears with conscious awareness.

I embraced the child; I cried, she cried, we cried. I held her in my arms. I *felt* her in my arms; I told her I finally got it, that it was her feelings I felt when I went into the depression just a few days before—and I understood how devastatingly frightened she was that I was about to leave her in the garbage, by completing my dissertation without having found her. I cried again with agony and with ecstasy, and I felt her cry for finally being recognized. She finally knew I would never leave her. After all of my training in alchemical hypnosis entwined with dynamic psychotherapy, which I used with literally hundreds of clients over the years for their healing, for the first time, I finally *felt* the healing of this painful shame in myself! In my work with others, I have found that many people who feel so very ashamed of them selves trace the shame to feeling painfully rejected by a parent during the changing of a diaper, and calling the child stinky, while sending out an energy vibration of great disgust for the child because of what he or she produced in that diaper. It really doesn't matter what the source of the rejection is; what matters is that any rejection is crushing to the tender core of the child.

***

What I had understood in my head regarding the healing path had finally penetrated into body knowledge and what I had not known in my *feeling-knowing* before, I had come to know. It was one of the most profound experiences of my life. This dissociated child-self was the reason I needed to write the dissertation. She was the missing piece. I concluded my dissertation in the early months of 2001 with this paragraph.

As this chapter comes to a close, another journey begins—the journey on the other side of the wall, along the path that has just opened into my future, wherever that may lead. I have much to learn about the little girl who lived in the garbage and joins me now on that journey. I suspect she may be the one who was responsible for so many of those behaviors that seemed to be coming from "some unknown part of me." I have no idea what will come from this, but I suspect it will be an interesting trip. We both have discovered that we are so, so worth all that it took for us to find each other, and that neither of us need be ashamed.

Hand in hand a fat lady walks with a little girl along a path formed by the very steps they take, singing and dancing as they share the experience of their new life together, moving into the distant sunset toward an unknown future.

***

It seemed as if years had come and gone since Alanza made the prediction about my weight melting away without my having to *do* anything, though only a moment in three-dimensional time had passed. I returned from a long journey that moved through the years of struggle with weight beginning when I was 19 and into my years in graduate school that took me along a path into the darkest and most hidden places within all the stories related to that journey. In a microsecond that took years to experience and 13 chapters to tell, my awareness returned to Manitou Springs in Colorado with Esther and the tattooed lady, who didn't seem to notice that I had been gone so long.

About this point in her reading, a puzzled look seemed to come across Alanza's face as if she was seeing something Esther and I could not see. She asked me that significant question, *"What does the number 3 mean?"* And when it didn't seem to match anything in my awareness, not my birthday, my address, no 3's in my age or the year of my birth, that puzzled look came back on her face. She told me that she saw a large 3 in front of me, but she couldn't see what it was trying to tell her…and I wasn't able to help her with an answer; so she continued the reading.

It wasn't until after the psychic's reading that I started to become aware of all sorts of 3s that were in my life. I am the third child of five children, of a mother who was a third child of five, and my mother's mother was a third child of five. My father was the eldest of three children and his father was eldest of three. My telephone number had four 3s in it and all three of my addresses, actually, did have 3's in them: my residence in Florida, my mountain retreat address in Colorado, and my PO box, in Florida. But it was clear to me that those were not related to the meaning of 3 that Alanza had seen. Instead, as I thought about 3, I knew it was communicating something much more important, though I can't tell you how I knew it, something to do with my future self that was connected to my past and present self, and to my way of looking at the world that is filled with 3s. And I knew this future self that was somehow connected to 3 would be a prominent part of my future writing.

Chapter Seventeen
NANKING AND AUSCHWITZ

Before we can live in the present with all of who we are, it may be necessary to return to the past to reconnect with parts of ourselves that we left behind. But sometimes those parts of us exist in different lifetimes…and in those cases, we must be willing to face whatever it was that kept a part of us from moving beyond that life into this one, and also, we must be willing to surrender our need to believe that this is the only reality that exists or the only lifetime we have lived.

A concept that is profoundly important to my perspective—formed from years of doing inner-work, both with myself and with many clients—is that the patterns that have weaved our lives are not limited to this lifetime alone, though events in this life act as a catalyst that connect to the past. Just as an event and our experience of it in adult life can find its origin in childhood, when we are willing to dig deeper, we can find roots that go into past lives.

As I was writing the previous chapter, my personal life experience in this lifetime drew me into remembering journeys I had taken into two past lives that allowed transformation of the energies in my life related to particularly dark and painful events in human history. The first had to do with the Japanese invasion of Nanking, China in 1937, and the second had to do with the Nazis in 1943. In both lifetimes, the lives were very short lived. In the course of 10 years, I lived three lives as little girls in three places of horror. In the first, I was a Chinese girl who lived just four short years in Nanking, and two years after that death, I was born into a Jewish family during Hitler's Third Reich. Again, I died when I was four years old. Just a year after the lifetime ended in

Auschwitz, I was born in Alaska to parents who participated in atrocities that would touch these past life memories for me, very early in this lifetime.

***

All through my life I had a strong interest in China. Although it is apparent that some of my interest in the orient came from my mother who wanted to go to China when she completed her nurses training in 1939 but instead went to Alaska where she met and married my father, my interest seemed to have come from some place inside me that was much deeper. I read books by Lin Yu Tang and Pearl S. Buck while still in Junior high school and when assignments in social studies courses allowed personal choice, I most commonly wrote papers related to China. I loved traditional Chinese clothing styles, and when I was able to buy my own cloths I often selected yellow and black color combinations or red with gold accents. My favorite dresses had high neck collars, and side buttons that later I was to discover were common in traditional Chinese culture.

When I was four years old, I began having a most powerful nightmare that invaded my sleep more times than I can count; the dream was exactly the same throughout my childhood and even into my adult years. In the dream, I was a child, alone in a large empty house that seemed to be my house though my child self in this lifetime didn't recognize it. Somehow I had come home and found everyone and everything gone. I stood looking out a front window and watched a double line of soldiers march up the road toward my house. A sense of terror filled me. I ran into a closet and climbed up slats to the upper shelf and lay quietly in heart-pounding fear. I heard the front door open and the sound of soldiers' boots as they struck the wooden floor echoed through the house...the footstep sounds entered the room where I was in hiding. From my hiding place in the closet, I could see out of a small crack because I had not been completely closed the door in my rush to find safety. I was shaking and trying to hold my breath to not draw attention to myself. I watched as the tops of heads came into my view. One of the men walked over to the window where I had been looking a short time before, while another man paced and then walked over to the closet and more completely opened the door. I could see the top of his tan cap as he looked to one side and then the other. I was fully focused on the top of his hat. Then, his head tipped upward and his black eyes looked directly into mine, and I went into total shock. It was that exact moment of his eyes penetrating deeply into mine that I would always wake in terror, and this ending of the nightmare was the same every time.

When I was a child, and even later in my teen and adult years when the same dream recurred, I had no idea what the dream meant; but, I remembered every second of the dream my entire life...I could draw the uniforms of the soldiers, the bayoneted guns they carried, the shape of the caps both from a distance and from the top down. I saw the leggings that went up to their knees and the boots. The dream images have remained so clear. One afternoon in the mid 1980s shortly after I began therapy to integrate my splintered self, I was watching a World War II documentary when the reporter began talking about the Japanese invasion of Nanking in 1937. Atrocities committed against the Chinese were captured on film by the Japanese invaders, and the footage was being shown during the program. When the film showed a mass grave and Japanese soldiers shooting Chinese and throwing them into the long trough, a cry...a profoundly deep howl-cry...erupted from the center of me as I pressed the side of my face against the television screen holding the sides of the TV in my hands. Mournful sobbing continued to flow out of me as I watched the horror unfolding on the screen of events so long, long ago. In a very short period of time, hundreds of thousands of Nanking citizens were murdered by the invading Japanese army.

Although the documentary was in black and white footage, I saw everything in color. The colors of my dream were superimposed over the screen. A few days later, I went to the public library to search for World War II books that might show Japanese uniforms and eventually I found what I was looking for. The uniforms worn by the men in my dream matched perfectly to the uniforms pictured in the book. The colors were exactly as I had dreamed them. The caps, the boots, even the leggings...exactly the same.

When I discovered that what I had dreamed when I was a little child was connected to something very real in history, I decided I needed to go back into the dream and allow it to continue so that I could know why this dream came to me when I was a small child. In this now lucid dream, I saw the soldier, whose head tipped back and looked directly into my eyes, pull me down from the shelf. He and several other soldiers raped me and then one drug me out of the house by the hair and dragged me down to an open pit. I was thrown in while still barely alive and landed on top of the dead bodies of fellow Chinese. Others were thrown in on top of me. And then the dirt came. I remember screaming and then only silence. It is my belief that my dreamtime recollection of the incident of my past life in China just seven years before my birth in Alaska was stimulated by a horrible punishment inflicted on me when I was four by my father for telling "a lie" to my mother when I told her that it was my daddy who hurt me "down there." My father tied my hands and feet, put me in a box, and put the box in the ground, and then buried the box. But obviously in this life, I survived the burial, and I hadn't lied.

This memory from the past life in China, just as the memory in this life of being buried in the box, required many therapy sessions and much journal writing to overcome the trauma. But the deepest healing took place in China during the time I lived there in the early 1990s. In the summer of 1991, Chinese David and I traveled from Baoji by train to Urumqi, in Xinjian Province, a city in the far West that had been carved out of the Gobi desert after Mao took control of China. And after a short stay there we went by bus to Kashi on the far western border. Most of our travels were in places not on the tourist routs and we stayed in hotels that would not have met even the 1-star rating scale in the US, but the trade-off was that we had the opportunity to touch China in its heart.

We arrived in a small Western city at the time of the grape festival and there was only one hotel left in the entire city that still had beds available for us. David was given a room with several other Chinese men, and I was given a room with three Japanese. When I walked into my room, I was quite surprised—as were they—and I apologized for the apparent mistake. I returned to the front desk and explained that they had put me in a room with three men, and asked for a room with women.

The clerk explained that this was the only available bed and if I did not want it, I could try to find space at another hotel. There were empty beds in Chinese women's rooms, but it was illegal for foreigners to be assigned rooms with Chinese. So, I returned to the room I was given, and asked if any of the men spoke English. One young man, quite tall and very thin, said he did, and I explained the situation. He translated the information to his friends, and we agreed that we would not dress or undress in the room, but would do that in the lavatory down the hall.

The young English speaking Japanese man and I began talking about our experiences in China, and he mentioned that he had begun his travels in Nanjing—the post revolution name for Nanking—since Japanese are particularly hated there. He became very quiet, and then told me, with tears in his eyes, that he believed Japanese must never forget what their fathers and grandfathers did to the Chinese during World War II. He said he had to go there to understand for himself the impact his ancestors had on China. And he added that he, and all Japanese, must carry the shame.

I sat quietly with him as he completed his story and then his head dropped in silent humiliation. I placed my hand on his shoulder, and told him about my past life experience in Nanking. I explained to him my belief that if we search history enough, we can likely find that every nation, every race, every group, at one time or another in their pasts committed some atrocity against another group of people…and that my belief is that we are moving into a time when we can seek forgiveness for our ancestors by forgiving them, forgiving us, and learning to never do what they did. His dark brown eyes began to mist over as he put his arms around me and asked forgiveness for what his ancestors did to the little child in that life. I told him that I forgave his ancestors and explained that through him, their souls could learn to be in the world in a much different way. Because he carries their genes and his learning transforms his DNA, theirs can be transformed as well, no matter where they may be in the Universe because they are genetically connected. This kind of DNA level transformation in him has the ability to send the transformation to all those who share any form of connection, through all time. Tears spilled from his eyes, as he understood the profound significance of what he had just done. We both cried and our hearts became forever connected.

I truly believe it was no accident that the only hotel room in the entire city that was available to me, was with three Japanese men who had come to China to remember what had happened in Nanking. I believe that the asking and giving forgiveness that this young man and I experienced together in a hotel room in the middle of the Gobi Desert has the power to transform all who were in any way genetically, or soulfully related to him and to me, and all that are in any way connected to them, too. The decades old hatred between the Chinese and Japanese can turn to heart connection, just as what was experienced between the young Japanese man and me.

***

Less than two years after my death in Nanking, I was born into a Jewish family in Hitler's Nazi empire. The memory of this lifetime came back to me shortly after meeting the man on the bus in Washington, DC. Following our deep conversation about my life going through unparalleled changes, and his strange departure, I went to the Holocaust Museum in D.C. only to become sick when I saw the photo of the glasses of victims of Auschwitz.

After having a near breakdown over seeing the photo, I knew I needed to do work with the feelings that left me in such pain. Just asking to be taken to the source of the feelings, led me to my life that ended in this most horrendous World War II concentration camp in 1943.

I was very young, likely about four years old when my family had gone into hiding in an attic of an old couple. It was a very dark and dingy space with almost no furniture. There was an old desk with dusty files and papers stacked up, likely the place where the family put old records that didn't need to be in the living space below. We were completely isolated from the outside world; there was not even a window to let in light. The couple must have gone away, and we had run out of food. My older brother offered to slip out to see if he could find us anything to eat, but my parents were afraid that he would be noticed and taken away by German soldiers. They decided to send me out to find food, figuring that no one would notice a little girl. I carefully made my way down the narrow stairs and into the nearly empty and very cold house. It looked as if the couple might have used their furniture as firewood because sawdust and wood splinters were strewn about, left as evidence of what used to be there.

I followed my father's instructions very carefully. I crawled over to the front window and looked out on the street to be sure there were no soldiers anywhere and then I opened the front door and stepped out into the unknown. I quickly walked down the steps to the sidewalk and continued walking for several blocks looking for anything that I might be able to bring back to my family when a nice man called out to me and asked me if I was lost. I told him that I was looking for food and asked if he could help me. He took me into a store and bought a bag of groceries and offered to help carry the food home. I was so very glad that I had found someone kind to talk to and we walked back to the house, back into the front door and to the closet where the narrow stairs went up into the attic.

The kind man left and I carried the bag up to my family, but instead of being happy for what I brought them, they seemed upset. They asked me lots of questions and I told them what had happened. My mother was frightened and thought we should leave immediately, but my father thought we should wait until dark. Before they could decide what to do, there was the sound of the sirens that got louder and louder and then there were sounds of boots on the wooden floor...the door crashed in and soldiers with guns came running up the stairs and took us away. But before they made us get into a truck, I saw the kind man who had helped me carry the bag of food. I looked into his eyes and my eyes asked him why he told on us. I wanted to see in his eyes that he was very sorry, but it was too late. He would not look at me any more. I knew I had done wrong, that what I had done had brought terrible things to my family and there wasn't anything I could do about it. It was all my fault.

I didn't see my parents or my brother after the truck ride. The memories from this life that filled my awareness came with a sense of great confusion and a felt sense of many who seemed really afraid. I remember being taken to a large room and strapped down on something and my body memories include experiencing electric shocks that reverberated through my body so powerfully that it felt as if I had been split into a million pieces. It was hard to follow any thought stream but I remember being told to take my glasses off and put them on a pile, along with glasses from lots of other people, and to remove my cloths.

Photo from www.shamash.org/holocaust/photos auschw01.jpg Vol I part 2, Picture #8271. Retrieved 9-18-07. Photo of Prisoner eyeglasses at Auschwitz # 14877 (1943) is reprinted by permission of the United States Holocaust Memorial Museum.

I have had body memories of being naked and being herded into the showers with many other women and children, and though I lost consciousness, but not before I watched others collapsing all around me, I know I didn't die, because I, also, remember being dragged from the room of horror into another place…an even more horrible place… where I was thrown into a fire while I was still alive…and I finally lost my life in the hissing of the flames.

And about a year later, in 1944, I came back into the life I have been living since then. I was born with a right eye that was weak, that rolled over into a cross-eyed position when I was tired, stressed, or frightened, and during those times, I lost sight in that eye. Just after I began school, my parents took me to the eye doctor who ordered glasses for me. When they arrived, they were wire rimmed with round, thick lenses, just like the ones that were in the pile in my last life. And from the very beginning, I hated wearing those glasses; they gave me terrible headaches when I wore them.

***

It wasn't until I completed writing *The Mask,* and did an edit of this volume that I discovered something totally unexpected. Three years after I met the man on the bus who told me the contract with my husband was complete and I would experience a very different life—one I could not even imagine—I had that dream about the reconstruction of our business office, where I realized that there was no place for me, and not long after that I left my husband. When I re-read the dream, I realized that the image of the unfinished stairs and the attic room Jake indicated as being my office was a duplicate of the attic space in that most recent past life in Nazi Germany where my family hid until we ran out of food. In both spaces there was not even a chair, no phone, no communication, no windows; both were dimly lighted spaces without a carpet, without any comfort at all.

In my waking life, near the end of our marriage, I tried desperately to communicate with my husband that our lives were headed toward ruin, but he didn't know how to listen to me…in the dream, he was so involved in his plans that he didn't pay attention to what I was saying. And in that past life, I have a strong sense that Jake was the German soldier who I believed offered to help me in my time of need, as he did in this life when he helped me with my physics problem and then with the blue blanket, and then in the German life, he turned on me, but wouldn't look at me, I believe to avoid letting himself know what he had done to me, something he repeated in this life and in the experience presented to me in my dream. He must have died shortly after that event, as did I, to be born into this one not long afterward. In this life, he was just 20 days older than me.

In the German lifetime that ended in 1943, before the showers, I was put through the horror of electric shock testing and then I was sent to the showers to be exterminated, but some kind of failure in the system prevented me from dying. I have the felt sense that someone fell on top of me and somehow that prevented the gas from killing me, though I was nearly asphyxiated. Still alive but unconscious when I was yanked out of the shower and loaded on a cart for disposal, I revived from the cold night air, as I was being taken, with the dead bodies of the others, to the dark place that housed the oven at Auschwitz. The terror that I felt in the reconstruction dream just as I stepped out of the door and into the blackness was the same terror I felt as I entered that very dark place and then was thrown into the fire.

Not until I did an Internet search to see if I could find the photo of the glasses online, did I discover the Jewish Network web site that, along with the photo, had a description of what was done to many children in Auschwitz when there was no room for them. Many were thrown directly into the furnaces to be burned alive. I was thrown into the flames with horror-stricken children who had not been in the showers and we died together in the fiery silence of our screams. When I read the article about people being burned alive, I was sickened, not just because it was an unbelievably horrible thing to do to human beings, but also, because I had experienced it in that past life and carried the memory in my soul's DNA. And, I believe it was that memory that caused me to become violently ill after I saw the photo in the Holocaust

Museum in Washington, DC in the mid 1980s, though at the time I had no conscious idea why.

***

There is such insanity in this whole belief system that so many of us have carried for eons of time, for myriad lifetimes as souls, that what we do to others will be done to us…and what others do to us, we will do back to them…and out of that belief, we have created much of the history of mankind. Without awareness of the connections when I first traveled to these lifetimes, and more recently while writing *The Mask*, I realized that these two lives that ended before I turned five were connected to past lives in which I had concluded that it was not safe to be a child; certainly these three lives verified that belief.

And in a horribly ironic way, the life that ended in Auschwitz was connected to the life I lived as the drunken man, who cared more about his own gratification than its effect on the woman he loved. That man who possessed my developing soul so very long ago, lived out the rest of his life—and many lifetimes to follow—trying to make up for what he had done, and the woman from that time tried lifetime after lifetime to get even for what I had done. The two of us went about creating our personal universes that were intolerably ugly.

That woman from so long ago held beliefs about herself that led to her becoming involved with someone as thoughtless as I was in that life; after all she was a wench, and at that time in human history, when a man possessed a wench, and treated her like his captive—someone he could do anything to because she belonged to him—she had the security of a place in the community, even though the community believed that wenches deserved to be treated with degrading disrespect. Over myriad lifetimes, Jake and I played out the roles of selfish man and wench, captive and captor, owner and slave, brought about by the lifetime that ended for her in a fiery death. And for me, I accepted being punished, lifetime after lifetime, because I believed that what I had done had to be made right. In a way, we both contracted to make right that terrible wrong.

What neither of us understood back then or in all the entangled life-times that followed was that both the wench and the drunkard created that life out of the beliefs each held about themselves…and both created the fiery death for reasons only our soul's know, and both created all the scripts for all the dramas we played out, each lifetime. We put on different age-appropriate wardrobes for each life, and essentially acted out the same storyline.

Even small details were repeated. In the life just before this one, I was taken out of the Nazi showers in a gas-induced stupor and discarded and soon that life ended. In this life, my father spun me around on a merry-go-round until I got dizzy and then he viciously raped me, which made me believe that the horror would never stop, and I decided to put myself to sleep by breathing in gas fumes, and in both lives, I survived the gas. In the life in Japan, I was buried alive after a horrible rape at age 4, and in this life, I was, also, buried alive at age 4 after that first horrible rape in the forest. When Jake took me out of the shower after spinning me around, making me disoriented and dizzy, he dropped me on the floor…and when he did that, a part of me knew that our relationship had ended, but what I didn't know was that it had ended before it had begun in this life.

The look that was on Jake's face was more of a possessed creature than my husband. I believe the look was the same one that was on the face of the "wench" so long ago when she realized that my thoughtlessness as the drunkard in that lifetime had cost her, her life. She had incarnated in many forms, and in this life, she was Jake; her hatred raced through the centuries to possess my husband. From this perspective, the Biblical reference saying that there is nothing new under the sun is not just a statement of eternal truth, but is a description of this particular way of being that will continue until we choose to wake up to discover that we have been reading lines in a long-running play and we decide to stop.

The problem with these long running plays is that when two people, two groups, two nations interact with this concept of getting even or making right something that was wrong, the one that is harmed wants to inflict more damage than was done to make sure the other really gets it and never again does whatever that offense was. And then the one being punished feels that the other needs to pay for hurting beyond the original suffering. This belief guarantees an eternity of payback, conflict, and drama that assures the continuation of the long-running theatrical performance.

Humanity can stop this insanity in two ways. The first way is that it can continue this pattern that keeps upping-the-ante until the payback is something so big that it destroys both sides, which would end the insanity with death of us all. *Or,* we can choose another way. We can stop this insanity by owning our responsibility for creating the drama that may have been going on for millennia, and ending the contract that can only lead to destruction. This is true for us, both individually and collectively; it requires willingness for us to become conscious of our responsibility for the drama and to become aware of where that contract is leading us.

We can take our focus off getting even, off of grasping or feeling guilt, shame, and anger, or seeking the destruction of the other, which really means destruction of ourselves because we are all connected, whether we choose to believe it or not. We can choose to focus on forgiveness of ourselves for being unconscious and playing such a winless game, as well as forgiveness of the other for being as unconscious as we have been in playing the game. Just imagine the world we can create as more and more of us take responsibility for healing our wounds by repairing the damages done from this and past lives that have affected how we live, within this life. And imagine how we would live if we allowed our healing to change the meaning of our collective history!

When I finally understand that I draw to me the energies that reflect what is in me, and when what is in me becomes conscious of being connected to all that exists, I experience being at peace, in harmony, and balanced. I know that I am safe in my world, no matter what might be happening in other people's worlds. And I know this because I am connected to all that is. When I transform, I create a wave that flows through the universe like a stone that is tossed in the water creates waves that touch everything in existence. Even if my fellow humans choose destruction, I am eternal and cannot be destroyed…so I am eternally safe. I lived two very short lives in war torn countries and among the beliefs that followed me into this present life was one that children are not safe. I returned to another place in which children were not safe…on some level, I believe I chose it to finally change that belief.

***

The collective result of the inhuman treatment that happened to me in China, at the hands of the Nazis, and in my childhood in Alaska brought me into a life where I finally lived into adulthood and decided to seek healing. And as I faced the pain of the past and brought healing to this and to past life experiences, I have been able to experience an ever-increasing awareness in my mind-body, my heart and soul, that I am safe. As I let go of life-long patterns that tried to keep me safe by being separate, including the pattern that used a fat body to maintain distance, I experience more and more moments of true peace…and that can bring Alanza's prediction into reality…in its own time. So, maybe another answer to Alanza's question about the meaning of three could have included these three lifetimes that came together to teach me what my soul needed to know.

***

Because I had not even thought about all this confluence of lifetimes or about the many "3s" that touched my life during the session, and she couldn't seem to see what 3 might mean, the psychic continued the reading and almost in passing, Alanza talked about my health. She reminded me to be thoughtful about blood pressure, maybe cholesterol, and diabetes. I knew that in spite of my weight, I have never had a cholesterol problem, and my blood pressure was consistently 120 over 80, with only very few slight variations over the years. But I told her that I would pay attention to any messages I might receive and be thoughtful of my health.

Near the end of the session, Alanza said she saw journals around me, lots of writing, and asked if I was a writer. I corroborated her vision, and said I had been writing and journaling for at least 20 years. With almost a gasp she exclaimed, *"Three! You are going to write 3 books, and somehow there is going to be a screenplay involved."* With great emphasis she exclaimed, *"This is the big chunk of money I have been seeing coming to you all during the reading, but I just couldn't see where it was coming from."*

A look of calm came over her face, as if she had just solved a very difficult and disturbing puzzle. I told her that I had believed what she had said about the books and a film based on the books, because I had know it was true long before—for a very long time, actually—but I just had no idea how such a thing would come about. With all the confidence that a psychic can have, she assured me that all of this *would* be happening for me. I would be coming into wealth; I was going to have the man of my dreams in my life and the excess weight that I have carried for most of my adult life would melt away. I would be living in a beautiful home overlooking the water…and…I would write a trilogy that would become a screenplay; and she assured me that I would be very, very happy.

It would have been very easy to dismiss the words of this tattooed lady as a creatively in-tuned charlatan who had discovered how to read people's responses and tell them what they wanted to hear…but I knew something important was happening that I could not dismiss and Alanza, the nurturing earth-mother, was simply reflecting back to me what I had known for a very long time.

Chapter Eighteen
BEFORE ALANZA...ESTHER

If you look back through your life, you might notice how not only the momentous circumstances, but also, little, almost insignificant events opened pathways that took you in directions you could never have imagined for yourself. Life is a series of these amazing events and the meaning you attach to them determines whether you live the path you walk from a place of power or a place of defeat.

As we left Alanza's storefront in Manitou Springs, I knew that the reading was a very important piece of my experience since leaving Florida in the late summer of 2006. I knew what the psychic had said was true, and felt a little embarrassed at being so confident about everything. I was amazed to think about how close I had come to not having this integral piece of the puzzle, when I resisted going on the vacation with Esther, and I can't imagine what my life would be like had I not gotten the messages the tattooed lady gave me. The background to this near miss goes back again to another side path that is important to my connection with Esther, and the rest of the story.

***

After divorcing Jake in 1989 and having lived in the People's Republic of China for nearly two years, I returned to the US in late 1991. My intention was to reconnect with my former husband and find out if the internal transformations I had experienced during the incredible time spent in the middle of the Middle Kingdom had allowed me to become strong enough to make a new relationship with him work.

Jake had been especially kind in the last weeks of my time in China by helping me out of a very difficult situation that erupted just as I was preparing to return to America. During my time in China teaching English in a college in Baoji, a town of 1.5 million people, that I often described as being 200 years West of Beijing, I was paid in *renminbi*, which translates as the People's Money. At the time, this money could not be converted to American dollars outside of China, so my translator, guide, and friend, David, arranged for a local bank to change the money I had saved into US currency. I did keep out a few hundred renminbi to pay for expenses I would incur before my departure.

I carefully placed the nearly $1000 in a beautiful embroidered money purse, and put it in the bottom of my handbag, and soon thereafter, I took a short trip to Xian, a few hours train ride from Baoji, for last minute arrangements before flying to Beijing. I decided to get my hair washed, cut, and styled in the capital city of Shaanxi Province the day before my departure and found a shop very near my hotel. One of the attendants could speak English, so I explained to her what I would like done and she led me to a the station of a lovely young woman who seemed to understand what I requested.

She took my jacket and purse and hung them up on a hook, and then walked me to another room to get my hair washed. Instead of leaning back into the basin, she positioned me in such a way that I was leaning into the basin—face first—as the young woman poured water through my hair. While she was shampooing, I saw in my mind an image of another young woman removing my handbag from the hook and taking my embroidered money purse. I didn't know what to do with the image, and decided it was fear talking to me...I didn't want to insult my hosts with suspicion, so I did nothing.

After a very thorough shampoo, the young lady led me back to the station, and as she performed her art on my hair, I completely forgot about the disturbing image I had a few minutes before. I paid her from the *renminbi* in my pocket and headed back to my hotel. I was exhausted from the day and called for a masseuse to work out the kinks in my neck and back. I nearly always pay for such services before the session instead of after, but when I reached in my handbag to get the American dollars to pay her, I discovered that not only was my money purse gone, but so, too, were my airline tickets. Of course, in that moment, I remembered the vision I had while my hair was being washed. Everything I needed to get back to the states was gone.

In near panic, I called my ex-husband, telling him what happened and he offered to buy my airline tickets back home and cover my expenses with his credit card. He was genuinely kind and his concern for my wellbeing was palpable. He, also, agreed to purchase tickets for China David, to accompany me to the US, but that is another story for another time. Perhaps, like me, Jake had changed during the time I was gone. A number of other unrelated obstacles occurred, and I ended up not leaving China until September 13, 1991, which was nearly two months later than I had originally planned. Between Hawaii and the mainland, somewhere over the Pacific Ocean, I made the decision that if he wanted to, I would be willing to reconnect with Jake, to see if we would be able to make a marriage work. Though the flight was 25 hours from Beijing to Seattle, the arrival was the same day as the departure because we crossed the International Date Line.

Jake picked David and me up at the airport on Friday the 13th of September and welcomed me home with a hug, but I sensed something had changed. Without really knowing why, I asked him if he was married. He responded with a simple, "No." But I didn't feel that I had gotten a complete answer, so I asked him if he was going to get married. He paused for a moment, and said, "Yes." He told me that he was going to Las Vegas the next weekend and would be getting married there.

Part of me was in shock…but part of me must have known it, though I can't explain how I knew. My former husband drove me to his office in South Seattle, and I used his phone to call the president of a Florida college to tell him David had arrived and was ready to continue his trip to Florida for a teacher exchange program. The president had offered both of us positions in his school when I returned to the states, but I was not intending to take it because of my decision to see if it might be possible to reestablish my marriage. With this unexpected information from Jake, I accepted the offer. Instead of going back to the life in the Northwest that I had left almost two years before, with mountains and forests, and fast running rivers, I completed the business of reconnecting to the states and then packed my car and drove from Seattle to Clearwater, Florida the same weekend that my ex was promising to love and cherish his new wife *'til death do they part.*

***

For the next 15 years, Florida was my home, but I had never really dropped roots there or made any deep connections, with the exception of three people, one of them was Esther. We met in the fall of 1992, just after my return from New Zealand, where I had gone to complete my training and certification as a counselor in Alchemical Hypnotherapy. Upon my return, I had two messages on my answering machine; both were from people asking if I did individual counseling. One had heard me talk at a local Religious Science church and the other was a student from the college for which I was employed the first five months I was in Florida. The college student had been in counseling with another therapist, but thought I could help him with issues related to women. I agreed to work with both, and my practice began.

One of the things I did at the beginning of my work was to give clients transcribed copies of their session notes to help them remember what occurred during hypnotherapy. The student often gave the notes to his other therapist, David from St. Petersburg, who happened to be the president of a psychotherapist's organization. He seemed very curious about my work and invited me to attend the Pinellas County Marriage and Family Therapist's monthly meeting even though I wasn't a licensed therapist.

I had mixed feelings about going to such a group, but decided to go in spite of my reservations. I had no idea that part of the group's beginning ritual was for everyone to stand up and introduce themselves, and I thought it would be best if I found a way to slip out because I had no idea how to introduce myself to these credentialed people, many with

MA degrees and some with PhDs in psychology. I had a BA in political science and history, and a certification as a clinical hypnotherapist. I felt so, so very out of place.

When it was my turn, I stood up and explained that I was not a marriage and family therapist, but was more of a spiritual guide who helped people connect with their essential self to bring spiritual healing to themselves and the world in which they live. My self-introduction was short, and I am not so sure how sweet…but after I seated myself, I remember a barrage of internal attacking thoughts. How could I have said such a stupid thing in front of these people who might want to report me to the state for practicing psychotherapy without a license? Even though that wasn't what I was doing, my work could have been construed as that and I was terrified I had brought on the wrath of the state by what I said, if not the wrath of the professionals. I couldn't stay present with the program and don't remember anything about the topic that was presented.

When the meeting was over, I turned toward the door to see if I could slip out quickly enough to avoid any confrontation. But as I quietly neared the exit to make my escape, President David stopped me to invite me to a party, and several women approached me, and handed me their cards, asking if there was a possibility that we could talk sometime. Several wanted to book sessions, and two wanted to know if I would be interested in being a friend; one of those women was Esther. I was dumbfounded!

The following week, Esther and I met at a restaurant in Safety Harbor for lunch. She told me that she had been struggling with whether to ask me to be her therapist or friend, and had decided that a friendship would be more meaningful, in spite of the fact that she felt I might be able to be of therapeutic support at the very beginning stages of her divorce. As we talked, we discovered that though we had very different life experiences, there were so many parallels in the general patterns that flowed through our lives and in the principles that were meaningful to both of us. Over the years, our relationship developed into a deeply meaningful friendship.

From the beginning of our 15-year friendship, Esther called almost weekly to invite me to come out and play, usually for dinner and a movie. She said that if she didn't coax me out, she was afraid that I would become a hermit...and I am quite sure my friend was right. I never did like mingling, going to parties, socializing in groups, or interacting with people I didn't truly know on a personal level, which made getting to know people on a personal level really difficult.

I moved five times in those 15 years, each time thinking that it was a simple relocation until the more complete move out of that state, which I felt sure was just around the corner. When it was time to sign a new lease, I did so, instead of buying a home, because each year was supposed to be my last. The major reason I didn't leave was because I had no idea where I would go. And then I began a program that took seven years to get both a Masters and then a Doctoral degree in psychology, and it didn't make sense to attempt a move in the middle of my studies.

At one point, when it seemed that my thesis had come to a complete halt, I interviewed with World Vision to take a job in Sierra Leone, a coastal country in Africa, during the time of a horrible attempt at ethnic cleansing, when so many people were being butchered and children were being maimed and dismembered with machetes. But the violence had escalated to the point that the organization had to close down their outpost, and I didn't go.

Those 15 years in Florida were filled with so many stories, so much growth and change, yet, I couldn't find the reason to leave the place with which I had never made a deep connection. Since my divorce in 1989, and my relocating to China, the move to Florida and then New Zealand to complete my training as a hypnotherapist, and my decision to get a doctoral degree in psychology, I had always followed significant inner guidance about what to do next in my life...but every year, I kept waiting for the directive to leave Florida, and it just didn't come.

In 1994, I had such a deep longing for the energy of the West coast that I joined a dear friend who rented a car—a beautiful apple red convertible—and we drove across the country. Connecticut David wanted to see a part of the US that he had never seen, and I wanted to put my feet in the Pacific Ocean again. Something in my body longed to be near the tall trees, the mountains, and the fast moving rivers and I needed to hear the roar of the Ocean crashing against jagged rocks, something that just doesn't happen on the Gulf Coast of Florida. It was as if something of great importance had been drained out of me during the years I had spent, without being rooted in the very flat, sea level land of the sunshine state; I needed to be filled again by rustic mountain energies and powerful ocean forces. I felt somewhat replenished, but the energies were not enough to get me through what would happen a couple of years later.

Following my father's death near the end of 1996, an event that had far greater impact on me than I had imagined it would, I experienced all the symptoms that felt like a heart attack. Still in graduate school, having no health insurance, and very little extra money, I couldn't go into the hospital. But when a dear friend who worked in the intensive care unit of a local hospital found out what had happened, he asked me to come to the hospital for special care. When I arrived, he ushered me into the private unit where his friends conducted tests that indicated I had experienced a heart attack. One young woman handed me a bottle of nitro tablets. With that in hand, I boarded a plane a few days later for Manaus, Brazil to attend an International Shamanic Conference that I had planned to attend long before. It was there that a miraculous heart healing occurred—but that is a part of another story for another time, although I do believe that this first healing in 1997 was what my hike dream referenced when I knew I had been down the path before, but had found another way that I believed I could find again.

***

In spite of my need to connect with the energy of the Pacific Ocean, with fast running rivers, and tall trees, I didn't want to return to the Northwest...at least not at that time. Having been healed but not yet recovered, I met that same friend in San Rafael, California a few months later and we drove along the West Coast again. I remember standing on a huge rock that jutted out into the Pacific, and as the sun rose behind me, and the ocean waves crashed in around my feet, I breathed in all that I could of the powerful energy, that seemed to go into the core of me and I felt it heal the exhaustion in my body.

Despite that deep calling to reconnect with the energy of the Pacific that my body so greatly needed, I felt no call that told me it was time to let go of the extremely shallow and ungrounded roots in Florida and go somewhere else. So I remained for another decade, getting my Ph.D. and developing my psychospiritual practice. Despite having spent nearly 15 years in that southernmost state, I still felt disconnected from any knowledge of where I was supposed to be.

In my last apartment that overlooked a nature preserve, which included a small lake filled with fish, large turtles, and a few alligators, I felt closer to nature than I ever had felt in Florida. I had 20-foot cathedral ceilings, and, for the most part, general peace and quiet in that space, but it was not enough. I painted my apartment fern green with accents of cucumber green, and covered my walls with beautifully framed, 18 X 24 photographs of the Cascade Mountains that I had taken on a trip to the Northwest sometime in 2005. I brought in large tropical plants and trees, creating an inner forest to match the green of the mangroves that grew around the lake and as far as the eye could see. I decided that if it wasn't time to be in the energy that my heart wanted, I could create the stage that would let me act as if I were there, until living in that energy would be real.

***

And then what I had been waiting for, for a decade and a half, finally happened. In the spring of 2006, following a night of dreaming I woke in the early morning with an unquestionable knowing that I had received my long awaited directive! Finally, after all those years, I knew it was now time to close my office, turn out the lights in my apartment and take to the road, but I didn't get any information as to where that road would lead. When I told Esther that I had finally received the message letting me know that this was the time, tears welled up in her eyes, and from a place of true friendship, she said, *"I am so happy for you...and I am sad for me."* Somewhere inside me, I was surprised that she really cared enough to cry because of my departure. In all those years, I had never really been able to take it in that she loved me.

Several months passed from the dream to the reality, as it required multiple levels of planning and moving, as well as tender explaining to the many clients who were working with me on significant life issues of their own. I moved out of my apartment in July of 2006, and moved in with another good friend. She had offered me a place in her home, which would become my legal residence as I traveled more or less rootless throughout the country.

***

One of the things I thought would happen after finding the child who was buried in the garbage was that I'd find a retreat where I could write. I had one book published, and 17 that were on my computer in various stages of completion, but I had never done anything with them. After I completed my dissertation, I knew that the near future would be about finding a way to bring life back into what I had written long before, and in doing this, I thought I might still find what had eluded me, and that was the key to releasing the excess weight I had carried for too long. From 2001 to 2006, instead of losing weight, I had had gone to a dangerous and all time high of 276 pounds. This seemed contrary to something I had known for years, that I would again be slender, and healthy. Years before, I had seen a vision of a slender older Sandy clearing her property of fallen branches and knew she was in my future; I just didn't know how to get to her.

At the time of my departure, the last day of August 2006, I didn't know if I would be returning or not, and if not, where I would end up...I only knew that I had been seeing visions of mountains, tall trees, and rivers for many years, and something in me knew that I needed to experience being in the high country. I thought it might be somewhere in the Northwest, very likely not where I had lived before, because when I imagined the familiar forests and mountains of Washington State, I didn't feel as if I was being drawn there. I had considered the possibility that I might find my home in Oregon, near David, or perhaps Montana, where I knew no one, although Montana was the state of my mother's birth. Thoughts of Alaska, the place of my own birth, abundant with forests, mountains, and rivers, crossed my mind, but the land of 24-hour darkness for a half of the year didn't seem workable for the rest of what I wanted in my life.

From August through November, I drove from the South East to the North West, and visited many places in the country. In my travels, I discovered that the mountains that had been speaking to me in my dreams had been the Rockies, the Great Divide between the Eastern and Western US, the backbone of our nation and particularly, the magnificent ranges in Colorado. In spite of all the personal work I had done in my life, and all the significant changes I had made, I knew that I was still unable to access the full power and strength of my own backbone. And that is what I needed to reclaim. My whole being told me that I would reclaim that backbone strength in these mountains.

I found the perfect place for a writing retreat, a wonderful little carriage house 8,300 feet above sea level, surrounded by mountains, many of which are higher than 14,000 feet. Although I have returned to florida every couple of months or so, and sometimes more often, as I write these words, I am still in the mountains. The morning sun is shining in my window, this very moment as I write, and birds fill the trees in the abundant pine forest that surrounds me. A small stream, which turns into nearly a river during mountain downpours and winter melting, flows outside my window, not 30 feet away.

This place is abundant with animals of so many species, except the human kind. More often than not, days go by without my seeing anyone except for the wild animals and my two domestic critters, Jenny and Rachael. Cars and trucks do drive by, now and then, on their way to or from the South Platte River, which is a 15-minute drive from where I live, with more traffic in the summer than winter. But for the most part, I am alone in nature.

I believe it is no mistake that there are so many things about the mountains of Colorado that remind me of my birthplace in Alaska, the place where I was so connected to nature, as well as the place where the abuse happened that broke my heart and weakened my backbone, the place, as Alanza had seen, where my childhood was stolen.

So often, on my walks with Jenny, my 11-pound Lhassa, the smells, the sounds, and sights of my mountain retreat instantly take me back to the wonderful beauty of the Kenai Peninsula where my family vacationed when I was a small child. For the most part, camping vacations were safe times and I dearly loved the nature that surrounded us. I recall the joy of feeding a baby deer a head of lettuce as her mother looked on from the edge of the forest. I was probably 6 or 7 at the time. I remember the sounds of the Kenai River as it rushed past our camping sites and the smell of the campfire burning fallen branches that my sisters and I scavenged from the forest floor. Nothing can match the smell of the evergreens the morning after a rain in the forests of my childhood. All this is coming back to me in the Colorado Mountains. The magnificent snow that was in great abundance my first winter in the high country allowed me to reconnect to my memories of the beauty of Alaska that was nearly lost to me because of the negative dark side of my childhood. And I have used this time to reclaim what I lost, including so many parts of myself.

***

For me, this has been a time of connecting: connecting with silence, connecting with peace, connecting with nature, and with myself. Winter gave me much opportunity for inner connection, as nearly every weekend for two full months there were snowstorms and blizzards that made driving anywhere a less than attractive prospect. This time period has been one that reconnected me with my interest in photography, which, on some magical level, allows me to look into the heart of nature and capture it on film in such a way that the photos seem to have a heartbeat of their own. Other than telephone calls and the occasional contact with my landlady, and the people in her life, my life has been lived in relative isolation since I came here in Mid-November 2006.

***

Though anyone who might have observed my life in Florida—or even before Florida —would very likely have said that I was not isolated, I was alone most of the time. In retrospect, it is clear to me that for most of my adult life, like my childhood, my experience had been one of isolation despite my living and working among many, many people. Over the 15 years that I lived there, I had developed a full practice in Florida, maintained contact with a number of graduate school friends, as well as kept in touch with a few former students that I taught in China and I have remained close to my dear translator and friend, David, who came to the U.S. with me, a story for another time. I participated in a number of professional organizations, gave workshops throughout the country and presented at conferences in the U.S. and every now and then, presented in other parts of the world. But my private life was spent nearly always alone.

Though I loved the people at work and my friends, any close and intimate contact, person to person, was rare. For most of my adult life, almost no one ever visited me in my home and when I visited anyone, I managed to go for only a few hours or on very rare occasions, a few days at a time. I had friends scattered all around the country and in a few other countries, but very few friends lived close to me. For a time, one friend moved in with me when she needed to pull her life back together, but I maintained a distance, without even knowing I was doing that. I suspect we were closer when we were not in close proximity. The other friends I did have in Florida, I seldom saw on a weekly basis, much less daily, with the exception of two people and Esther was one of those friends who did not allow me to maintain isolation.

***

Even though it shouldn't have been, it was a surprise when I got a call from Esther in the early spring of 2007, just a few months into my mountain experience, asking if July would be a good time for her to come visit me for 10 days. As much as I love my friend, when she said 10 days, I felt a tidal wave of hot adrenalin flush throughout my body as if I were under attack. Almost instantly my mind began a frantic search for any reason to say I wouldn't be able to accommodate her, without sounding horrible. However, I responded as if there was no wave going on inside me, and I asked her when would be good for her. Her first choice was from the 12th to the 23 of July...and, of course, I noticed immediately that would be 12 days, not 10...Again, I said nothing. She wasn't counting the travel days. But I was.

As I began working with my summer schedule, I sent her an email to let her know that my mother's birthday was on the 11th of July and I was planning to be with her. I explained that though I could likely find a flight to get back in time for her arrival on the 12th, a visit at that time would probably not work. So Esther changed her plans to vacation here from the 18th to the 29th.

Weeks went by and I didn't contact my friend, but as July came closer, I was feeling more and more anxious about her coming. She left a message in early June, saying that she needed to get her tickets and wondered if I was OK with the dates we had picked. Of course, I was not, but I couldn't tell her that I didn't want her to come. I tried not to think about it, but whenever I did, I felt ashamed for being like a bad person, certainly not a good friend.

For nearly my whole life, I have been generally cooperative, willing to do what other people wanted me to do, so much that I seldom was aware of my own likes or dislikes. I had come to believe that what I liked was to please others. I didn't know that I didn't have any preferences until I was traveling with a co-worker from our office in Washington, DC to Williamsburg, VA for a conference back in 1985. In passing, he commented that though we had known each other for a number of years, he really didn't know me, and he began asking very basic questions. What kinds of films did I enjoy the most? What was my favorite music? Favorite book? And when I couldn't answer, he asked more simple questions, such as my favorite color, favorite food, or favorite time of the day? I think I was more astonished that when I went inside my head to find the answers there was nothing there. Only then, did I realize that, to my knowledge, no one had ever asked me those kinds of questions, and I had never asked those kinds of questions of myself, either. There really was nothing there!

That was a life transforming road trip. For months, I thought about my co-worker's questions, and then I went in search of my preferences. Four years later, I was divorced, which was one of the most difficult things I had ever done in my life; by the time I was ready to end the marriage, my then-husband finally decided that he wanted to keep it. This whole experience caused me to become aware of my preferences, but it was still difficult to own them and draw them to me, especially if it looked as if my moving toward what I wanted would hurt someone else. My solution to never having to experience this kind of pain again was to simply not get too close to people to prevent hurting them with my preferences.

One of the things I learned after being in the mountains for a time is the importance of being authentic and speaking my truth about what I want and don't want. When confronted with Esther's questions about her vacation, I finally got it that the most loving response was to be real, and to be real, I had to be true to myself by saying what I wanted—or didn't want—and this seemed to be the perfect opportunity. My focus had been on writing, not on increasing my practice, and expenses had gone up, resulting in more money going out than coming in. Taking 10 days for a vacation seemed just not workable. And that decision was what I finally communicated to Esther in an email, a decision that was an almost insignificant event in the whole scheme of life, but it took me in a direction I could never have imagined for myself.

Chapter Nineteen
A LONG MESSAGE TO DAVID

Knowing we have choice is a necessary part of choice. Before "Yes" has meaning, we must be able to say, "No." And before we can say, "No" with meaning, we must be able to say, "Yes." After we learn how to say what is real for us, we can choose whether we want to say yes or no.

In the many years of our friendship, Oregon David and I have learned to be deeply honest with each other, and authentic communication has become the central feature of our relationship. After receiving an email from him asking what was happening for me, I responded in a long message, sharing my immediate experiences and what had taken place around the vacation plans with Esther.

Hi David, Today has been quite a day. The Hummingbirds have been flying into my space, hovering close to my head and making eye contact. They are so delicate, so powerful, and so playful. I don't think there is a creature that is more heart opening for me than these small birds. Oh, my! Just as I finished that last sentence, one flew in towards me with tremendous speed and then stopped only a few inches away from my face, which caused a huge rush of adrenaline in me.... and then she flew back out to get her meal. How fortunate I am! I am still laughing and feeling the rush.

So, getting back to my day, I barely slept over the last few nights and woke this morning feeling so very exhausted. My sister visited me recently, which was good, but was, also, challenging, since I am not used to having people in my life on a daily basis, especially for what feels like long periods of time. As my sister's 5-day visit was coming to a close, I just couldn't envision spending 10 days with a friend who planned to stay with me in mid July. After much struggle, I sent an email message to my friend canceling the plans, with what seemed like very good reasons, including my low income over the last two months, and the cost of the other trips I had to take. Though I had a sense that there was more to it, it was easy to focus on the issue that could "eat me up" the most and that was the money issue.

When she first mentioned a vacation a few months ago, I remember feeling a shock go through me. Even though I don't have a required "schedule" in my life, I am used to how I organize my days, and such a visit would really throw that off. My immediate response was to feel her suggestion as an "invasion" rather than something joyful. But I love my friend and didn't want to offend her so I said nothing, figuring in time I would find a way to adjust to the whole idea.

I told her I would check into things we might do, as she was interested in perhaps going to Utah or Arizona to see the Grand Canyon and she wanted to go on a hot air balloon ride. But every time I began to check, I became frozen. Along with this, I needed to make decisions and plans about going to Seattle, Florida, and Connecticut this summer; but I hadn't made those arrangements, either.

It was clear that something was blocking me on several fronts because I was doing nothing about developing workshops that I hoped would redirect my practice and increase my income, something I need if I am going to support myself. I had glimpses of a future time when I would be making presentations all over the country, and doing experiential workshops, but just haven't been able to pull anything into focus. Even though I have dropped down by 70% in my income in the last couple of months, I've been doing nothing to change it.

I have been frozen in my writing, one of things I wanted to accomplish when I left Florida to find a place where I could access the creative juices. Ideas would come that felt so important but after the initial inspiration, nothing more would flow. I have had so many starts and stops that the whole thing has felt ridiculous…but any attempt to force myself to develop the ideas put me into a place of feeling so distressed. My thoughts became confused and any sense of direction was lost, as if whatever was there had scattered into a thousand pieces and there was no way to pick them up and make any sense out of them. I couldn't find any connection, no thread, and no stream to catch and follow. So finally, I gave up trying. I figured that something would make this untenable situation change.

I couldn't see how I could enjoy a vacation…really what seemed like someone else's vacation…with all these circumstances looming.

The last night of my sister's visit, I was so exhausted, I went to bed early and dropped into the first deep sleep I had been able to find in days. Sometime after midnight, a blood curdling series of barks from Jenny wakened me. Still in shock from the abrupt waking, I turned my head toward the window in my front door and I saw a figure silhouetted against the porch light. The knob turned, the door opened, and the person entered my tiny space. I screamed in that half-asleep/half-awake way…that was almost muffled by dreamtime, and I was filled with frozen terror.

My sister began to apologize for waking me. She urgently had to use my bathroom, because the bathroom in the 5th wheel trailer where she had been staying wasn't working. My body was frazzled from the late night scare, but we both laughed it off, and she went back to her living space across the yard. But, I couldn't get back to sleep. The experience touched too many childhood experiences of being invaded in the night. Instead of fighting it, I got up and corrected a couple of students' papers and finally crawled under the covers around 5 AM. Needless to say, I was a wreck the next morning. One of the things I did before going back to sleep was to send an email to my friend canceling the "vacation" in July.

I felt relieved by my decision, but was concerned about how she would respond…and of course, she was very unhappy with me, as I could tell from the response she sent the next day. In my cancellation message, I had offered to talk with her if she wanted and she simply gave me times she would be available the following day. I was very anxious as the time for calling arrived…I did some energy grounding with a crystal, which helped somewhat, but I still had a very restless night and a most unproductive day.

When I called her, she didn't recognize my voice, at first. She said I didn't sound like me and asked how I was. I told her that I had really been doing quite well up here in the mountains, but recently had felt like I was just treading water, not going in any direction and trying to keep from going under. When I said that, I began to feel waves of emotional pain.

She told me that she had felt very badly about my canceling our time together; I had given no indication in previous conversations that there was any trouble and she had to do a lot of grounding work because she was so upset with me. She told me that she believed my decision to cancel was not about all the reasons I had mentioned, but was really about my feeling threatened by the thought of spending so much time with her.

I began to speak again, but my throat felt as if fingers were clenching my neck, pressing in so tightly that there was no air. I tried deep breaths, and then told her what I was feeling. I must have sounded like a small child. When she gave her assessment, I knew she was right, I knew that underneath all the reasons that were true, there was a more fundamentally true reason. And I felt so, so badly that I still had problems with people being too close on a personal level.

She asked me if I had been working with anyone to get to the bottom of this, and I explained that for some time I had intended to talk with a friend in Seattle, who does psychic counseling, actually since my trip to Seattle in the spring when my family thought my mother was dying. But I was frozen in that, as well.

There were still lots of things up for me that were all intertwined in feeling frozen, and I knew concerns about my friend's visit was just the tip of the iceberg. Two weeks before I got that call from my sister last spring telling me that I had better get home immediately if I wanted to see my mother again, I had been on a liquid fast, that not only made me feel so much better, but had resulted in the loss of 17 pounds. I was so happy about my body changes. The day that I left for Seattle was the last day on the liquid fast. But over the five days while I was in Seattle, all the weight I had lost, had come back, despite the fact that I hadn't eaten that much, but the little that I did eat was unhealthy. I couldn't make myself go back to eating healthfully after returning and that scattered confusion overtook me. It was terrible. I kept thinking I would get through it, but that just didn't happen. Since then, I had planned to make the call to Anne, but didn't.

I told Esther that when I got off the phone with her, I would call Anne, to see if she would have time to work with me, and I committed to calling her back to let her know what was going on.

Immediately upon hanging up with my Florida friend, I called Anne. But when I called, she didn't recognize my voice either, something that never happened in the 20 years I have been working with her to uncover deeply hidden psycho-spiritual issues. I explained that my throat was raw, and that what had been going on caused me to feel as if someone had clutched me by my throat and the fingers were squeezing so tight I could barely breathe. Like so many other times when I had a great need she was available, and this time was no exception; so we did a phone session for an hour and a half.

After filling Anne in on what was going on, she paused for a moment to sense my energy and start her work. She began by telling me that though what I was experiencing seemed huge to me, in fact, it was only fine tuning old thought patterns and responses, which had been with me for so long that I didn't even know I was responding in any particular way. Anne reminded me that procrastination, as I was doing in treading water in so many arenas of my life recently, simply happens when energy is not aligned with desire. Procrastination is a response that provides a message to look within to see the misalignment and to change, but instead, I have used it to beat myself up and feel badly about myself.

Instead of allowing my energy to align and support my desires, I learned very early, like others who self-sacrifice, that I had to adapt to other people's energies and desires. Anne explained that I had learned how to attune myself to other people by matching them, which can be both a gift and a burden. It is a gift when used to understand people, to have empathy, and to communicate; but it is a burden when I lose myself by disconnecting my energy from my desire and aligning with theirs…it is a burden when I give up my power and take on the false belief that I am vulnerable and can be taken over by others, something that makes me feel invaded and powerless to stop the invasion. In my professional relationships where there are strict boundaries, I was able to use the gift because I was not personally involved, but in personal relationships this attunement had been a burden, since I hadn't developed healthy boundaries around myself with regard to personal relationships.

As I am writing this to you, I am getting flashes of my life, when I did this…my, oh my…I did this a great deal. I can see, now, how empty it is to give up me to please someone else. When I did this, I was left feeling numb and they were left feeling alone…because I was not there; I was just an extension of them. I recall years ago describing what this felt like as me being nothing but a reflection of a reflection, with no substance at all, as if Sandy did not exist. And energetically that was correct. I relinquished the organizing principle deep within me; I abandoned the action that defines me as being the unique Sandy and gave it to someone else…so in essence, I became the other person instead of me.

I remember how I so seldom expressed my wishes or desires. I discovered a way to find out what other people wanted and agreed with that. If someone pressed me to make my wishes known, I would scan them to find out what they wanted, even when they didn't say it, and then choose what they wanted. Most of the time, people were happy to get what they wanted without having to compromise. I prided myself in being flexible, with a side benefit of having others want to be with me, but the reality is that we both lost me, and what we experienced together didn't feel real.

If being flexible was too intolerable, my answer was to isolate as the only way to protect myself and that is what I have done the better part of my whole life. Anne pointed out that nothing in the world let me know that there was any other choice in my personal relationships… It was either open to being invaded or withdraw into isolation to prevent being invaded.

As a child, I learned to hold back my own energy, to keep it from vibrating at a higher level. I learned to repress my own desires as a way to not feel the hugely disturbing feeling when desire and energy aren't in alignment, and in doing so, I lowered my vibration to match those around me. Because I felt that my abandonment of myself made me "bad," I tried to make up for it by being even better in the eyes of others, which meant cooperating, pleasing, being more flexible, and abandoning myself even more…what a vicious cycle.

Since the pattern of self-abandonment was so embedded and almost always unconscious, I chose isolation and felt invaded by anything that threatened to come into my space…not because someone or something was actually invading or even asking me to change my vibration, but because I would go on automatic pilot and give me up when someone got too close to me, whether or not someone expected it of me, or even wanted it.

This belief in powerlessness, of losing myself, is a lie because I know I am powerful. Anne reminded me that this is coming up now, by the circumstances I have drawn to me—my family, my sister, and Esther—so that I could clean up this little inconsistency in my automatic patterning that does not match the truth of who I am. Anne said that my essence was proclaiming that it is no longer acceptable to me to not let my essence shine, to not be my whole self and to not teach by my being, and to not heal by my being. This unacceptable pattern of losing myself, of relinquishing my power had to go!

As I see this, what I need to do is to stop using my ability to match as a burden and focus on using it as a gift. I have grown enough in my spiritual understanding to know that I draw to me all that comes into my experience by focusing on the energy of whatever I draw…I know this deep within, and this truth doesn't match the lie that I can be invaded by anyone. Anne reminded me that nothing could happen to me that I have not matched.

I thought for a moment and realized that I really had been excited about going on a vacation. But what was frightening me was that if I went with this friend, I would let go of myself, of my protections, and I would hate myself and the vacation, or if I let her get too close to know me and express my wants for the time together, she would end up finding out who I really was, the me that I always felt like I had to hide, and she would hate me. Some part of me felt that the essence of whoever I am is unacceptable. I really thought I had worked with this issue and brought healing to all the little Sandy parts of the past, but apparently there was something still unhealed. I understood that it was really not my friend who would think such awful things about me; it was me projecting my own self-disgust onto her as if those thoughts were hers and then felt I needed to protect myself against her rejection by isolating myself.

Anne reminded me that to heal this low energy vibration, it is necessary to acknowledge the reality of what is being experienced in the moment, which opens the door to what I prefer to feel, and then to focus on that. When I do that, immediately, I begin to draw what I want to me because I am a creator…I am creating my world out of what I believe and focus my attention upon…I know this…I KNOW THIS. I know I have known this for a very long time…but in this area of my life I have not lived what I know. Now, I get to.

As Anne and I were talking, a hummingbird flew into my space from the open window and hovered right above me, just as when I started writing to you. Anne magnificently pointed out that the hummingbird coming into my space delights me; it is not an invasion, because there is no resistance, no loss of power. I do not give myself away to this lovely creature, or feel threatened by its presence. She said that it is possible for me to feel this way about everything I draw to me when I focus on what I want instead of what I don't want.

What a great metaphor! To me, the hummingbirds represent beauty, flow, movement, harmony, playfulness, connection with the universe, and they are the embodiment of the embracing of life, pleasure, and joy. They are expressing an energy that matches the energy of my essence that I don't access enough. I am impressed with how powerful the hummingbirds are even though they are so very tiny. This is why I drew them to me and they are not invading by coming into my room.

Just as I wrote that last sentence, another hummingbird flew into my window and looked at me…this is so, so wonderful.

Anne explained the process so clearly…when something comes to us that is from a lower vibration, and we match it, for whatever reason, we experience the energy. If we go into fear and resist it, we immediately begin to engage it, which causes us to focus on it even more, since we can't engage without focusing. The focusing causes us to not just match it momentarily, but to lower our vibration and we lose connection with the higher vibration that pleases us. In that lower vibration we believe we are powerless because we believe the vibration that does not please us has captured us. We believe in powerlessness and let go of claiming our power to draw to us what we want. We perceive it because we match it and then because we feel it, we believe it is real. I know I have known this for years, if not decades, but I needed to hear it, reflected back in Anne's words in this context.

The value of having myriad vibrations, some we prefer and some we don't, is without these choices we would have no way of knowing what we do prefer. It is by seeing what we don't want that we know what we do want. And knowing what we want and receiving it brings conscious pleasure. Without the contrast we would be unconscious regarding the pleasure and the choice.

We create by allowing or we can create what we want…it is all in becoming aware of what we prefer and then focusing on that…in the focus we vibrate at the level of our preference and that is what creates it. And the hummingbirds continue to play outside my window…every now and then coming in a bit closer, and I would swear that they smile at me. Anne reminded me again that we don't have to adjust to others to be acceptable; that all the non-acceptance I experience—or believe I will experience from others if I don't match them—is simply my focus on non-acceptance in myself.

I smiled at what I had managed to create to bring all of this to the front for healing. Esther had mentioned that she wanted to come visit me from July 12 – 23. My mother's 91st birthday was July 11th and my family wanted me to be there to celebrate and one of my good friends said he would be getting married in Florida July 7th, and my own desire was to spend a week or so with friends in Connecticut. I haven't seen them for a year and a half, which feels far too long. I couldn't see how I could do all of this without it costing so much in money and in time. And I didn't want to have to put Jenny and Rachael in a kennel for a month. I was trying to please everybody and find a way in it all to please myself but couldn't…so I froze and was unable to make any decisions at all.

I wanted to expand my work to increase income, as this current situation of spending more than I am earning is unsustainable. But to go out into the world, which for me meant matching other people's vibrations and giving up myself was too painful, so I became scattered and confused …and did nothing.

The shift I needed to make was from trying to "solve the problems" related to all the external demands, to focusing on what I prefer, which automatically lifts my energy vibration to the true nature of my essence. This higher vibration then draws more of the higher to me and supports the desires of my heart. The rest just naturally falls away.

This is such a simple message, and, yet, it can be so difficult to grasp. The simple solution is to allow myself to focus on what I prefer, allowing my energy to match my desire, while releasing fear of what I don't want…and I need to remember that if it hurts, don't do it… But like many other humans, I learned, if it hurts, find a way to numb it and do what I believe I must, anyway.

I asked Anne to notice my energy field to see how it looked after all of our work. She paused for a moment and then said there was still some red anger energy around the belief in powerlessness. She commented that anger was not a bad thing…in fact, anger is necessary as a tool to step out of powerlessness, with a "Hell no, I am not going to do that anymore" attitude. She encouraged me to see anger as my ally in that it challenges the programmed pattern, which is based on the belief that I could create safety by giving up power.

I explained that I didn't want to get stuck in anger expressed as self-defensiveness, which supports a subtle belief that I can be overtaken and lose my power. In my heart, I know that overtaking only happens when permission is given. I choose to use the energy that we call anger, not as attacking others as a way to claim power, but as a way to propel me to claim my right to focus on what I want in such a way that I allow myself to experience what I prefer. This anger energy, shifted in its focus, can be the energy that embraces life, that loves the experience of being me, and that has no need to blame others for taking something away from me that they can't take unless I let them. This I prefer. My red energy is there to help me learn that I can be strong and passionate. It lets me affirm the right of others to be strong, as well, without either misusing that strength to control the other.

Something that I had not mentioned to Anne, but I knew was there, was that I was still beating myself up for having lived in the mountains for as long as I had without having lost the weight I believed would result from connecting with mountain energy. I have known for years that my weight is related to all of this giving up of my power. And this is a whole new discussion. It occurred to me that I fill up my space with my body when I don't fill up my body with myself.

It feels as if all of what has happened here in the mountains has been about me claiming myself, claiming my power, claiming my backbone. I knew that when I first came, I just didn't know how my reconnection with my true self would play out and I felt so abandoned by myself, as well as by the Universe when the opposite seemed to be happening.

What I now see is that I drew all of this to me, to more fully claim my power. It will be interesting to see what happens next. Love, Sandy

***

After the phone session with Anne was completed, I wrote the long message to David, and then I called Esther to tell her that I decided I wanted us to go on the vacation together. I explained to her what had been going on for me…and how her request for a vacation had brought up so many unresolved issues, ones that I was not aware of until the work I did with Anne. We mutually decided to reduce the time by a few days, and I confessed that I might have difficulty with having too much together time and trusted that we could both communicate to the other if we needed to isolate. She accepted that I might need to take time out for myself or for any client who might call, as that was much needed income for me and help for them.

Both decisions—to cancel the vacation, and later to take the vacation—were important. Before a *yes* could be meaningful, I had to be able to say *no*. If I had not said no, the likelihood is that I would not have been able to uncover deep wounds and bring healing to them, but also, I would not have discovered the subtle but powerful structures of isolating that had unconsciously ruled my entire life.

There are times like these that I am amazed at the inconsistencies in my way of being in this world. I could divorce my husband, leave my country, and live for nearly two years in the very middle of a country where I was the only foreigner in an entire district of several million people, but I struggled to tell a friend that I had concerns about her coming to visit for a few days. I could travel into remote villages and sleep on community beds with a dozen people, and share hotel rooms with fellow travelers whom I had never met before, but I couldn't bare the thought of sleeping in the same hotel room with a friend. I guess life wasn't intended to make a lot of sense.

In the weeks that followed, I enjoyed putting together plans for the eight days, not counting travel days. We would explore places in Colorado that I had not visited because of my tendency to cocoon myself and not come out unless it was necessary. Searching the Internet, I discovered all sorts of places of interest, not just for Esther's visit, but for other friends should they decide to come sometime in the future. And maybe, some of them could be places I would visit on my own.

Chapter Twenty
THE VACATION

Life is a risk. Don't allow unfounded fear to hold you back from experiencing the magnificence of life!

From the time I was in the 8th grade and learned about Pike's Peek in my US history class, I wanted to visit the mountain that was so important in the westward movement, and I found a way for us to do that. Esther wanted to challenge her fear of heights so we decided to take the Cog Railway up the 14,110-foot mountain to the very top, and we, also, planed to take a ride in a hot air balloon. Our schedule included lots of mountain driving, to go to hot springs, hidden high country mountain towns, as well as festivals and fairs.

It was so good to see my dear friend when July 20th finally arrived. From the first day, Esther and I took advantage of every waking moment of her eight-day visit. Saturday afternoon, the day that I picked her up in Denver, we went to see *Harry Potter, and the Order of the Phoenix*, something that was a tradition for us since we had gone together to the other four Potter films when I was in Florida. What seemed to be the central theme in this film was that each of us must come to terms with the fact that we possess both good and evil and we all have a choice as to which one will characterize our lives, a lesson so appropriate for what was happening for me in all of the issues and challenges around darkness and light, power and weakness, speaking and not speaking and so much more at that time in my life.

I believe that many people who have chosen, or want to choose good, are terrified that evil exists within them and so many spend their entire lives trying to prove, both to themselves and others that what is true—that the dark side exists in them—is not true, or they live their lives in agony believing that no matter how much they want to be different, they are by nature evil. If they believe in their evilness, they may endlessly seek some form of salvation, which somehow never seems enough, or they succumb to evil, choosing what seems natural, instead of recognizing that it is *choice,* not evil that is natural, and good and evil allow choice. In the meantime, lives are lived without connecting to living, or lived in a frantic search for something that can never be found. Human beings so often label anything that seems favorable or familiar, as good, and anything that seems to be unfavorable or not understood, as evil. These were the thoughts that were on my mind as Esther and I finished watching Harry Potter that first day of our vacation.

Our first excursion after her arrival was to Pikes Peek. After Esther's heroic cog rail ascent and descent, we found a parking spot in Manitou Springs and began peeking into shop windows to get a flavor of this quaint mountain town. We both paused for a moment at a storefront that advertised psychic readings, and it was clear that Esther wanted to go in. I was willing to go with her to see if the reader might have time for us, which brings us back full-circle to where we started, with Alanza and her predictions of abundance, joy, and writing.

***

The next day, after having gone up to what felt like the top of the world and then visiting Alanza, Esther and I visited the Cave of the Winds, also, near Manitou Springs. Though commercialized with floodlights revealing interesting shapes and shadowed openings into the darkness and despite the tour guide repeating the same non-spontaneous scripts about the caves, the experience was well worth the entrance fee. Part way through the tour, we were directed to look at a ledge where thousands of coins and other sparkling objects were piled up like the rounded top of gold and silver in a treasure chest. A flood light revealed the glistening treasure, all protected by a Plexiglas shield to prevent plundering by unconscious or uncaring visitors.

The guide told the story of two young women who had ventured into the caves back in the 1800s. Still unmarried at 19, and concerned about becoming old maids, they removed their golden hair clips and placed them on a ledge as a request to the God of the Cave to help them find mates. Apparently they both found wealthy partners and were married soon afterward.

The story of the young women's luck spread, and as years passed, more and more people who entered the cave added objects of value or coins on the "altar" hoping that good luck would come to them. The legend that was passed down to this very day, said that if you toss a coin or something of value on the shelf and it remains there, you will have a year of good luck, unexpected wealth will come to you, and if you want to find a mate, you will find one within the year. However, if in tossing your coin, yours falls to the ground or causes others' coins to fall, you will have two years of bad luck, and if you are in a relationship, it too, will fall to the ground and fail just like the coin.

All during the tour, I had been trailing behind, taking photos of the rock forms, the many stalactites and stalagmites, the deeper openings within the caves, and whatever else drew my attention. This cave altar was no exception. The group had moved on, with no one taking the challenge to throw a coin onto the pile. I positioned my camera to catch the sparkle of the treasures when the thought came to me to throw a coin onto the heaping treasure pile. I was almost surprised by a second thought that warned me not to risk two years of bad luck. Although I really don't believe in legendary blessings and curses, I was surprised by the intensity of the second thought. I dismissed it all as silliness...and then another thought arose. *"Life is a risk, don't hold back from life."*

So I pulled out a coin and tossed it on the pile. My coin did not fall, and did not cause other coins to fall. Again, I smiled. I could hear the tour guide in the next room ask if everyone was there, and I turned to join them. But before moving forward, I looked down at the cave floor to be sure I wouldn't trip on anything. Right there in front of me, I saw a folded dollar bill not two feet away. I reached down and picked it up. To my surprise it was not a 1-dollar bill, but a 10-dollar bill. What an immediate return on my action! Though part of me dismissed the find as a very fine coincidence, another part of me believed that my decision to take a risk had opened me to another Universe where money and good luck would come to me easily. And I thought about the session with Alanza…

Interesting things began to happen since I met the fortuneteller, and in another way, nothing really happened at all. One of the last nights Esther was with me in Colorado we were scheduled to see ABBA, one of my all time favorite groups. The concert was a rain or shine event in the open-air Red Rocks amphitheater, about a half hour from my mountain retreat. It had been raining most of the day, so we brought umbrellas and assumed we would be experiencing the rain part of the *rain or shine* concert. As we drove through the town of Morrison on the way to Red Rocks, the traffic signals on the main street were out and the Friday night tourist traffic was nastily congested. We made our way through the streets and up the mountainside where we were directed to park in the lower lot, which meant a long hike up to the theater.

Wind turned our umbrellas inside out, and in spite of the weather we were about to leave the parking lot and take the long path up, up, up to the magnificent outdoor theater, when a young man called to us, suggesting that we might reconsider the climb. He was with a group of twenty-something tailgaters singing along with ABBA songs barreling out from the car stereo. They looked as if they were having a very good time in the rain. The one who called out to us, told us that lightening had stuck the transformer that provided power to the theater, which meant likely there would be no concert. The young man said it would be pointless to walk all the way up the hill only to find out that the concert would be cancelled. The climb was long and steep and it was obvious that there were no lights anywhere; so we heeded his suggestion, and decided to wait.

After a few minutes, Esther asked me if I wanted to go over to join the happy tailgating party, and we did. The group of seven, 3 women and 4 men, most of them in their late 20s or early 30s, and one man, who appeared to be in his 40s welcomed us. They offered us cookies, fruit, and beer. We accepted the first two offerings and they gave us water. They didn't seem to care that we were older as they included us in their party. The one who told us about the power outage said we were the only ones who listened to them, so we deserved to share in the fun and food. Everyone else that they had warned chose to walk up only to have to wait in a long, long line in the cold rain and wind.

We stayed with the happy group for over an hour while everything that could be done to repair what a lightening strike had destroyed was being done. We danced and sang with them, and finally, an official came through the parking lot to tell us that that concert was off. Esther and I said good-bye to our young friends, hugging the girls and shaking hands with the young men. I shook the hand of the older man and thanked him for the hospitality. As we walked toward my car, it occurred to me that the older guy, a big teddy bear looking man was probably about 45. I thought of Alanza...and smiled. It wasn't that I thought that this would be the man I would run into in a grocery or bank line, a few months later, but I realized that for the first time in years, I was actually looking at possibilities; I was opening my heart to a hidden dream that I had carried since I was a young woman, to have a man in my life who I loved and who loved me, a man who would love to receive the card I had purchased when I was 21...that said, *Grow Old With Me, The Best is Yet To Be.*

I realized that the singing and dancing to ABBA music was something I had never done quite like that before, not with a group of people I didn't know, and certainly not feeling so connected to the experience as I had that night. I had sung and danced many times before in my life, but most of it was done from a place of disconnection from my authentic self. The experience felt like I was opening to what had been stolen from me...many decades before...and again, I smiled. All of this felt like a beautifully choreographed metaphor risking opening to and celebrating life.

Chapter Twenty-One
REFLECTIONS ON CHINA

Be willing to allow the dream that speaks to you—the one that lives in your soul and doesn't go away–to find a place in your heart until you see the door that can take you to the Universe where your dream lives. And then, find the courage to go through the doorway.

As Esther and I began the half hour drive from the Red Rocks Amphitheater to my place, higher in the mountains, I mentioned that I had been thinking about the book that Alanza said could become a screenplay and asked my friend how she envisioned its beginning. I had thought about it, on and off, from the day that Alanza put words on an idea that had been in my mind for years. Esther's immediate response was that it should open in China and the nearly two years I lived in that country after I divorced Jake back in the 1989. Certainly, that was a powerfully transforming time...and to think that those nearly two Universe-altering years of my life began as a dream I had when I was in psychotherapy.

***

In the mid-1980s, I had begun counseling, in search of a way to repair a marriage that was crumbling from the inside out. I didn't believe in divorce but divorce seemed the only answer to the problems that were causing me feel as if I were dying on the inside. My heart had been deeply sad for too many years and my soul felt too lonely to continue living as I had been. I had begun to connect with my dreams that seemed to hold many answers for me. Many of the dreams had been precognitive and some of those precognitions where about the ending of my marriage, something I just couldn't face in waking reality.

Other dreams gave me glimpses into my future that I didn't know were future dreams until they happened.

Sometime in early 1987, I woke from a dream with a single image that etched itself into my memory. That image was of many bubble balls, the kind that children blow from a soapy liquid, but the bubble-balls were large enough to contain entire scenes; each was different, and I was in all of them. At the forefront was a bubble-ball with a group of Chinese people who were around me, and it seemed to be a joyous occasion. Behind the first bubble were others that contained scenes from what seemed to be places around the world. I saw one of me in India, in Africa, and the others were in lots of other countries that I can't recall. My waking thought was that I was going to China…and later I would be going to those other countries.

The feelings from that dream image were powerfully strong, but I had no idea how such a thing was going to happen. The more I tried to dismiss the dream and the feelings that were connected to it, the more the images from the dream seeped into my waking life. More than a year had passed since the dream, when a friend called to ask a favor. I was able to help with his request for at-a-distance healing, and when our conversation was complete, he said, *"Now that you helped me, is there anything that I can do for you?"* Without any hesitation, I told him that I had had a dream the year before, which left me with the clear feeling that I would be going to China, but I had no idea what to do about it.

His immediate response was to give me a suggestion to get a job in a travel agency as a way to find out the details of traveling to a country, which at the time was just barely opening to foreigners entering its borders. I hung up the phone and picked up the newspaper—this was before the advent of the Internet. I opened to the job opportunities section and looked under travel agents. There was one position advertised and I called to find out if it was still available. The man who answered the phone told me that he was the one who was looking for an agent, but unless I could get there within the next hour, I would have to wait for an interview until he returned from a trip to Germany.

Without changing clothes or doing anything to enhance my appearance, I jumped into my car and drove to the address in Georgetown, which was about 30 minutes away from where I lived. When I stepped out of my car, I realized I was wearing sneakers, overalls, and a t-shirt; my hair was in a ponytail, and I was wearing no makeup, not exactly the ideal presentation for a job interview.

I hurried into the travel agency and introduced myself to the owner of the company. He ushered me into his executive office and began asking all sorts of questions and a short time later, I had the job. He told me that my training would begin when he returned from his European trip, but in the meantime, I was supposed to send his secretary my resume, and return the application form that he gave me as I was leaving...and a few weeks later, I received word that my training would begin the following week.

The first day of the class, one of the senior agents approached me during the lunch break and mentioned that he had seen my resume and thought he might have the perfect job for me, if I would be interested. But before I could answer, he asked me if I wanted to go to China. My immediate reaction was to squeal with delight, and in the next breath, I contained myself and asked for details. He gave me the telephone number of a woman, who was recruiting people to lead tours of professional Americans through China. She scheduled an appointment with me the next day, which was the last day of her interviews. At the end of the appointment, she shook my hand and told me that normally it was not her policy to tell people that they had the job until she had time to return to her office and go over all the candidates, but she wanted to let me know so that I could begin preparing for my trip to China. I never took the travel agency job, but near the end of 1988, I was traveling as "guide" through the amazing Middle Kingdom with a group of medical researchers.

The last stop on the tour took our group to a teaching hospital, in Xiamen, Fujian Province, where I met the director of the medical training staff who spoke English. He inquired as to whether or not I might be interested in coming to China for an extended period to teach English to his staff. If nothing else, this experience let me know that my dream was not about me traveling through China, but it was about actually living there. So his invitation seemed to be the fulfillment of my dream. He gave me all of the required papers that would grant me an official invitation to come to China, a necessary requirement for any person going there at that time. It would have never occurred to me that I could teach English in another country. Although I did have a BA degree and had been a teacher, my focus was not English.

The value of this single trip to China was not the experience of going to the Middle Kingdom, but rather the discovery that traveling through China was not what my dream was directing me to do. I knew that I was being led to live there, and this first trip let me know that I could teach English as my *entrée*. By going with the group, I had made discoveries about what I needed do to enter this Eastern country that had drawn my attention from the time I was a small child. I left with the forms that would allow me to return, and actually live there.

***

After returning to the US, I became more deeply engaged in psychotherapy, not only dealing with marriage issues, but with childhood issues that were becoming prominent and were making life very difficult. As much as I tried to focus on filling out the paperwork, I just couldn't complete it. I would begin and then be interrupted by a phone call, and when I returned, the papers would be gone or some other situation would occur that needed my attention and the papers would end up with newspapers or journal notes, all of which distracted me from the task I had so fully intended to do. One time, I searched everywhere for the papers, and they were not to be found. In total frustration, I communicated internally, saying that if some part of me knew where the papers were, I would really appreciate it if she would tell me. I saw an image of the garbage basket in my kitchen, and when I looked in it, I found the papers at the bottom of the basket, tucked under the plastic lining.

Weeks turned into months. As June 1989, approached, I still had not filled out the paperwork for the fall of that year. My chances of getting all the clearances in time for the September classes seemed remote, but I could not make myself do what something inside was blocking me from doing. While alone in my apartment on the 4th of June, not understanding much of anything at all that was happening in my life, I turned on the television and saw images of horror going on in China. The student revolution had just begun...I was in shock. I remember going to the television set and wailing...so, deeply...as I watched what felt like my brothers and sisters under attack in Tiananmen Square by other brothers and sisters. Something in me ached so deeply for what was happening in the land that I had loved all my life. It seemed as if the country that had just begun to open, was now closing down, and it would not be safe for me to go there to teach, or to find out what had drawn me there all my life.

I went into a major depression and didn't leave my apartment complex for a number of weeks, except to buy dog food when the supply was gone or to go to my weekly therapy appointments. I ordered in food when I was hungry, which was not a regular thing, as some days I had no interest in eating. I spent most of my days sitting in my bamboo Papasan chair staring into emptiness. Newspapers piled up in my living room, not even removed from their plastic bags. My trips to the garbage bins took place in the middle of the night as I walked my dog...a time when I would not have to interact with any human being. I couldn't watch TV, and just listening to the radio put me in overload...so I sat in silence, day after day.

One afternoon, in late August, I got up from the Papasan chair that had become my daytime home, and began to clean up my apartment. I removed all the newspapers from the plastic sleeves and made one big pile to take to the recycle bin. In a few hours my place was tidy and I was ready to throw everything in the trash. After a few trips to the Dumpster, all that was left was the pile of newspapers. I still can't explain why I did what I did next...but nonetheless, it is exactly what happened.

I picked up the stack of papers, and removed one from somewhere in the middle of the pile. I opened the paper and pulled out a middle section from that paper, and took it to the bathroom. The rest I took to the paper recycle bin. When I returned to my apartment, I filled the tub with water and splashed in a soothing bubble bath liquid, stepped in and I lowered myself into the hot bubbly water. After allowing myself time to relax, I picked up the newspaper section and began to read. There, in the section I had selected out of the one newspaper rescued from the huge stack of papers, was an article about a China teacher-training program. Western Washington University in Bellingham, Washington had developed a program to train people to become English teachers in China, but because of the Tiananmen student uprising, the numbers for the September class had dropped from over 90 people down to less than 10. The article indicated that the program was open to people who were still interested in going to China to teach.

I leapt from my hot bubble bath and ran to the phone. The article was from a few weeks before, so I had no idea if the class was still open. I caught the director of the program just as she was leaving her office for the weekend, and she faxed me the application form for the class that was to begin shortly. She encouraged me to fax back the information by Monday to meet the deadline for enrollment.

***

A few weeks later, I was sitting in a class of ten people, studying basic Chinese language, history, geography, and culture. The class was intended to not only prepare the participants for teaching in China, but the program placed teachers into colleges and universities in that country. As the program neared its conclusion, I received two invitations from universities in coal-producing areas in China, which I turned down. Somehow, I knew neither place was where I was supposed to go, though I didn't know why. The hospital in Xiamen that had invited me the year before did not have connection to Western Washington University, which meant that neither my school nor the hospital could participate in the placement process.

Another problem was that administrators in many colleges and universities in China didn't know if it would be considered politically correct to engage a Westerner as a faculty member, since earlier that year, students who were protesting many government policies had demanded democracy in line with the West. Any school that might appear to be leaning toward Western thought could experience retaliation much like what had happened during the terrifying Cultural Revolution, three decades earlier. As a result, there were far fewer placements of English teachers being made.

Just as our training was coming to a close, one of my fellow students received an invitation from a college in Baoji, Shaanxi Province, in the very center of China...and with the invitation, was a letter that described the school. My classmate gave me the letter, and when I read it, I knew that this was the place I was supposed to go, but he, not I, had received the invitation. I have no idea how I knew that Baoji was supposed to be my school, I just did. Nothing made sense to me.

Weeks passed...and winter had turned the college campus to white; it looked like there would be no new invitations coming until the next year. This all felt so wrong because I felt strongly that I was supposed to be in a college where I couldn't go. I drove to the campus just before the school was to close for Thanksgiving, and went to the office of the China Teacher Training Program. As I approached the office, the young man who had received the invitation to Baoji, was just leaving. I asked him how he was doing and when he would be leaving for his tour in China. He told me that he would be going the first part of February, but that he was not going to Baoji, after all. He had received a second invitation from a school in Xian, which had offered him a slightly higher salary and took that offer instead.

With a very full heart, I wished him a wonderful holiday, and hurried into the office. I literally begged the director to send my vita to Baoji before she left...and she agreed to stay a bit longer and fax the material to China. After the holiday break, I found out that I had been accepted. It took a few more weeks for all the paperwork to be completed, for my visa to be approved and arrangements to be made for my overseas travel.

***

Before the coming of spring, in 1990, my plane landed in China, and deep in my soul—as I left customs and entered the bustling airport in Beijing—I felt as if I had come home. Shortly after arriving in China, I met the young man, whose English name is David, who was assigned by the authorities to be my translator, traveling companion, and protector, a job that carried the grave responsibility of making sure that nothing bad happened to me. China David became my dearest friend and confidant and I found out later that he was the person who had written the letter that let me know Baoji was the place I was supposed to go. The time I lived in China was the most profoundly transformative period of my life up to that time, but that, too, is another story for another time.

In late January, a little short of a year of my being in China, I was invited to a middle school in the high country of Shaanxi Province to give a talk to the students and teachers. It was blustery cold and I dressed as warmly as I possibly could. My translator and friend, David and I made it through the snow covered mountain roads to the school and found that the entire student body had been assembled in an open field; all were seated on wooden benches awaiting our arrival. An outdoor stage had been built and we were directed to step up on the stage and invited to approach the microphone. I gave a speech to the students about dedicating themselves to their dreams and working hard without quitting. I talked to them about allowing their dreams to weave together with the dreams of others to create a beautiful and profound China. It was a powerful experience as students and teachers listened to my English and then to David who repeated my words in Chinese. Many of the children had been studying English from the time they first entered preschool, but most of them, as well as their teachers, had never heard the language spoken by a native speaker.

After I finished my talk, I stepped off the stage and began shaking hands with the students. They had just that very day received their school year books and they were collecting around me to get me to sign their annuals in English. It was a lovely time, almost a time of celebration. I stayed with them until the lead teacher announced that they must allow the American to go into the building to escape the cold.

My translator and I returned to Baoji and a short while later, perhaps a week or two, I heard a knock on my door. David had brought me a packet of photos he had taken over the previous few weeks, including the ones from our trip to northern Shaanxi. We sat down and looked at the photos, remembering the events that each represented. Very nearly the last photo was one he had taken when he was still on the stage and I was in the crowd of students and teachers, with them smiling and handing me their yearbooks to sign.

I stared at the photo in total disbelief. The snapshot he had taken, the angle, the perspective, was exactly the same image that I had seen in the bubble dream almost three years before. In the dream image of me in 1987, I was wearing the winter clothes I had on in 1990, which included a long, wool-knit coat, not unlike a woman's version of the tweed coat Jake wore the night he came to my door bearing gifts so many years before. And in 1990, I wore a knit head cap exactly as it was in the photo. I had purchased that coat in 1989 in the states, without realizing that I had already seen what I was looking for in my dream and felt driven to find just the right coat, but I had no idea that is what I was doing at the time. The hat I was wearing, however, was not one I had purchased. It was given to me by a friend as a departure gift to keep me warm in the frigid cold that swept across China from the Siberian Plains, and it, too, was exactly what I had seen in that bubble image in the dream. My friend had no idea that I even had a bubble dream much less an idea of what that dream-cap looked like. This amazing experience was only one of so many others like it that I had in China...some of which I had shared with Esther, so it was understandable that she might imagine that a screenplay about my life could begin with China.

Chapter Twenty-Two
THE ANGEL LADY

No matter what is happening in your life that seems not survivable, you will survive; no matter how alone you may feel…you are never alone. You are eternal; you exist through all time, and with you, always, is the essence of all those who have loved you, all those who do, and will ever love you. And with you, is, also, your future self, who has already survived and moved into a more whole way of living. When you allow your future self to guide you from where you are to where you will be, you will know the truth of your survival; and when you allow all who love you to support you, you will know what it is to release loneliness.

Esther's idea about the opening of my book beginning in China sounded good, but somehow, I couldn't find the way to pull together all that seemed to belong in a book from that place in my life. Though I could see my China years as a separate book, I couldn't see how to weave the story into a more expansive work that on one plane was not only about my whole life, but also on another plane, was about all of us. I didn't know how to go back and explain the threads that led to my being there while trying to tell a story that took place in the middle of my life as a beginning point. Confusing! Maybe if this book were supposed to have begun there, I would have seen the connecting threads more easily.

For years, I had been trying to write a story of my life, one that had the ability to reach beyond myself, but I struggled with a way to begin it…maybe because there were just too many beginnings. I thought more about a possible beginning for this first book of a trilogy that Alanza predicted and on the drive back to the mountains from Red Rocks, I considered the idea of starting at the end of my life, writing about the Sandy I have seen in flashes, who is an old woman of 92, that I believe I will be when this life is finished. Then I could allow the thread of stories of the past to form as a way to explain the path that led me to old Sandy. I played with this idea for a while as images of my past experiences with a Sandy of the future flowed through my mind; however, most were not of the old woman, but rather the images involved experiences I had when I was a child and future Sandy visited my child-selves of the past to help the little girls survive difficult times: interventions I believe that allowed me to be here now.

***

Though I had been connected with what I came to identify as my future self since I was a very young child, my first awareness of the idea of a future self came to me during a particularly difficult time in my therapy process in the 1980s. Prior to that experience, I believed what I now know as my future self was a separate being. As I child, I called the being that visited me and brought me comfort, the *Angel Lady*.

For those of you who have never experienced going deeply within to access the many aspects of yourself, including many parts of you that may well experience life from a different time, this concept of past self and future self can be confusing. Imagine that when you were a child, you lost someone or something that meant the world to you, maybe a much-loved pet. The experience may have been so painful that in the moment of the greatest pain it felt like you would not be able to survive it. One of the ways we get beyond such deep pain is to move through it, which would have required us to feel the pain, acknowledge what happened, say good-bye in whatever way we could and move forward with an expanded understanding of life...one that includes great loss, and death.

If a child doesn't go through the pain, but looks for any possible way to avoid it, the child-self splits off from the pain and buries the heart-broken part deep inside, disconnecting from the experience and then grows past the painful time into a generally functioning, but not whole adult. A small part of that person is still living in the past with the pain, not knowing how to move through it or expand understanding about life. This stuck part believes that life is about painful loss, which is not survivable. Another part of the self monitors the adult to be sure nothing will touch that buried pain and terrifying belief about life. Perhaps the adult will take on anti-pet attitudes, such as: pets are dirty; pets are unhealthy; pets stir up allergies, pets cost too much. And though any or all of these might be true, they are not the deeper reason, which is, *"If I get a pet it might die and then I will experience too much pain and I don't want to ever feel that way again."*

The deepest pain that the person is avoiding is the fear of death, which will find a way to return in the adult's life until the fear is faced. If this adult does get a pet or finds someone else to love, the adult relationship can include experiences that could touch upon the fact that life includes death. When loss or fear of loss occurs again, a door can open from the space in the adult's life that accesses the place of the past where the child that was left behind has been buried, maybe even for decades. When the pain is finally faced, experienced, and released that aspect of the buried self can be rejoined with the adult self and the functioning but incomplete self can now be more complete. The belief that life is about painful loss that is not survivable, and the opposite belief that life is about avoiding loss, moves to a healthy understanding that life holds many experiences that are joyful and sad, and includes loss and death of those we love, and we can survive the pain of loss.

Since we all have multiple experiences with pain in our growing up years, it is possible that we have many aspects of ourselves buried in the past, and as a result we have many defenses that prevent us from experiencing full lives. All the things that we resist experiencing, or that we intend to do, but don't, could be evidence of part of ourselves trying to protect us from feeling pain, perhaps useful at one time, but likely no longer useful because it limits our lives. As adults, we can face what felt like death-causing pain when we were children. When we go back into the past to rescue the child self from the pain, on some level, we are allowing the present to enter the past to allow transformations to happen. There are some that would say that the "going into the past" is metaphoric, and does not actually happen in linear time. My experience suggests otherwise.

***

When digging deeply into the buried emotions regarding the breakup of my marriage, I began to access parallel emotions related to the trauma of my childhood. I discovered that the agony in my then present life, opened the door for me to connect with events from my past, in which child parts of me remained stuck in a time lock, experiencing trauma as if it were still going on. I would go back to the child and help her become free of the damage of the horrific events by intervening and providing this aspect of myself, my adult understanding to help her release what was happening and invite her to let go of the past and join me in the present. Almost all the time, when the past event was confronted, and the child was allowed to move through it and join me in the now, whatever physical or emotional pain I was experiencing in the present would fade away. If I was sick, this healing process allowed me to become well, because there seems to be a significant link between emotional pain and physical illness. There were so many incidents where parts of me were trapped in the past, and the intervention resulted in such profound freedom in my mind and body.

Because I came to recognize that the roots of present problems are in the past, the idea of intervening into the past to heal something in the present made complete sense to me. And as I unraveled more and more of my past, I discovered that my child self had been able to access other realities when something in her world was too overwhelming. Called dissociation in the field of psychology, this ability allowed my consciousness to experience itself as existing beyond my body and traveling to other places where I learned to see the world much differently than what is common in the Western World. Though, at first, the understandings were from a child's view, later, my interpretations of the Universe based on my *"out of body"* experiences became more complex.

***

When I was very small, a woman I called the Angel Lady, began to appear to me. No one else could see her, but I came to trust her ability to keep me safe in the most life-threatening circumstances. At times, she would simply appear, sit there on the end of my bed, and tell me things that gave me courage to keep going when everything in me wanted my life to end. Other times she came to take me by the hand and lead me to what some call alternate realities, where at least a part of me learned more than I consciously know, even now.

But, as I grew into my teen years, through the learned pattern of dissociation, I had not only forgotten my childhood, I had forgotten the Angel Lady, too. However, when I was 15, I remember sitting on my bed on the third floor of my family's Seattle house, working for hours on a pencil drawing of a woman. I recall that my oldest sister asked who the woman was, and I told her I didn't know; but there was such intensity about wanting to get it perfect, something I couldn't explain. I drew the curls that surrounded her face with special care. I don't know how many times I drew and erased those curls until each hair was in its perfect place. Each line, each shadow, each fold, and curve had to be exactly right and the pattern on her clothing had to fit some perfect likeness, as well. It was as if I had some image in mind, like a picture that captured something with great meaning, and I wanted to reproduce it perfectly.

The woman in my drawing was wearing a loosely fitting gown with leaf patterns in the fabric, and there was something about her that made me feel safe. I carried that picture in my notebook through high school and kept it in a special folder at home when I was in college. I often pulled the drawing out to look at it when I needed something, though I don't recall knowing what that something was that I needed. That picture was my most important possession, until I was a senior in college. In that year, a fire consumed the third floor of my parents' home, and everything I owned, including that picture, burned. By the time I was an adult, most of my teen years were forgotten as well, just like the vast majority of my childhood, and it remained locked up in the hidden recesses of my mind until I began therapy in 1986; though I had forgotten many other things, I never forgot the image of the woman I had so carefully drawn when I was 15.

Something amazing happened in that extremely difficult time after I had left my husband but was not, yet, divorced. The man that I had met—the one with whom I had become intimate, and resulted in the shattering of my life, as I had known it—had become my lover and his home had become a sanctuary for me. The house was in a private community, with tree-lined streets, where children could play outside and feel safe. The house was large but cozy. He had overstuffed brown leather couches and chairs with soft woven comforters and rust colored throw pillows that he had purchased on one of his treks through India. A large wool rug with deep earth tones added to the coziness. He had a magnificent Indian drum in the corner and a painting of an Indian shaman over the huge fireplace mantle. His home was so richly mas-culine, but with warmth that allowed the feminine to feel protected. The living room opened to a well-manicured back yard encircled by tall trees, and the upstairs master bedroom overlooked a beautiful meadow where horses grazed, birds sang in the trees, and butterflies flittered in the flowers down below. For me, this place felt like a home in the Garden of Eden.

Though we spent a fair amount of time together in that house, there were many times that I went there when he was not home, as a retreat where I could feel safe and alone. This was a place where I wrote in my journal and did inner work; and so often, before I knew I could go back to rescue these child parts, I sent images of his house, his yard, flower gardens, and images of the horses in the meadow to the little girls of my past who had no flowers, who had nothing of beauty in their lives. On cold evenings, when I stayed with him, I enjoyed watching him care-fully construct the kindling and logs, and light the fire in his fireplace and I recall sending that picture back to the little girl who shivered in the musty dead smelling basement somewhere in the 1950s. I sent the picture of the meadow to the one that believed she would die the time I was buried alive in a box when I was just 4.

***

One morning, after having spent a peaceful night in that cozy house, I was sitting on my lover's bed. I was wearing his black cashmere bathrobe, feeling safe and deeply cared for. I watched the sun making lace-like shadows on the window as the wind played with the tree branches in the backyard. When I looked up toward the sun peaking through the trees, I saw a reflection of myself against the glass, as the sun had turned the window into a momentary mirror. My hair was down, loosely falling in waves around my shoulders and the robe was slightly pulled back away from my neck. Shadows of the lace-like leaves cast patterns on the bathrobe. It was a picture that remained for the briefest of moments but captured the peace that was in my soul as I had never before known.

To my total shock, what I saw in the window was a replica of the woman I had drawn nearly 30-years before. The hair, casual and forming a waved-frame about a face that I had drawn as a teenager, matched exactly the image I saw reflected in the window. Even the robe that was pulled back with folds in it was exactly the same as in my drawing. The leaf patterns I had so carefully drawn on the robe were actually created by the sunlight casting leaf shadows on the robe. It had to have been sometime in 1958 or 1959 that I carefully drew this portrait of someone I didn't know back then, but in 1987, I knew, with no doubt in my mind, that I was the woman that my teenage-self had drawn. I believe that at 15, some part of me was driven to record an image of the woman in the window, a woman who would not exist for almost another 30 years, but she existed in the teenager's mind. I believe the young girl's drawing was the way my future self—higher self, true self, whole self, eternal self, my being, my essence —used to help the current Sandy understand that all aspects of me had a connection through time.

The woman in that beautiful sun filled moment had hope and peace in her life, at least when she was at her lover's home. The adult Sandy looking out the window in that second floor bedroom was a woman who knew what it felt like to be loved, to be valued and seen, when my teenage self felt unloved, not valued, and not seen. I can't tell you from any traditional understanding of space and time how this happened, but I do know that it did.

It was that event that caused me to consider a non-conventional under-standing of time…in which past, present, and future were simultaneous. Much later I came to understand that if my adult self was going back to rescue my child self from life threatening situations as a way to heal current difficulties with roots in the past, and my child self knew that someone she called the Angel Lady had come to protect her, which gave her strength to live through impossible situations into the future, then the past was impacting the present and the present was impacting the past. But another important part of all of this is that my future self, drawn by the teenage Sandy, had, also, made connection with and impacted the past, at the time that past was present for the teenager.

Not long after this experience, I found myself in my adult life in an extremely heart-wrenching situation. I had no way to know what to do… so I called out to my future self to help me find my way out, just as I had done for little Sandy, as my child self's future self. I began asking my future self, the one who had found her way to full healing, to guide me to her, just as I guided my child self of the past to the present me. Not only have I benefited from this understanding of time, but also, many clients who have been open to consider alternative paths to healing have benefited from asking guidance from their future selves.

This understanding of Angel Lady in past, present, and future became a profound aspect of my perspective of who I am…of who we all are…and it has transformed my life.

Chapter Twenty-Three
SELA

What would your life be like if you embraced the idea that you are a multi-dimensional being and far more than you think you are? What would it take for you to consider such an idea?

Seven years after that amazing experience of seeing my reflection in the window, another event shifted my awareness of myself even more significantly; I met Sela. In those intervening years, I had finalized my divorce, lived in China for close to two years, relocated to Florida, and went to New Zealand to complete my training and certification as a clinical hypnotherapist. Though I was aware of some "presence" throughout my life—especially from the time I began working with another David, who was my psychologist in Seattle—I didn't come to know that presence as Sela until just after Christmas in 1993. Prior to that time, I didn't know her name, other than Angel Lady, in childhood, and my spirit guide, later on, but I came to understand that from her, I learned to enter the alternate realities, to move above the categories of time and space, and manipulate the flow of energy.

My first conscious awareness as an adult of an entity that was looking out for me arose in a most unusual way. I had been seeing a body therapist in Clearwater, Florida for a number of months as an adjunct to my psychotherapy. It was not uncommon for this gifted body therapist, also, named David—I will call him Clearwater David, since I seem to have collected quite a group of significant people in my life with the name of David—to tell me that there were angelic presences in the room directing his therapeutic process with me. On occasion, it was not unusual for both of us to sense the spiritual presence of guides and helpers, and now and then, the presence of people who had passed on but were coming back to help me through particularly difficult releases.

In late December of 1993, a spiritual presence let herself be known speaking first with Clearwater David, telling him that she had been try-ing for years, for decades, to talk to me directly, but I was too stubborn to listen. She said her name was Sela, and until I was willing to listen to her, she would communicate to me through him. At the time, this David was more open to that sort of thing than was I. She told him that she wanted me to get to know her. I was extremely skeptical at first, but was willing to listen. Her basic message, besides giving me her name, and letting me know she was the one my child self, called Angel Lady, was to ask me to be aware of her. After the session, I went to my mailbox and found a Christmas card from a friend I had not heard from in several years, one that I believed had not had room in her life for a friendship with me anymore. It had heralding angels on the front, and a statement that she missed the connection that we used to have.

During that Christmas season, I received a number of presents from friends scattered all over the country; absolutely every gift I received was an angel. It seemed that I was being given a magical message that Sela was an angel. In time, I was to discover that Sela was not a separate being, one that I saw as an angel outside of myself, but she was con-nected within *me*. She is the infinite me, the essence of me that flows through all of my lifetimes. She is the whole me that is connected with all the planes, with the Highest, with the Universe. She had been send-ing me thoughts, visions, pictures, experiences, and understandings all my life; I just hadn't attributed any of that to her in the past. Sela is the one who knows healing energies and taught me to stop my blood from flowing during surgery and so much more. It took some time for me to connect all of this. And though I knew her, I really didn't know her...

Sela traveled with the angels in alternate Universes, she knew how to see through time and space; she could be in one place and be seen in other places at the same time. She helped me in times of disappoint-ment, even as a child. Sela was the Angel Lady that came to visit me when I was too afraid to live. She breathed into me to revive me after that horrible experience of being buried in a box. She, also, allowed me to fulfill wishes and needs that seemed important to a little girl, and later to a woman.

One such incident happened in Alaska when I was 10 years old. From the time I was in the first grade, I looked forward to the fourth grade picnic. At the end of each year, the fourth grade children were permitted to travel by train 30 miles from our town up to a little town called Moose Pass in the beautiful Chugach National Forest in the Kenai Mountains. While children in the other grades were in school, fourth graders spend the entire day playing, splashing in the glacier river, and having lunch provided by the mothers. In the afternoon the children returned to Seward, on Resurrection Bay by train.

My family left Seward in the fall of my fourth grade year, long before the picnic, and I was so deeply disappointed that this experience was taken from me. While in Anchorage, 120 miles away from Seward, I went to the picnic anyway, or at least a part of me did. Only one of the children spent time with me; the others didn't seem to know I was there. I remember the magical taste of the hot dogs and potato chips, and the taste of coke from an icy cold bottle that had been cooled in the glacier river that was our playground. At the end of the day, the children all got on the train just as raindrops began to make ripples on the river's surface. The picnic was such a clear memory for me, but there was no way I could have attended, not in any traditionally accepted way. Much later, when I was reviewing my life's history, I realized my family had moved before the picnic had occurred; I remembered I didn't get on the train to go to or leave Moose Pass and the picnic spot. At that moment, so many years later, I understood that I had attended the picnic in an altered state called bilocation. My Sela-self had taken me.

Another incident similar to the picnic journey occurred decades later while I was in China. The week I separated from my husband, Sara came into my life. She was my amazing little Lhassa puppy who sustained me during the worst time of my adult life and in several instances she was responsible for my not exiting this world. We were deeply bonded. One of the most difficult things I have ever had to do was to leave her when I went to China; she was not quite three years old. A lovely couple I had known for a little over a year agreed to keep Sara while I was gone. I knew she was having difficulty adjusting to life without me from the letters my friends sent, but they assured me she was improving. After about six months, I began feeling intense worry about her. One day my worry pulled me into altered state and I found myself walking down the hall of my friends' home in Seattle. Sara came bounding out of a bedroom and leapt into my arms. I felt her wiggling body against my chest and her wet tongue on my face. I looked into her eyes and explained that she needed to be a good dog. I told her I had not left her forever. I would return and take her back. She settled in my arms and in that moment I was back in China.

Upon my return to the states, over a year later, the man who had cared for Sara, cautiously asked me if I had come to the house one night when I was in China. I was astonished by his question and asked, "Why?" He told me that he had seen me for a microsecond, walking down the hall toward the room where Sara slept, and that she was a "different dog" after that night. Prior to that event, she had been so bad that he and his wife had taken Sara to a dog psychologist. The couple came close to divorcing over their differences of opinion as to what to do with her. Following my visit that night, Sara was an "angel." He told me that he saw me in physical form, but that somehow I seemed different, like he could see through me, yet, he knew I had been there. I smiled and told him that I had come, but was surprised that he had seen me. Without knowing why, the moment he cautiously asked me that question, I felt as if I had been caught. Now I know that it was Sela's energy that took me to Sara.

Sela was able to see inside people's bodies and help them release blocked energies, or loosen tightly spinning energies to heal what was wrong with them. Her vision could shift intensity and see inside bones or muscles, and could observe the working of systems, and could see the movement of molecules. She could ride internal energy waves, whether they were light or matter and could find the spaces between the particles that took her from one reality to the next. Sela could go backward and forward in time and often gave me dreams that later would occur in waking life exactly as I dreamed them. She was able to read energies of people and know their thoughts. I was always aware that I had to be careful with others not to disclose that I knew what I was not supposed to know, and had to consciously shut off knowing what didn't seem OK to know. If people didn't want me to enter their space, I didn't.

Another time, I had been working with Seattle David for almost three years when I inadvertently discovered that he was moving. I found myself in altered state walking through his new empty house. I wrote about the house, describing it in detail and then asked him at the next session when he was going to move. With a look of puzzlement on his face, he told me he was not moving. I was stunned. I knew it was his house and that he would be moving, but I knew that he wouldn't lie to me. A few months later he announced that he was moving to the midwest. He had just made the decision. I asked him if he had picked out his house yet, and when he answered affirmatively, I began to describe the house I had visited in the vision a few months before. It was the same house.

Sela's awareness of events beyond time and space became more apparent as I recorded my visions and dreams in my journal and then, weeks or months later experienced the exact events. Often, I knew there was a message in the dreams or visions, but I couldn't understand the meaning until the "future" event happened. There were times I knew what was happening in other places just when they were taking place.

One early morning, a few months after I had separated from my husband, I woke from a deep sleep knowing there was a fire engine at my husband's and my business, though I didn't see a fire. I jumped in my car and drove 17 miles south to the office, but outside there was no fire engine, only his car and the car of his secretary. I hurriedly entered to find the floor flooded with water. I asked where the fire engine had gone. He looked at me with surprise and answered that it had left perhaps five minutes before; he wanted to know how I knew. I told him I saw it in a dream and I wanted to know if he was OK. Apparently there was a malfunction in the fire alarm system causing all the sprinklers to turn on, and though there was no fire, the fire station was alerted. So that was why I saw the fire engine but no fire. As usual, he seemed very uncomfortable when this kind of thing happened. He looked at me with questioning in his eyes and asked if it wasn't that I saw it in the dream but my dreaming made it happen. I was devastated that he believed I would do such a thing. That kind of response may well be why I chose not to know much of what I knew.

As I reflect back to a much earlier time, I remember an event that occurred shortly after my family moved from Alaska to Seattle in the mid 1950s. My parents took us to a minister's home up on Capitol Hill, a place none of us had ever visited. It was a large, mansion-like structure in the historic section of town. When we walked in, I knew the house, though I had never been there before. I stood in the entry that opened four stories upward to the crystal chandelier that hung from the vaulted ceiling. Everyone else had gone into the sitting room. I joined them, and in a moment, feeling a bit anxious, asked the minister if I could go up to the top floor to see the library. He looked perplexed and asked how I knew there was a library up there. I was embarrassed and shrugged my shoulders. The minister gave his approval and I scampered up the several flights of stairs. There on the top floor, was the library exactly as I knew it would be. I stood in the center of the small library, looking all around what seemed to be a place in which I had felt safe in some distant past; a peace filled me and I returned to the others in the sitting room on the main floor. No one asked me anything about it and my parents never mentioned the incident.

***

When I first met Sela in my conscious awareness as an adult, in December of 1993, I asked her why she had come into my life. At the time, I was not able to hear her with an inner hearing, something that I later developed, so I used my Motherpeace Tarot card deck to find her response. Through the cards, she helped me see that she had come to help me face all of my fears even my fear of her and to allow what frightens me to be my ally. She explained that she is the one who knew I was ready to ask the questions about her, and she was the reason for my asking the questions.

She told me she came to help me learn to connect to my body. For the vast majority of my life, I, or at least parts of me, were able to connect to the higher levels of existence, but I had not learned how to fully be in my body. Sela explained that I needed to connect with the physical world, the world my body lives in if I am going to teach what I came to teach, which is my deepest conscious awareness that justice prevails, that the human experience of the Universe that has gotten greatly out of balance will be brought back to balance. I know this is what my heart believes. That is why I don't feel afraid of the social, political, economic and environmental chaos that is present in our world. I know that all chaos is simply a reaction to the fear that created the original actions many, many generations ago, and continue to be replicated…and this can be changed. I know our world can come back to a natural balance; I need to gain the courage to teach it. I am not the only one teaching this message.

She explained that because of my childhood, I withdrew from my body, and from my feminine energy. Part of what she was here to help me do was to release my lack of receptivity to and compassion for masculine energy, my reluctance to surrender to the feminine, and my resistance to embrace my shaman-spiritual knowing. She said that I hold people with my eyes open because I still believe that I cannot trust men, and I believe that I am not safe with women; a way of being that doesn't leave a whole lot of people with whom I can connect. She, also, told me that she came to help me find a new name and to help me bring spiritual power into the physical world. At the time, I thought that having a new name meant that I was going to learn how to identify myself as the feminine shaman, but several years later, I learned that her statement about my name was much more literal than I could have imagined.

***

I had been in graduate school for a little over three years when I signed up to take a year long training course in imagery and healing, taught by one of my professors, Jeanne Achterberg known internationally for her work in imagery and healing, especially related to cancer and Frank Lawlis, known for his work that integrates complimentary and alternative medicine into hospital settings, and both well known in the field of psychology. Jeanne taught the anatomy and physiology portions of the course and how imagery could influence healing, a core teaching in her many books, and Frank led the group of nearly 40 people in the shamanic rituals.

On September 18, 1998, Jeanne and Frank began the third of the four weekends of imagery and healing training. This fall weekend session at Santa Sabina in San Rafael, California was dedicated to studying the images we hold of who we are. We were led through processes and given information that would help us understand the relationship of those images to our health. Officially, this is called psychoneuro-immunology. As we collected together the first night, 30-some participants in this yearlong study-group were asked to reflect on the previous few months to consider what each of us might be bringing forward in ourselves that deserved to be named. Dr. Achterberg told us about the importance of "taking on a new name" from her own personal experience and then she proposed, as our first experience, a shamanic journey to find a new name. We were asked to consider what part of ourselves needed to be recognized. I felt my heart smile at the synchronicity of what we were doing because I had been considering actually changing my name, going beyond the intent of the experience, but since I had been unsuccessful in finding a name that suited me, I decided to find out where this experience would take me.

The lights were dimmed as nearly three-dozen people closed their eyes, and allowed the sounds of a rattle and drum to take them into trance state. Within a few moments, I found myself dropping into a tunnel that took me on the swirling and looping of a downward spiral. I have no idea how much time passed; it could have been a few seconds or an eternity.

Then, without expecting a shift, I felt as if a gigantic eagle swooped down from the heavens and lifted me into the night sky. It took me over an ocean and up the side of a cliff onto a plateau area atop a mountain and it dropped me in a circle of beings that seemed to have come to assist me in discovering my name. As I looked around at those in the circle, I recognized some as guides I had worked with while on other journeys and other's I had never seen before. They were the oddest collection of beings I had ever seen. There were angelic creatures with smooth-skinned faces that seemed to glow from an internal light source standing next to rustic looking beings, deeply creased, weathered-faced shamans in animal-skin clothing from all over the ancient world, and wise men and women that seemed to be from past and future times. Though no one spoke, I sensed something important was about to happen.

I was taken through many experiences in my past and then based on those experiences, I asked the circle of beings if my new name should be from one of those times, but instead, I heard that my new name is to be Sela. I felt myself pull back and resist taking on that name. I knew that on December 30, 1993, a little less than five years earlier, this magnificent guide told me during a body therapy session that her name was Sela, which she said was a Hebrew word and meant hark as in: "listen...turn your head and listen to what is being said." It, also, has the meaning of something solid, something that can be built upon, like a rock. Not knowing Hebrew, nor hearing that name before, I asked a Jewish friend who acknowledged that the translation was correct. Later, I found that there is another meaning, which refers to something that is forever; Sela goes on without end.

From that time on, Sela has participated in numerous healing journeys and has been calling my attention to many ways of seeing and knowing that I didn't understand before. At first I had considered her to be a spiritual guide and in time came to know her as my spiritual self on a "higher" plane. She seemed to be beyond the physical, but had the ability to intervene and influence my experience in this three dimensional world. When I asked again if I really was being directed to take on Sela as my name, the strange group of spiritual guides affirmed the accuracy. They told me my new name was from this day forward **Sandy Sela-Smith**.

I was told that my parental given name San Dra, which split the power of the name, was to be Sandy, given by the circle. It is to be one name instead of a divided name, as it had been from my birth. Sandy is a derivative of Alexandra that means *a helper of people*. I was told that my last name is to remain the same; that was the name I selected when I was married; it was my name of choice. A *smith* is one who shapes and transforms things, metal, leather, and…souls. They told me Smith is to be connected with my spiritual name, Sela, one who points the way to a higher vision by entreating people to listen to a grounded truth, a truth built on the rock. Together my new name means *one who helps people transform by offering a new way of seeing, hearing, and knowing truth*. I looked around at the beings in the circle and accepted the name they had given me. In accepting the name, I felt my whole body open to Sela, the part of me that I needed to recognize as me. In later years, I came to understand that Sela is the aspect of my unique being that resides under the mask, my unique mystery that is in union with the great mystery.

An amazing tingling filled my entire body as if every cell had accepted being Sela. Ecstasy filled me in that moment, and a shift in the sound of the drum and rattle pulled me back from the deep place. I knew that when I returned to Florida, I would go to the courthouse and apply for a legal name change. The first step in being an authentic teacher is to live in integrity with what is known, to be an example without words, to give power to the words, so I knew I needed to follow the directive I had been given. On October 12, 1998, less than a month after that amazing experience in alternate reality, I entered the judge's chambers in a Pinellas County Courtroom, and San Dra Smith became Sandy Sela-Smith in this 3-dimensional reality. But this didn't happen without sorrow. While waiting in the corridor to be called before the judge, I sat quietly on a wooden bench, looking at a paper that had the name I had used for so many years. I wrote San Dra Smith on a blank page as a tear fell; I realized this would be the last time I wrote that name as something that identified me. It was like a death, a funeral for who I used to be. And though there were tears before, when I left the chamber with my new name in hand, I felt a sense of expansion, a feeling that a birth had happened.

As my connection with Sela continued, I realized I was afraid that if I accepted who she said I was—*a channel, a magician who contains and disperses energy*—that I would somehow become destructive if I did this from the dark side, a place of ego, instead of a place of love. Her job was to work with me on this. Sela needed to make her self know to me to help me free myself from beliefs that grew out of the lies that kept me from knowing the truth. I needed to clear out the lies that held me back from experiencing my true power.

What I have come to know is that every one of us has a "Sela" counter-part. I am sure that there were some aspects of what I wrote about in my past that you understood because similar things happened to you. Part of the reason I became more conscious of all of these things, was due to the deep inner searching that I had to do to heal a particularly difficult childhood. Had I not had to heal such deep wounds, I might have done what most people do when they have pre-cognitive dreams or when other "strange" things happen, such as when they think they saw what they couldn't have seen. I would likely have pushed them away, too; I would not have acknowledged them or maybe even not have remembered them.

Taking the name, Sela, as mine, didn't mean that I would fully step into being Sela, but it was the beginning. I had to overcome the fear of being myself in the world, a fear I had carried for many years.

Chapter Twenty-Four
OWNING THE MAGICAL CHILD

It is not unusual for some significant person in your life to have rejected your wonder and greatness when you were very young, even if it was only once and for a very short period of time. After that rejection, it is not uncommon for you to reject your own wonder and greatness. Those who rejected you were rejected, long before, by someone else, and to accept who you are would touch the pain of what happened to them. They avoid feeling their pain by passing it on. What would your life look like if you decided to embrace your wonder and your greatness?

My reluctance to know my own power, to feel my backbone, and live my life from the place of recognizing who I am in this world, had been something that I lived with my entire life and a reluctance that I have been especially aware of since I lived in China. It was there I began to see the problems that could come with being myself. Beside my lifelong attraction to the Middle Kingdom, one of the things that drew me to China was an ancient energy healing practice called Qi Gong. Though I had been aware of energy healing since I was a small child, my adult awareness was stirred when I, myself received an unexpected energy healing in my therapists' office five years or so before China became a part of my life.

I had just begun to connect with incidents in my childhood when, during a therapy session, Seattle David asked if the child-self we were working with had anything she wanted to show me. Using an Ericksonian technique, he said that if she had something to show me, she could lead me to a door and behind that door would be whatever it was she wanted me to see. She led me to a curtain, rather than a door, and then pulled it back like you would a shower curtain. But, before I could register what was there, everything went black. A shock wave exploded in my chest that flipped me back in the recliner chair, and I lost consciousness.

When my eyes opened, Seattle David's hands were floating above me, and I asked what he was doing. He explained that he was not really doing anything, but that I was doing it. Not understanding his answer, I asked with greater emphasis, *"What are you doing?"* His response was to ask me what I was feeling. I told him that I could feel heat in my chest, heat in my heart, and asked a third time, *"What are you doing?"* He explained that he was reflecting my own healing energies back into me and I was feeling them as heat. I must have had a very puzzled look on my face, and knowing that I had come from a Christian background, he asked me if I remembered that Jesus and his disciples healed people with their hands. Of course, I remembered reading about that, and he explained that he was doing something like that.

After a few minutes of receiving whatever was happening, the session was over, and I reassured Seattle David that I was feeling fine. When I left his office, I was aware of how bright colors looked. I don't think I had ever seen flowers look so beautiful. Everything seemed more alive. I drove to West Seattle where my 92-year-old grandmother was living in a nursing home. She had withered away from a strong 5'9 woman to one who likely wouldn't have stood much over 4 feet tall if she could stand. Bed-ridden for some time, my tiny grandmother was always in great pain. When I walked into her room, she greeted me with a half smile and told me that she was exhausted from too many nights of no sleep. I asked her if she wanted me to see if I could help her, and she shook her head in the affirmative.

I pulled up a chair beside her bed and felt my arms rise up, without my lifting them myself, and then my hands began to float over her body as if they had a mind of their own. They looked like they were doing what Seattle David had done just a short time before. And then they simply stopped and dropped down to my side. I was a bit surprised by the experience, but thoughts of myself disappeared as I watched the changes in my grandmother's face that, now, looked so peaceful. She turned her head and looked into my eyes with a softness that I had not seen from the first I knew her. Then she whispered to me that she was tired and wanted to sleep. I asked her if she wanted me to come back the next day and she nodded a barely visible yes as she slipped off into sleep.

The next day grandma greeted me with a cheery voice. She was alert and happy, and told me that she had slept wonderfully the night before. I noticed that red spots that had been on her face the day before were gone. For years she had been plagued with skin cancer and had many white spots where the cancer had been removed, but apparently because of her age, her doctors must have decided to let the new red spots do whatever they were going to do. For the next few days, I continued to see her and each time I asked her if she wanted me to help her with my hands. Each day she said yes.

One day, I walked into her room to find two of my aunts and an uncle who had come to see her, and the three of them were arguing about what to do when she passed, as if she were already dead. They didn't seem to notice or care that she was very much awake and could hear them. She had a very angry look on her face, something that they didn't seem to notice either. I asked her if she wanted me to leave, and she said no. So I waited for my relatives to leave, and I pulled up my chair beside her again. I asked her if she wanted my hands to do what they did, and she nodded, yes. While all this was happening, I told her that I really didn't know what I was doing and wondered if she knew. Again she nodded, yes, and closed her eyes. After only a couple of minutes, grandma said she was tired and wanted to sleep. So I kissed her good-bye and whispered I would come back the next day after church.

After services, as I was driving home to change, I was gripped with sadness. For some unknown reason, a wailing sound emerged from the deepest part of me. The sound filled my car, and likely, the whole freeway, as tears poured down my face. I had no idea why this sadness had come over me. After putting on more casual clothes, I drove the 20 miles from my home to the nursing home, and when I walked into my grandmother's room, her bed was empty. Though in retrospect, it was very clear what had happened, even from the wailing cry on my drive home, nothing seemed to compute in that moment. I went into the hall and asked the nurse if they had taken my grandmother to the lunchroom. I wanted to know where I could find her. The nurse asked me to identify myself and then said she was sorry that no one had told me that my grandmother had passed away earlier that day… just about the time I was driving home from church.

I drove over to my mother's house wanting to ask why someone couldn't have called me to let me know that my grandmother had died. My parents knew that my grandmother and I had become close, but instead of expressing my distress over what seemed like a lack of concern for my feelings, I simply told them about finding the empty bed. I, also, shared with them about the energy healing and how grandma had finally been able to sleep and about the red spots that had cleared up. But instead of being happy that her mother had died peacefully, my mother seemed disturbed and told me not to say anything to anyone about the healing, though she did say she was sorry that I found out the way I did about my grandmother's passing. She didn't explain why no one had called me, but asked if I would give the eulogy, and I agreed.

When I met with the minister who was going to provide the services, I told him about the peace that my grandmother felt in her last days, and the powerful experience in my therapist's office that seemed to have provided a catalyst for me to do the same thing for my grandmother. He asked if I would make an appointment with him after the funeral so that he could do an exorcism to help me get rid of whatever it was that had taken me over. He believed that while it might be possible for something like this to happen on a one-time basis, it was not good for ordinary people to get involved in this kind of thing. And like my mother, he advised me to not talk to anyone about what had happened. In spite of the fact that my mother's minister and my mother believed there was something wrong about what happened with my grandmother, I knew it was not bad; in fact, I knew that there was goodness and *godness* in it.

***

Not long after this experience, I read a book by John Chilton Pearce called *Magical Child*. The basic premise of this book is that children are born with amazing, magical abilities, but our culture erases those abilities by discouraging them instead of being open and encouraging them. The single passage that struck me so deeply had to do with a man who was in a terrible accident with his young son. While the father was not badly hurt, the son was thrown from the car, and his arm was deeply gashed that cut into an artery. As the father rushed to his little boy's side and saw the gravity of the situation with blood gushing at every pulse of the boy's heart, the father shouted an order to his son's arm to stop bleeding…and the blood stopped. If the blood had continued to gush, the child would likely have died before the ambulance had arrived, and certainly before getting to the hospital. The attending physician was seriously puzzled and had no explanation as to why the child had not died at the scene of the accident considering the severity of the wound, but didn't know how to take the father's explanation into his medical worldview.

Of course, the moment I read that passage, I knew it was true. A few weeks after having read that book, I was scheduled for minor surgery, and did what seemed natural. I talked to my skin and muscles, just as the father had talked to his son's artery, when he shouted, *"Stop Bleeding!"* I knew the procedure that was going to happen, and explained it to the cells that were leaving, as well as the ones that were staying, and then told them that when they felt the pressure of the knife, that was the signal for the blood vessels to stop bleeding, and when the remaining tissue was fully reconnected, that would be their signal to allow the flow of blood to resume. Even though I was sedated during the procedure, the doctor told me afterward that I kept asking him if I was bleeding, and he kept saying, *"No."* He asked me what I had done to stop the bleeding, and based on the look on his face, I suspect he didn't believe me, either.

A few months later, I heard that Matthew Manning, a healer from England, was conducting a training workshop in Seattle and I registered for his course. He worked with terminal cancer patients and had demonstrated an amazing rate of remissions. The medical system didn't understand how he did what he did, but when they determined that they couldn't help a person, many London oncologists provided these people with contact information for Matthew, just in case he could do something. I learned a great deal from him, and began practicing simple processes with people I knew. It was very easy to help people release headaches, and relieve pain. In time, I began helping with more complicated physical problems.

While at a spiritually focused conference sponsored by the Unity church of Seattle, a woman who heard about me asked if I could help her with a knee problem that had plagued her since she was a child. At that time she was on a swing going very high when she lost her grip of the ropes and fell, which did major damage to her right knee. Though most of the damage healed, she always walked with pain, and if she was on her feet too much, her knee became painfully swollen. I allowed my hands to move in whatever way they wanted, and stopped when they stopped. The woman stood up and began to cry. For the first time since she was a little girl, her knee didn't hurt.

A man, who was nearby observing what was happening, asked me if I could help eyes that were in pain. I told him I didn't know but was willing to try. He had been working with chemicals and an unexpected accident caused the caustic liquid to spray into his eyes. He had been to a specialist who had given him ointment, which didn't stop the constant grainy feeling that left him with headaches and a very frustrated disposition. I asked him to sit and then gave my hands permission to move as needed. Again, as before, when my hands dropped down to my sides, I knew whatever had been happening was finished. The man opened his eyes, blinked a number of times and asked what I wanted from him. He said the irritating grainy feeling was gone and so was the headache. I didn't want anything except maybe his agreement to live his life with greater joy. I don't recall knowing why I said that to him.

Unlike the negative responses from my mother and her minister, positive reactions came from people who were on a more spiritual, rather than on a religious, path. I was not usually open to exposing myself to the criticism of people who would reject what I was doing. Though there were times that I sensed an opening, and would send healing energy toward strangers I met in lines at the grocery or counters in department stores. Sometimes, I simply sent healing energy to all the people in cars on the freeway as I was driving, knowing that those who were receptive could take it and those who were not could let it pass by. In retrospect, most of the time I felt good about what was happening, but there were times I didn't feel so good. Those times happened when I began to feel like I was somebody special because of the healing that happened, and when I did work with people with that thought, I felt sick afterward. It would take many more years for me to really get it that I was not doing the healing, but, as Seattle David had told me long before, the recipients are healing themselves, all I was doing was reflecting their own healing process back to them.

***

Without conscious awareness of the reason, part of what drew me to China was to learn more about Qi Gong, a part of the ancient Chinese healing tradition. When I first arrived in China, I met my translator, David. He was the amazing young man who had written the letter describing Baoji, the letter that caused me to believe that Baoji City was the place I was supposed to go. As I wrote earlier, I ended up there, and David and I became dear friends. I told him about my interest in Qi Gong, and within a few days he introduced me to one of the professors at the college who was in training to be a Qi Gong Master.

Professor Tang was a gentle, yet spirited man who had a reputation for being a *seer*, as well as a Qi Gong master in training. His rich black hair, always well groomed, was thick and made him look taller than he actually was. He was shorter than I, maybe by two or three inches, and his body was dense, though not fat. His black eyes sparkled with compassion, but there was always a sense about him that he was up to something. We became friends, though I felt I needed to keep him at a slight distance.

The two of us were like apprentices, practicing on each other, neither of us really believing in what we were doing, though both of us wanted to believe; yet on a deeper level, we seemed to know the reality underneath our disbeliefs. There were a number of times that I sensed his presence in my small unit apartment, as if he were spying on me and one day he told me that he was practicing mind travel and had been coming to visit me in my apartment. I chided him for not asking permission and set up an energy wall that would prevent him from entering or seeing anything. Though I really didn't believe in energy walls or in his ability to see from a distance, I felt as if I was setting boundaries in a world that still seemed so unfamiliar to me.

One afternoon, Tang arrived at my door to announce that he had arranged for me to meet the circle of Qi Gong masters with whom he was studying. The professor had borrowed a bicycle for me for the trip and the two of us headed out of the college compound to meet these old masters of Baoji. He led me through the neighboring village compounds and to the now dry river that separated the city from the countryside. We wound our way through temporary gardens and around soft spots on what had only weeks before been the very wide river bottom. We maneuvered our bikes past sharp boulders and rocky debris that had been left behind when the raging river stopped raging, and we made it to Baoji city.

There was something almost surreal and trance-inducing about that experience of making my way through a place that would exist, as it was, only a few more weeks and then it would be gone when the rains returned and the raging river would rage again. And yet, in some strange way, I was walking through a thousand generations, all alive in the people who were busily tending their gardens in 1990, living millennia-old life-patterns of farming in the in-between time of the river's pattern. After climbing up the riverbank, we traveled along back streets and main thoroughfares, weaving our way around heavily laden bicycles, goat drawn carts, animals being taken to market, as well as duce-and-a-half military trucks, busses, and cars, all making their way on roadways without lanes, to finally arrive at the local Qi Gong clinic where the masters often met.

Professor Tang asked me to wait in an outer room while the masters discussed what to do with me. A beautiful old man emerged from the back room. He must have been in his 90s and couldn't have been a more perfect picture of a Chinese healing master. He had long gray hair that was tied back in a traditional braid and a long thin mustache that flowed into a thin beard. He carried a photograph, which he held out in front of me. Tang asked me to look at it and tell the old man what I saw. At first it appeared to be a photo of some kind of altar or shrine draped with a Chinese-red velvet cloth. On the altar were four glass objects that, somehow, reflected back the camera's flash in a way that seemed blinding. But then, I noticed something very strange in the shadows behind the four objects. I saw a number of ghostly looking figures. My first response was to try to figure out how the light was creating the illusion of figures, but as I gazed more deeply into the photo, I could not help but be surprised at what seemed to be emerging. The surprise must have shown on my face because the old man asked Professor Tang something and the professor directed me to tell him exactly what I was seeing.

The more intently I looked, the more I saw that the photo was filled with faces, with transparent images of figures as if stacked one upon the other going deeper and deeper into the blackness behind the glass objects. I felt as if I had entered some trance where I was seeing things that have always been there, things that most eyes have learned not to see. Many of the ghostly figures looked as if they were suffering and crying out from some in-between place, while others looked as if they were simply observing me observing them.

After many questions and answers for what seemed like hours of translations, the old man returned to the back room and in time he emerged again with the other old gentlemen. They invited me to join their Qi Gong circle. The old man told me that I was a powerful person with great abilities but I played with energy as if it were a toy. He offered to teach me how to use it as a tool. He told me that the masters were interested in my understanding of energy because they believed that I knew it differently than they did. They didn't know if my difference was because I was a woman or because I was a Westerner, or maybe both, but they hoped that I could teach them what I knew as they taught me what they knew.

The months that followed were amazing…and a story for another time, but there is one experience that belongs here. One evening, while preparing for my teaching classes the following day, I heard the sound of sirens and saw flashing lights outside the window, followed by a knock on my second floor apartment door. Mr. Tang was standing straight and as tall as he could look, surrounded by a number of uniformed officers. I was told to come with them. Being in post-Tiananmen China, was frightening enough, but being taken by the police, without explanation, was even more terrifying. With flashing lights and sirens, the entourage of several official cars left my compound and drove through the streets of Baoji. As we sped away, the professor explained that I was being taken to a large hospital where the police chief lay dying of cancer. He had been given Western treatment, followed by treatment from a long line of traditional practitioners and healers, and as a last resort, they decided to see if the foreigner could help.

We arrived at the hospital, unlike any hospital I had ever been in, in the West. The dimly lighted hallways were covered with dust and spittle; the smell of unfiltered cigarette smoke permeated the air. I was escorted into a room where a dozen or so family members huddled together to say good-bye to the beloved Liu Chin, while provincial officials waited in the background, perhaps anxious for the moment when power would transfer to the next in line. Liu seemed to have difficulty breathing. It was hard to comprehend that this man, just a few weeks before, had been a leader whose words could mean the difference between life and death to any who now stood silently at his bedside.

Liu Chin had been one of the most powerful men in Shaanxi Province, China; but, pancreatic cancer robbed him of his former strength, and impending death left him with little but memories of who he used to be. His skin was a sickly yellow, and his stomach was swollen so tight that it was apparent he was in excruciating pain. His yellowed eyes, though sunken in dark and shadowed sockets, were not at all empty.

They seemed to be filled with the kind of quiet sadness that reveals both pain and acceptance of what is about to happen, a sadness that no longer needs to grasp at the hope in the eyes of others as a last frantic effort to cling to life. His legs and feet stretched beyond the gray sheets, and his body, though frail and thin from the months of struggle, seemed to fill the hospital bed indicating that he was a much bigger man, even in his dying, than most Chinese living in health. I didn't know much about him, other than the fact that he was a very important government official, whose very name was both feared and revered.

Professor Tang, the only one who spoke English, cleared a space and signaled to me, indicating that I should come forward to begin using what the Chinese considered my special style of Qi Gong energy healing on this dying man. Fear of what might happen to me should I fail to bring healing to him dissipated as Mr. Liu turned his head and looked directly into my soul. I nodded to him and he to me, as if we had known each other a very long time.

I closed my eyes and stood in the presence of Mr. Liu's energy. I felt my hands raise and begin to float, making infinity sign movements above him as if my fingers were communicating in some unknown language with his body. So now, in China, in the hospital room of an important political leader, my hands were floating and I still had no idea what I was doing any more than the time I had asked my grandmother if she understood, when I didn't. I felt like a fraud perpetrating some unholy hoax, wondering how I ever got myself into this situation—and then my hands stopped moving and dropped to my side.

No words were spoken as Professor Tang escorted me out of the room and to the awaiting government car, along with an entourage of the six or seven police cars with flashing lights and sirens. He opened the door for me as I slipped into the back seat; I waited for him as he returned to speak to a group of people that had followed us from the hospital room to the exit. After a short period of time, he slid in beside me and directed the driver to go; the lights and sirens accompanied our exit from the hospital compound.

We rode for a few miles in silence before I asked Tang if he could tell me what had taken place in that room. I expressed my concern for what might happen if Mr. Liu died. Tang assured me that I ought not to worry because the officials knew that it was too late for Mr. Liu. Because he had been to Chinese doctors trained in Western medicine, as well as visited by a number of traditional doctors and Qi Gong masters, by the time they decided to check out the American to see what she could do, they knew it was too late, so no one expected the impossible of me. But he told me that the officials and masters watched what I had done, and determined that I really understood principles of healing energy. Of course, my conscious self was very confused and discounted the information as coming from less developed people who believed in magic, because I believed I must have been tricking everyone, including myself, into believing this hoax of energy healing.

There was a part of me that had fully accepted the reality of energy healing; I had seen so many amazing recoveries in the two years between grandma's good night's sleep and healed face, and Liu Chin. But there was another part of me that believed all of this "energy healing" as a mind game played by gullible desperate people who wanted to believe that the healers were magical. And the healers were perpetrators who took advantage of the desperation. The two parts of me, the one that believed and the one that saw this as a hoax, warred in silence on the trip back to the college.

A few days later, I received a call informing me that an official car would be picking me up again. Apparently the swelling in Mr. Liu's stomach had almost completely gone away and his toxic yellow complexion had turned to near normal. He had asked for another treatment from the American. This time, my translator, David, accompanied me to the hospital, along with the police cars and sirens.

I entered the room and was immediately ushered to Mr. Liu's side. I smiled at him and he smiled back and then he closed his eyes. My eyes shut, as well, and a moment of silence was followed by the now familiar sensation of my hands raising in the air and floating a few inches above his body without my controlling them. I became aware of lots of talk in the background, as Mr. Tang was telling everyone to not speak a word of this to anyone. He told them that the American belonged to Baoji and if word got out, I would be taken over by the peasants or officials from other places. I felt heartsick by what I was hearing.

It was flattering to be held in such favor, but I knew that I really wasn't doing anything. A person could get well or not get well and if I were given credit for them getting well, then I would be blamed if they did not. I had not reflected on that experience and my overhearing the conversation, until years later. I am very sure that Mr. Tang was speaking to the others in Chinese, since the only other one in the crowd who knew English was my translator and he was with me. But I know that I clearly heard and understood the conversation he was having with the Chinese people who hovered in the back of the room. I cannot explain how that happened.

***

When I felt my hands drop to my sides, I looked at Mr. Liu, and asked him if there was anything else that he needed. He asked everyone in the room to leave, his wife and children, his relatives, and all the officials—he wanted only David and me in the room. After they all left, he slowly revealed a secret that he had held on to since he was a young man. When he was just 19, he had fallen in love with a college sweetheart and had asked her to marry him, but his parents had disapproved of the union because she was from a lower class. His father held an influential position in their unit and arranged for the girl to be sent away, and Liu did nothing to stop his father. Later, he married a woman approved of by his parents, but he held onto his feelings of guilt his entire life for not honoring his first love. He cried and the tears turned to deep sobbing for his youthful behavior. After opening his heart and speaking the truth, he was able to forgive himself for being so easily persuaded to do the "socially" acceptable thing. His face reflected a beautiful peace after finally speaking of what had oppressed him for so long and releasing his life-long sorrow. He thanked David and me for listening. He turned away to sleep as David and I left him alone in his room.

A week went by and I was asked to return for another treatment. Neither David nor Tang were available to come with me this time, so all I could do was communicate with my eyes and send love in the form of energy while connecting with the wave patterns above his body. Again, I was delivered back to my unit with an entourage of police cars, flashing lights, and sirens.

Several weeks went by and no one spoke of Mr. Liu. At a gathering of Qi Gong masters, as if in passing, Mr. Tang mentioned that Mr. Liu had died. I was broken hearted and began to cry, something that Mr. Tang seemed not to understand. He told me that Mr. Liu was dying when I met him and it was just a matter of time…and his time had come. After my initial feelings of mournful sadness, I became frightened. I asked if the officials or the family blamed me for not saving him, and Mr. Tang assured me that I had nothing to worry about. But I had come to understand that what Tang tells you is more what you want to hear than what is necessarily the truth, so I was not reassured.

A couple of months later, Chinese David and I stopped into a downtown restaurant and found two of Mr. Liu's sons having lunch. They asked us to join them and told me that they were grateful that their father had died in peace and without pain. I gleaned from the conversation that they were not angry with me for not saving him—they had never expected that.

Though this was one of many such experiences in China, it taught me something that went deeply into my being. I saw the danger of becoming recognized as a healer and believing what others might believe me to be, as something special, someone who is more than they are. The truth is that as human beings, we all have these abilities, and certainly we all heal ourselves, though we might think it is someone or something else who is doing it. When we get cut or have a break in a bone, it heals because our bodies are agents of healing. If anyone else had been drawn to the opportunity to study with someone like Matthew

Manning, as I did, or had a health crisis and someone used their hands as Seattle David did with me, that person might do the same things I learned to do. Healing is in our DNA. But most people don't choose this kind of path that for some reason my soul chose. And that is OK. I didn't choose to be a great cook or a great artist, or any of the other life paths that people choose, and that is OK, too.

I have been aware for some time that I would someday become a recognized leader in the field of healing, if I wanted to be. Another psychic, many years before, told me that I would decide if I would make that leadership in a limited or in a world arena. The decision was up to me, and her words felt true. Sela let me know that she was present with me to help me find comfort in whatever decision I would make.

As December of 1993 was coming to a close, Sela told me she was coming, along with angels, to act as guides for what it is that I came to this world to do. She said she had been waiting for a long time for me to be able to connect with her, and told me that 1994 would be a year of great changes, of doors opening beyond my expectations. Just six months later, not only did I experience a magnificent transformational healing with personality integration, but I was accepted into graduate school to begin what was to be a most profound 7-year educational and spiritual journey, that ended with my earning a Ph.D. and acceptance of my magical inner-child, something that I had struggled with so profoundly for most of my adult life.

Sela finished the question I asked her by saying that she made herself known to me so I might experience conscious awakening, and reconnect with happiness. With a refreshed spirit, I would be able to fully open to my purpose in the world. At the time that I recorded this message from Sela, I found myself hesitating and realized that I still held beliefs that I needed to protect myself from being noticed in the world. After hearing Sela's answer to me, I wrote the words that were reflected in the last Tarot Card I had drawn, *"I guess what it is time for me to do, is to ask the creator to give me courage to step beyond the hesitation and trust the special star that is emitting a benevolent ray of light, and let it take me to wherever it is I am to go."*

Sandy Sela-Smith, Ph.D.

I discovered that Sela has always been a part of me and I have always been a part of her. She is myself who moves into the future and sends messages to the present in dreams, thoughts and visions. She leads me to places where I can lift the curtains that had, in the past, separated me from what I knew and helps me remember what I had forgotten. Sela is myself who works with clients and supports them as they retrieve parts of themselves lost when personal power was stolen in their pasts and as she has done for me, she helps them reclaim what is theirs.

Sela is that part of myself that continues to teach me, cajole me, chastise me, and love me into higher knowing, into my future self. She presents me with synchronous events that allow me to discover patterns that were difficult to see, but could be seen more clearly when viewed from a distance. The more I work with others, the more I know that every one of us, including you, the one reading these very words, has a part like Sela. And everything Sela has given to me, your equivalent has given to you or is waiting to give to you, if you have not made that connection. Sela, and your counterpart to her, exists in the magical child and returns to those who have disconnected from that child, to help them reconnect when they are ready to know who they truly are.

Chapter Twenty-Five
308 AND 111

Do not dismiss the synchronous, unexplainable, and unusual events that you experience in your daily life and in your dreams. Sometimes, the parts of you that live on the different planes and in the different Universes are doing all they can to speak with you. Be open to the communications and notice what meanings seem to fit the harmony of your mind, body, and spirit in the moment you first know there is a message. If you misinterpret the meanings, as long as you remain open and unattached to those meanings, new communications will come to you to guide you on your way.

A few years after I met Sela and then discovered that she is the "me" that exists on all planes—the "me" under the mask, that is in union with the mystery—a series of events happened that I couldn't explain by any conventional means. The four events began and ended with computer anomalies that my Mac computer technician was unable to explain either, and sandwiched between those two computer events were two dreams that seemed to be uncannily related to the two other anomalies.

The first computer malfunction caught my attention because I had never had anything like it happen before. I was writing a paper for the Psychology of Shamanism course regarding the shamanic experience of time, in which past, present, and future are interpreted as being no different. Shamans were able to travel into the past or future the same as they did in the present. While I was writing a paragraph explaining this concept, about 8 in the morning, I noticed my computer clock showed

2:45 pm. I had been writing for some time and neglected to do a save of my document. Fear exploded in me that I might lose everything I had written. I did a quick save, and breathed a sigh of relief when no crash happened. Then I attempted to correct the time problem by clicking on the time and date at the top of my computer, but instead of showing the correct date, which was Thursday, January 11, 1996, it showed: Tues. November-1-39. I recognized the reversal of the 11 and 1, but also, was aware of the synchronicity of writing about past, present and future, being simultaneous events, when a past date was flashing on my computer in the present, for no apparent reason.

Wondering if something important might have happened on 11-1-39, I waited until the afternoon and called my parents who were on the West Coast to ask them if they knew what they were doing in November of 1939. Both of them did their best to remember, but really couldn't say much in detail. My father thought that he may have been preparing to leave his university in Tacoma, Washington to go to Alaska and my mother was in Nurses' training in Portland, Oregon, still a year away from her graduation, and relocation to Alaska, where she met my father. There seemed to be no intuitive hit for me in their comments. After my call to them, I closed and saved the document; but instead of showing 1939 as I had thought it would, the date of my document was recorded as Tuesday, November 1, 2039. It was not the past, but the future. I was puzzled by such an anomaly.

I called my computer technician, who couldn't explain what might have caused such a strange occurrence, especially because the Mac I had at the time was programmed up to 2019, and if someone tried to input a 2039 date, the computer would not take it and the system would revert to 1939.

I reopened the paper, to answer the last question for the course, which asked the student to consider, based on the literature from the course, whether or not the student believed him or herself to be a shaman. I debated about answering the question in the affirmative, even though I believed that Sela certainly met the criteria, and though I was still struggling with the concept that she is me, I decided to own what I believed was true. I wrote:

My own initiation, which lasted for nearly a half century, was the initiation overseen by Sela, my inner spirit guide, my higher self, my Angel Lady, my self who lives on all the planes. Sela came to my awareness from the time I was buried in the box when I was 4 and believed I was going to die, which fits the beginning initiation ritual for people who receive a call to be shamans. This initiation, like that of most shamans, used the illness caused by malevolent practitioners to allow for a leap in consciousness to multidimensional perception. The malevolent people of my childhood were the abusers who created such terror that I divided into over 250 parts and fragments, described in modern psychology as dissociative identity disorder. Because living in awareness in my body was intolerable, I willingly left my body behind to fly to the other realms. My Sela aspect taught me to travel the unseen paths and become a technician of the sacred.

My illness became a vehicle to higher planes of consciousness. As a result, I feel far more comfortable in the alternative realities than I do on the Earth plane. I agreed with the "higher realms" to remain in 3-dimensional reality because of an internal belief that I have a purpose to accomplish though my intention was always to leave as soon as that purpose was fulfilled. I had no desire to attach to or identify with life here. Instead of coming from an awareness of the physical and connecting to the spiritual, releasing the limiting categories of the physical and discovering the oneness of the spiritual, I was connected with spiritual awareness, experienced life without categories, and had to discover how to live within the categories of the physical. What is happening to me, as my initiation period appears to be coming to a close, is that I am discovering that I can hold both worlds. I discovered that the physical world is not evil, and it is not just an illusion, as I had previously believed. Now, it seems that I am ready to open to the message that Sela gave me just about two years ago. She told me I would be learning how to be in my body and that I was on a vision quest to find a new name, to bring spiritual power into the physical. She told me that I was letting go of rejection of the shaman and opening to embracing the feminine, a significant enough act with which Richard Tarnas ends his most provocative text, The Passion of the Western Mind, that is a vision of humankind's spiritual renewal occurring with the embrace of the feminine. Perhaps, the new name that I have resisted since this journey began but now embrace more willingly, is acceptance of myself as feminine shaman.

In order to include this information in *The Meaning of Three*, I retrieved this material from my shaman paper and when I copied the answer I had written that held this statement, I noticed that the page number of my Shamanic paper was 111, a number that, over the years, has held significance for me, somehow connecting me to the bliss of the eternal.

In January of 1996, I copied the paper to my computer with the odd date and saved it on a disk. I went back into the system and corrected the date and time to match what the rest of the world was showing. In the 16 months between two computer anomalies, the first recorded above and the second that will be explained later, my life was filled with more than I could have imagined. I completed 15 course units in six months when the normal completion for an entire year is 12 units. Shortly after that, my father died from an eruption of his aortic aneurism, which sent me on a journey that lasted for nearly a year during which time I was unable to complete any more courses. I had a heart attack while completing a most heart wrenching process of disconnecting emotional ties to my former husband. Not long after the heart attack, my sweet Lhassa, Sara, became ill with what was diagnosed as congenital heart failure, something she didn't have until I had a heart attack. My precious heart companion suffered for months, and despite all my work with her, she died in the spring of 1997, which lead me into the darkest of depressions, perhaps worse than the depressions a decade earlier when my life was falling apart. While all of this dark energy of death and dying was spinning in my life, I had a dream.

In the dream, I was in a school building, returning to teach. It seemed to be a combination of my high school and the high school where I taught for 12 years in the early years of my adulthood in waking life. This place, however, had very thick walls—adobe-like construction—and seemed very solid. The building was very old with lots of halls. Some of the same people from the 1970's school were there in this new-old building. I walked into the office to let them know I had returned. It seemed to be a parents' night, where parents had come to find out what their children would be learning by following their child's schedule, going from class to class every few minutes. At one point it seemed as if the periods were every 20 minutes, but perhaps each one was every 7 minutes.

I walked up to where my former classroom, # 308, had been and dis-covered that another section had been added on to the building, while I was gone, and I found out that I would be teaching in the new wing of the school...I went into the addition by way of another thick hall and found my new classroom was # 111. The entry door seemed to be wooden; it had a rounded top, sort of Spanish style. My classroom was a very large lecture hall. The door opened at the back and top of the room. Descending steps had rows of seats beside them for students to sit, much like a college lecture hall. I walked down the stairs to the podium.

Somebody wanted to talk with me about something that seemed trivial, at least it felt like a distraction because I had only a few minutes before the first people were to come in and I had not prepared what I wanted to say...I had no idea what order I would be teaching my classes; although I knew I would be teaching U.S. and World History but was not sure what else. I was aware that I had classes for the first five periods, my 6th period would be my free period and I had a 7th period class, though I had no idea what I was supposed to cover in that class. I felt anxious that I still didn't know what to say because I didn't know the order or content of what I'd be teaching.

The bell rang and parents were sitting in my classroom. There were parents, as well as younger children in the room...one of the little boys was very upset because he had to go to the bathroom and he couldn't find where to go. I took him by the hand and walked him down a hall and into a room that had a bathroom in it. I left him there and turned to go back to the lecture hall, but became aware that I could hear the child urinating. As I re-entered my room, now quite a distance from the bathroom, the sound of the urination became extremely loud. I even sensed that water that had been splashing up from the toilet was splashing me as I walked into my class.

Even though I didn't know what I would be teaching, I began to talk. Then I became aware of a hissing sound, like a steam kettle. It was coming from the wall behind me...I noticed a hole in the wall and steam was coming out of it. I asked all of the parents sitting on my right to move to my left just in case the steam blew up the wall. I didn't want any of them to get burned. I was aware that a number of the parents were parents from my teaching days two decades before.

I started to tell them about all the years between my teaching that had ended in the 1970s and my present life that led to this classroom, but I was concerned that they would judge me for having divorced Jake. Eugenea, one of my students from the 1970s, was there and had not changed at all. When she was a student, many years before, she had been very upset with me for not just telling students what was right and wrong... my style was to have them think through things and develop their own opinions. She sat down in a seat in front of me, looking exactly like the 17-year-old girl from long ago. She seemed to be putting her shoes on and then asked me if I was going to teach from the Ten Commandments this time. She told me she was orthodox and wouldn't be able to take my class if I did it like last time. I was puzzled because I thought I taught from a more liberal perspective than had been the foundation of the Christian school where I taught for 12 years. I felt confused by her comments.

Then the steam began to make the wall pulse. It looked like the pressure from behind the wall was about to explode, so I directed everyone to leave the room. Remaining seemed dangerous. Water began to pour out of the side of the wall and then gushing water began to fill the room. It was coming from the hole, as well as flowing from the entry door down the descending steps, like a waterfall. As I left the room, I hurried to the office to tell them of the problem in my room. I think I stopped off in several rooms on the way...I got the sense that the people in my room were homeroom parents and that actual classes had not yet begun.

I wanted to tell the office to make an announcement that room 111 had flooded and I would meet the people for classes in another room, perhaps in a large foyer or something. But a number of periods had passed somehow without my being aware of it. I had taken more time than I thought on my way to the office. I was concerned that the people had gone to 111 to try to find me, not found me there, and gotten upset. By the time I was ready to return to my classroom it seemed like 5th period had started. If that were true, I thought I could use 6th period to prepare for 7th even though I missed the first five groups that would have come to my empty classroom. I felt a sense of hesitation in returning but decided to return to the classroom and teach. I woke feeling very confused. I wrote the dream down, but didn't take time to look deeply into it, since so much was on my mind.

***

Two months later, I had another dream. In the dream, I was walking on an extensive, sandy beach that was filled with gravesites. I had the intuition that I was expected to get into one of the sites but was hesitant. Though there was no one physically with me in this dream, I was aware someone was walking with me toward my resting place. I looked at all the graves and told the one who was with me that I didn't like the idea of going in a box in the ground. I told my companion that I had already done that when I was little and I didn't want to do it again. I said, emphatically, "*You know how I feel about that.*"

My attention then focused on another place. It was a bed made of sand with sideboards and was above ground. I walked up to it and noticed inside it had a sand mattress and a shell-shaped pillow made of sand. I was not bothered about resting there. Someone had been boring a number of air holes in the bottom of the sandbox, which made me feel better. I was aware that when I got in, a top would be placed over me. I asked my companion what would happen if I wanted to get out before the designated time. The answer I heard was that I would not be able to get out sooner and felt some discomfort. I saw two digital read-outs in the sand. One I looked at, the other I couldn't see very well. The

289

read-out I saw said 2:45. I scratched the sand numbers to make them something else, perhaps attempting to change the time in the sandbox, but I am not sure if I was successful. I woke up wondering the meaning of this dream. But didn't take the time to work with it.

A few days later, mother's day, May 11, 1997, while writing about the experiences related to my growing understanding of human develop-ment, I checked the upper right corner of my screen to see the time. I had an afternoon client and didn't want to be late. I had guessed it was about noon, but the time showed 2:45. I jumped up out of my chair, ran to the bedroom to get my clean clothes together and prepare for work. I hadn't eaten yet, nor bathed so I had much to do in a short time. I couldn't imagine where the time had gone. When I looked at my kitchen clock, it said 12:30, not nearly 3 in the afternoon. This made no sense. I went back to my computer and looked at the time again; it still showed 2:45. I clicked on the read-out to see what date it showed. It was Tuesday, March 8, 37. I stared at the date in amazement.

Then, the whole top menu began to flash black to white. It flashed for the next couple of hours. The time began to change from 2:45 while the date remained the same. When the time read 3:36, I closed the document down, which was saved on my computer as if it were March 8, 2037, 3:36 PM. In that moment, I remembered the sandy grave dream from a few nights before in which I the changed date/time read-out, which began with 2:45 that I thought I might have changed it in the dream. Immediately, it occurred to me that because this was a dream of a sandy grave, this might be the time this life ends. I did a quick computation and discovered that on that date, I would be 92-years-old. I recalled that my mother's mother lived to 92 and my father's father lived to 92, as well.

Then I remembered the dream from a couple of months before about the school. In that dream about the new teaching position I was to take in room 111, I was told that I had to go past my old room 308, to get to the new addition and my new room. The 3-08 that was flashing on my computer in black and white, matched the 308 I had to pass by to get to 111. As I studied the "111" dream more thoughtfully, I wondered if 11-1-2039 was the date of my birth into my next lifetime, and if the room that pulsed and exploded with water was the beginning of the birth process into that new lifetime.

I called my sister to tell her about this most recent set of circumstances, partially out of a wish to have her understand me, and partially to tease her because she had a strong resistance to the ideas of past lives, future lives, and to some degree, at times, this life as well. She was silent for a moment and reflected to me that "308" was our house number on 6th street where the majority of the trauma of our childhoods happened. I had completely forgotten. I began laughing and crying as something inside seemed to be reminding me that everything is multiple leveled and is all connected.

***

The significant 8-day vacation trip with my dear friend, which had begun with the encounter with Alanza, had come to a close, but I didn't know that Esther's parting words would play a significant role in another series of synchronous events. As she was carrying her bags to my car, Esther asked if I would check out the red spots on my forehead and around my temples that she had not noticed when I lived in Florida. She seemed concerned, and to be honest, I had hardly noticed them. I told her that I would make an appointment.

Chapter Twenty-Six
THE "C" WORD

The Western world has carefully split who we are into many separate pieces and each small thing is studied as if it were disconnected from all the rest. Illness, like everything else is placed in a box and dealt with, without understanding that it is related to everything else in us. What impacts us in our spirits, influences our thoughts and emotions, and what is held in our thoughts and emotions is manifested in our bodies. We are one being, whether we choose to notice it or not.

It is likely that had Alanza not recommended that I pay attention to messages about my health, I might have dismissed Esther's comment about the red spots. But instead, three weeks after Esther's departure, I was in the dermatologist's office, being checked from head to toe for anything that might look questionable. Of course, the most obvious were the spots on my face, most of them on the left side and a few others on my chest, just below the clavicle on my sternum, which the doctor identified as being pre-cancer. He used a high-pressured gun to spray liquid nitrogen on the 17 spots and then explained that the spots would scab over, dry up, and fall off, removing the pre-cancer tissue and leave only clear pink skin that needed to be protected from the sun, preferably with makeup, to avoid them turning into permanent dark spots.

As the appointment was coming to a close, I asked the doctor if he would look at a well-hidden spot on the external skin of my vulva because it had been feeling irritated, as if there was an exposed cut. It had been biopsied a couple of years before and found to be benign, and was examined visually a few months before this appointment by a gynecologist who did not see it as a problem at that time. But something didn't seem right to me about it. This dermatologist decided to take a biopsy just to be sure all was well, and said he would get back to me about the lab results the next week. I knew these problem areas—on my face and on the external skin of my vulva— were related to the rape incident when I was about 6, because images of the incident that I wrote about in chapter 16 had been invading my thoughts for a number of weeks and seemed to come to me every time I felt the irritation in my pelvic area or the tenderness of the spots on my chest and face. I knew that unresolved issues on the emotional level affect our health and was glad I was addressing the problem.

Though many men had sexually abused me in my very early years, that one event seared me like a branding iron, and seemed to hurt me more deeply than the rest. That was the one perpetrated by the man who reeked of alcohol and rancid sweat, who dripped his perspiration and saliva on me in the process. He was the one who made me feel as if I were garbage and part of my child self split off, remaining in the garbage for decades until I found her just as I was completing my dissertation in 2001. I guess the fat lady and the little child who walked hand in hand into the sunset had taken me here.

After the appointment in the late summer of 2007, I had taken a trip to Connecticut to visit another David—we can call him Connecticut David—and his partner, Ben, both of whom have been my dear friends for years. I usually visited there at least twice a year, but I had not seen them for close to two years. We had spent several days together, enjoying the beauty of that northeastern state and I had all but forgotten my visit to the dermatologist when my phone rang while the three of us were in the kitchen. The doctor, himself, called to let me know that the biopsy had come back positive for cancer. He gave me the name of an oncologist to schedule a consult so we could decide what was the next best step. He wanted me to take care of getting an appointment as quickly as possible. At first I was stunned when I heard the "C" word, but then I slipped into that calm, "in-control" place and began to ask all the right questions, though I am not sure if I heard the answers. Because of its location, he felt that an oncologist who specialized in gynecology would be best, and I agreed to follow up.

Though part of me was terrified, I felt as if everything was going to be just fine, and there was really nothing to worry about. I assured David and Ben that I was OK. We had planned to go out later that afternoon to enjoy the sunshine, so before leaving, I applied a layer of makeup to cover the scabs that had by that time turned from red to black. However, the scab in my eyebrow had only partially lifted, and looked quite ugly. The black spots were very hard to camouflage with any makeup and I felt so, so awful. My distress was clear to David as we were preparing to go, and he encouraged me to calm down. Without intending to do so, I started to cry. David put his arm around me to comfort me and commented that it was not like me to show such vanity about a few marks. At that point the tears turned to sobs. I told David it wasn't vanity; it was shame.

I told him about the little girl from long ago who was so very afraid that people would be able to see that she had become garbage…and that she tried everything she could do to cover up what happened to her, and now, the spots on my face, where his sweat and saliva hit me, feel to this child in me as if they are exposing that shame. The tears I was shedding and the shame I was feeling were coming from the child. All my attempts to mask the "garbage girl" caused my face to break out in cancer, and my attempts to cover the shame of my pelvic area had failed, as well. David hugged me and tried to reassure me that I had no reason to be ashamed; but while my adult therapist-self understood what he said was true, my little child-self did not.

I spent the next few days reminding the inner-child that she was not garbage and that I loved her. I was able to do some internal work with all of this, but nothing went very deep. Throughout the rest of the time with David and Ben, a few hours would go by without any thoughts of cancer, and then the word would invade my mind creating fear and tension that I tried to push aside, but never completely. My dear friends offered to do a shamanic ritual with me to invite healing, and the day I left, Ben took a sage bundle, lit it, and covered me with the precious cleansing smoke while David read a chant used by Native Americans for centuries. At the close of the ritual, Ben gave me the remainder of his sage in case I wanted to continue doing more healing work with it back in Colorado.

I left feeling loved and cared for, and returned to Denver feeling more committed to work with more traditional methods to bring healing to my body, but I wondered if I should, also, consider the medical system. Not only was I struggling with what to do about seeing an oncologist, and all that might mean; but also, another frustrating thing happened. I had stopped losing weight, something that had begun almost immediately after Esther left until my return to Denver. I had lost nearly 20 pounds, according to Alanza's prediction, it was just melting off, and then no more melting happened. Something in me knew that the child who had come to the surface again did not want me to lose more weight. The more I attempted to communicate with her, the more I got in touch with huge rage, and the more rage I felt, the more my entire body ached. The two places that hurt the most were my right eyebrow, that pulsed with a pain that felt as if it went into my right eye socket bone, and my genital area; now no longer limited to the one cancerous spot on my vulva. The pain had spread to the entire pelvic region, sometimes almost overwhelming pain. Every time I felt an unusual body response, a pain, an irritation, a quiver, my thoughts immediately took me to a place where I believed that cancer was spreading and taking me over. My ear began to ache, and I thought cancer had settled there because of the thousands of hours of phone clients whose voices went into my head through an earpiece. I fell into a depression and wondered if I was going to die.

After struggling for a few days, I finally emailed my Atlanta friend, Bill, to see if he could work with me; however, his voice mail message said that he was traveling out of state for a family wedding and wouldn't be available for another week. I considered calling Anne, my Seattle psychic friend, but she had been working with her own concerns with her husband's cancer, and at the time and it didn't feel good to bring this to her. When outside help didn't seem to be possible, I wondered what I could do for myself. At one point, I visualized the little girl, and despite all the previous work I had done with her, apparently part of her was still stuck in that hellhole of a place where my father had taken me when I was barely 6 and sold me to that filthy man for his pleasure. I cried for that child of the past, and felt myself touching her face and chest to wipe away the man's body fluids that had dripped all over her. What I did for her felt important, but didn't seem to touch the depths of what I needed to do.

Within a few days of being back in the mountains, all of the facial pre-cancer spots had healed, but one; the one in my right eyebrow remained irritated and painful. When I did an internal check, the answer that I received was that this was the first spot that his saliva hit when the filthy man's body fluids splashed on me. Though I have had other cancers and pre-cancers removed from my face years before, the one in my right eyebrow was the first to appear two years earlier as a red patch, and back then I scrubbed it off, all the way down to raw skin. But then it came back as a red and scaly patch that dried and I pulled it off like sun burned skin. It remained red and looked more like a birthmark that went from tender to being dried and scab like, and I would pull it off again, time after time in the months that followed.

What began to concern me was that the tissue beneath the skin on my right eyebrow had become painfully sensitive even without touching it, and the red spot returned. All the while, my entire pelvic region felt inflamed and was very painful, as if I had a very bad infection. In spite of wanting to work with this on deeper levels since I returned to my Colorado mountain writing retreat, I couldn't find access.

After it was clear I couldn't work with Bill or Anne, I got a flash image of a ceremony I wanted to do with little Sandy. I found the perfect place, a clearing between my carriage house and the stream. The clearing was very near a grove of sunflowers and yellow daisies, which seemed perfect because yellow was the little girl's favorite color. The day that I got the idea seemed like the perfect day to do the ceremony. My landlady was gone and the man who lives in the basement of her house was gone, and there was no one anywhere near. I could be free to make whatever sounds might need to explode out of me from the child. Not long after I saw the ceremony in my mind, I took Jenny out for her walk and saw a cluster of daisies on the road that little Sandy wanted me to cut for her, so I returned with a pair of scissors and cut them. The image of the ceremony included using the earth to form a little child, surrounding her with flowers, and then lovingly caring for her wounded little body in earth-form, which seemed to be a genuine way of connecting with that part of me still in the past and bringing her healing. I was just about ready to begin doing what I saw in my mind, when the basement renter returned and started chopping wood right outside my carriage house. I put the flowers in water and sighed for the interruption. And then my landlady and her boyfriend returned home, which made the idea of having a private ritual, impossible.

I let the idea go, but felt a great amount of internal disturbance. By the evening, my eyebrow and pelvic area seemed to be screaming with pain and I didn't know what to do. I tried to write, but that came to nothing. I felt very trapped; I am sure much like little Sandy felt when she was left in that God-forsaken place so long ago. That night, I had the most restless sleep that I can ever remember, tossing and turning for hours at a time and then falling to sleep only to wake 15 minutes later, unable to return to sleep for an hour or so, and then falling asleep again for only a few minutes. That went on all night, and I finally got up at about 6:30 AM.

I was aware of how angry I had been feeling. With all of the pain in the bone under my right eyebrow, I wondered if perhaps cancer had actually migrated into the bone because I hadn't taken care of it when it first appeared. I wondered if there were other problems in my pelvic area because of the extreme pain and wondered if maybe a part of me was trying to leave this world and decided to use cancer as the way out. I knew that the idea of not being here has been an ongoing thought that never really went away at least from the time that I tried to asphyxiate myself when I was 8, though it did leave my waking consciousness for long periods of time. But whenever difficult experiences crossed my path, the thought would reemerge that I didn't want to be here, and I would long to "go home" with home being in some other world, not this one.

For some time, I had been aware of how very little of traditional life excited me. So much of how I experienced life was from a place of "going through the motions" without feeling much connection. I knew that when there is no joy in life, that life withdraws from me. I didn't want to die, but I wasn't excited about living, either. I am very sure that is what my child-self felt after that most horrible event when I was 6. After years of doing this deep work, I have become aware that when my emotions drop into low places or go *over the top*, far more exaggerated than what is warranted in the present, this is an indication that something from the past is pushing into the present for healing. But at the time, that awareness didn't help.

After having been thwarted from doing the ceremony the day before, I wanted so much to do the ritual the next day, but friends of my landlady from out of town, were coming to stay for two weeks, making my plans to form a little Sandy from the Earth and perform a ritual over her seem like an impossible idea, at least not in the place that seemed so perfect to me. Like too many other things in my life, my path to healing seemed to have been stolen from me, too.

Chapter Twenty-Seven
THE EARTH CHILD

When it feels as if the world has turned on you, notice the ways in which you have turned on the world and on yourself. Let yourself open to the message that exists in the events and experiences in your life that can take you to some part of you still stuck in some painful place in the past. Notice that patterns once seen and released will set you free to reconnect with your whole self and your world in the present.

As far back as I can remember, I have believed in natural healing and knew that once I found a way to access, express, and release emotional pain from the past, and in doing so, release the thoughts that originated in the past, the root causes of the illness would fade, and the illness itself could dissolve. This is what was on my mind as I began the ceremony for the child of so long ago who was so brutally treated, and never allowed to heal.

That morning, the sky was dark as rain clouds had been drenching the earth since dawn. To my surprise, no one was home, and the friends had not, yet, arrived. While rain gently fell, I used an old broken shovel that I found beside the stream to collect moist earth to form the body of a child. I kneeled down into the dirt and my hands began to sculpt a head, little shoulders, arms and hands, a torso, and little legs with feet, and then I began to carefully sculpt a face. The earth beneath my hands seemed to take on the energy of a child, and I began to feel the presence of little Sandy, as if somehow she was transported from the past and was with me in the present in this earth-child form. Feeling more connected to that little girl from the past than I had ever felt before, my heart began to ache and tears fell down my cheeks and mixed with the raindrops. I placed the yellow wreath of flowers around her head, and just as I completed forming the face, the rain stopped; a small opening in the clouds appeared in the darkened sky and sun poured over the earth-child, the yellow flowers, and me. Feeling as if Spirit was sending this beautiful ray of sunshine, I began to cry, again. I placed my hands on the earthen-face as if it were the face of this small child and through my tears, let her know how deeply sorry I was for all that happened to her. Energetically, I felt as if not only had she come to the present for this ceremony but on some level, I had gone back in time and was bringing comfort to a very badly traumatized little girl.

As I touched her chest, in the same place where the man's sweat and saliva had dropped on my child-self so many years before, tears flowed abundantly and the heat of the sun caused rivulets of sweat to fall from my face onto the earth-child that I had formed. Something about sweat falling on her again pierced my heart and I began to sob uncontrollably. As I spoke to her through the sobs, a drop of saliva slipped from my mouth and fell on the earth-child's brow and then on her chest. More tears fell. I needed to change the energy of invasion from so long ago, so I took the wetness of my own saliva and sweat and smoothed it into the earth-child that represented little Sandy. I told her this was our sweat, our saliva and our tears, and they would bring healing to her, to me, to us. I told her she could release the saliva and sweat of that hateful man, and let it melt into the earth as she received the sweat, tears, and saliva that came from my love.

I spat into my hand and began rubbing the spittle into the earth-child's eyebrow, making mud from the earth and giving it permission to heal the inner-child and to heal me. In that moment, I remembered the story of Jesus spitting into the dirt to make mud that he rubbed onto a blind man's eyelids, which allowed the man to see. I spit into my hand again and mixed it with the earth around the earth-child's vaginal area and invited the child and me to release the man's energy...and to open to her own spirit-filled energy to flow into all the spaces and places inside where the man's energy used to be. As my present self opened to the healing, I gave permission for my own angry energy to be released into the earth.

I took the sage that Ben had given me, lit it, and allowed the smoke to cover the earth-child and I repeated the words of the sage ritual—the same ones that Connecticut David had said over me not long before—and allowed the smoke to perform a cleansing.

The words were beautiful:

> From the element of fire comes this smoke, which is air
> From the element of earth grows this plant, which is water
> I call upon the elements and the blessings of spirit to please
> cleanse this area, this space, this being…
> For the good of all.

***

In that moment, I knew that this healing I had invited into me was not just for me to embrace, but also, my healing would be something to share in healing others. I stood beside the form of the child in the earth and began to sound a tone that arose in me spontaneously…it was very powerful and loud as it filled the space where I stood and flowed into the canyon between the mountains on either side of me. A number of birds seemed to come closer to see what was happening, and I am sure the animals and trees felt the vibration of that healing tone, as well. I spontaneously sent the sound in the four directions and above me and below me.

When I completed the sounding, I became aware that the man, who raped the little girl so long ago, wanted to feel a sense of connection, but his anger didn't allow him to know how to connect with other humans with love, so he misused his energy to force connection with someone too little to prevent his overpowering her. His anger indicated that he didn't get to experience connection in his own life, not even with himself. In that moment, I knew that I wanted every part of me to be connected to people and I wanted intimate connection with a special someone. I made a choice to open to love, and to release any anger that could prevent love and intimacy from happening.

After experiencing the power in the energy release, a thought came to me that it might be good to take the earth-child form to the little river that flows so near my carriage house and release it into the water. And though the thought might have been a valuable completion of the ritual, there was something inside that didn't want to do it. Instead, it felt right to allow the form to surrender to the elements and return to the earth in its own time. I turned to leave the ceremonial site when the man who lives in the house next door drove up near where I had just done the ritual. I felt a mild adrenalin rush and with it came an almost frightening thought, telling me that I needed to cover the evidence of what I had done, perhaps by scattering the dirt and sweeping away the flowers. Who knows, maybe in some past lifetime such rituals would have led to unthinkable punishment or death. I didn't want to bring fear energy into what had just happened, so I breathed into the fear and released it. If anyone came upon the site and wondered what it was, I knew I could explain it in a simple way that would not generate fear in them. I left it as it was.

***

Later in the day, I heard the sound of the All Terrain Vehicle outside my window. I looked out and saw my landlady's boyfriend driving by below my window with the ATV attached to a trailer he uses to collect fallen limbs and trees on the property, which he then chops up for winter firewood. His path between my house and the river, as far as I could tell, went directly over the ritual site. A trip to the site soon afterward revealed that tire tracks had run over the dirt that had been my earth-child. As I stood over the form that still held enough of the sculpture to be identifiable, I was struck by the reality that no part of me remained in the dirt, it was just dirt with yellow flowers slightly askew and even they were beginning to release their identity as flowers, and dissolve into the earth.

***

Standing there, in front of what had been the earth sculpture, representing my child-self, I remembered inner work I did on the phone with my Atlanta Alchemical friend, Bill, in 1999, when I was struggling with financial issues that connected to so much more. In the process of doing deep work, I found myself entering awareness from many lifetimes ago. As that 1999 conversation began, Bill and I were filling each other in on what was happening in our lives, and I told him that I was in financial despair. The disastrous year of 1996-97— my father died, my sweet-dog Sara died, and I had a heart attack—disrupted not only my graduate studies, but it, also, greatly impacted my private practice. My earnings had dropped to below poverty level, and I used my credit cards to survive. The negative down cycling put me in such deep debt, causing me to drown in bills. For the next two years, I was borrowing from one credit card to pay another, something I knew was insane, but I didn't know what else to do, and the debt kept increasing. I felt as if I had been disconnected from the Universe and had no sense of purpose or direction.

I was exceedingly lonely and my body ached for its emptiness. In those years of study, and then the disaster of 96-97, I had gained so much weight that the potential for a romantic relationship that I thought might heal the loneliness was less probable than it ever had been before, even if I had wanted one. Clerical problems at my graduate school had prevented me from getting my Masters degree when I had expected it, which blocked my getting a full mental health license. That, in turn, seemed to prevent me from developing my practice to a point where it could support my life and change the direction of my indebtedness. No matter where I turned, everything felt hopeless. I felt utterly helpless to change what was happening in my life. Bill responded with five simple words: *"Sandy, whatever happened to Surrender."*

Bill always has had a way of saying exactly the right words at exactly the right moment with the power to penetrate all the levels and layers and get right to the core of whatever was happening—this was an example. Those words brought up heaving sobs, releasing energies that felt as if they had been stored in me for lifetimes. For far too long, my life had been characterized by one struggle after another, never finding a place to rest; I had been too terrified of what might happen to allow whatever was in process to just happen. After all, whatever was going to happen was going to happen, whether I struggled or not. But when Bill spoke those words, and the deeply buried cry was allowed to come out, I felt my body surrender in a way that I can't remember having felt it do before.

***

After hanging up the phone, I lay prostrate on my bed, completely surrendered, and surprisingly went from a state of total exhaustion into a state of bliss, of connection with Creator, Universal Love, Great Spirit, The I Am. It was a surrender that allowed every cell of my body to vibrate with a light so brilliant all I could feel inside me was radiant white. It was one of those powerful moments when everything inside me became aware of its connection to all that is me, and all that is me knew that I am connected to all that is. This kind of feeling holds a knowing that I am eternally safe, even if it might not look like it in the outer world. In surrender, I let go of worrying about outcomes and know, whatever comes, I am able to handle, no matter what it is. Somehow, in that moment, it seemed as if my vision had been made so clear; I knew that in the center of surrender and acceptance of what is unfolding is ultimately the peace that comes from love, union, knowing, safety, and release into rest.

Following this amazing experience, though I couldn't explain why, I felt compelled to turn on my computer and log onto my Internet email. There was a message from a professor at my graduate school, giving information about a job in Africa. World Vision was seeking someone to do psychotherapy with people in Sierra Leone who had been traumatized by the horrible civil war that had left in its wake unfathomable human suffering. Immediately, I emailed my interest and my resume. Somehow it felt providential that my surrender brought me into contact with a position that might provide me with direction and purpose, as well as the financial support that had been missing since I took that step into the darkness over a decade earlier.

I was invited to Washington, DC to interview for the position and received the recruiting office's recommendation for the position in Sierra Leone, as well as for one in Kosovo. I understood that whichever came through first would be where I would be sent. However, because of the escalation of conflict in both countries, the positions were put on hold for a few weeks, and then for a few months. I was aware that a part of me remained surrendered to accepting whatever would happen trusting that what I was to do would open for me, while another part of me began to question the meaning of the surrender. It was apparent that I could no longer avoid the financial bankruptcy that I finally had to file. Even when paying the minimum credit card payments, I owed far more than I was earning and I had no savings or credit left to handle the indebtedness.

Again, I had to surrender. Months of inner conflict finally gave way as I walked into the attorney's office and signed the legal documents for bankruptcy. This was followed by weeks of agony waiting for the court hearing that would decide whether or not I could legally declare bankruptcy and two months of tension waiting to see if any of the creditors would challenge the petition. I began living more and more out of the part of me that lived in depression and questioned surrender.

***

Financial resources were dwindling. Yet, I was given powerful signs that my needs were being taken care of. The previous year, I had submitted a proposal for a conference presentation to the United Kingdom's International Society for the Study of Dissociation in Manchester, England. My proposal was accepted, but after all that had taken place in the interim, I had no idea how I would pay for the trip. Two friends, out of the blue, sent me checks; one was for $1000 and one was for $500. I left for London with $1500. The trip cost me a bit more than $1499. I came back, literally, with 2 pence in my pocket. Not long after that, my computer developed a problem that would cost $481 and some odd cents to repair. I knew I needed my computer to work properly, so I approved the repair and within a few hours of that decision, several old clients called to schedule tune-up appointments.

Six hours of sessions at $80 per hour, the amount I was charging at the time, gave me an unplanned $480. These kinds of situations continue to amaze me. In all of this, I knew I would be OK, but I still felt underlying anxiety, a tension that seemed impossible to shake no matter how much trust was there. This is where I was when Bill called, again, "just to talk."

***

Our conversation flowed in and out of subjects, in which we both shared common interest, including our therapy practices and the themes that seem to be present in our clients processing. I mentioned that since I made the decision at the Saybrook Residential Conference to center my dissertation research on a heuristic inquiry into surrender, especially related to weight loss, every one of my clients, old and new, had come into the office with surrender issues.

We talked about the meanings of these kinds of synchronous events and then he asked me what kind of personal work I had been doing lately. I was aware that there was something close to the surface that needed to be worked on, but instead, I told Bill that I had placed whatever was going on within me on a shelf inside my head an inch above my right eye. As I spoke, I felt my inner vision looking in the direction of the container on that internal shelf. I explained that I seemed to have been in a holding pattern, and was not sure I would have time to get into the emotional components of my work on surrender. I had been frustrated because I was not able to focus enough to do my essays, a requirement of my graduate school for advancement to candidacy, which means being a PhD, ABD—all but dissertation—though I had been reading a great deal and I had several major pieces of writing in various stages of completion, none of it was tied together. I felt frustrated and somewhat stagnant, but still was aware that something was moving on the inside. It seemed that the inner movement would somehow stimulate the outer movement.

When Bill inquired further, I told him I knew something was on the very edge of happening, but I just didn't know what it was. I kept repeating, *"I just don't know."* I felt an energy pulse begin to form in my chest and throat as it was pushing outward and upward. I allowed myself to identify the energy and expressed it to Bill, and in the speaking, tears welled up in my eyes. I told him that even though I trusted in my mind that I would be taken care of, no matter what happened, it was exceedingly painful to always feel so much on the edge.

I went into that state where I felt myself speaking to God more than Bill: *"Why is it that I always have to just barely make it? Why do I have to live life always without anything in reserve? I am not free to run like a little kid in a field of grass, with the wind blowing through her hair and her jacket billowing out with no cares in the world. Why can't I run free? Why can't I rest in comfort?"* By this time the tears could not be repressed. *"I have lived all my life like this, never really able to rest."* Tears turned to painful sobs and the sobs tumbled into choking spasms. I whispered to Bill that this felt very old, like some distant past lifetime.

As I spoke, I kept seeing an image of an emaciated body, a collection of bones so nearly ready to fall apart, with muscles struggling to hold the bones in place. Another howling cry expanded from my throat all the way down to my feet as it completely overtook me, causing my whole body to writhe in excruciating pain. I told Bill it felt as if these were my bones in another lifetime where I was dying of starvation. When I allowed my vision to increase, I could see that I was in Africa; I was a black woman, wasted away with only a thin layer of muscles holding the bones together. I didn't want to die. I felt those thin muscles contract tighter and tighter until all the energy was condensed and turned inward.

Bill quietly whispered *"release"* and then this frightened, struggling African woman let go and died. A cry erupted from me so deeply, that I knew I was touching something that had been buried an exceedingly long time. The cry that felt as if it had been held inside for centuries moved its way to the very center of my body. It seemed as if those intricate muscles that hold my bones together finally released the tension that had been there my whole life, and apparently for lifetimes. Bill, in that inscrutable way, responded with *"Hummm... scared to the bone!"* I felt another wave of tear-filled energy wash through and out of me. That African woman was as terrified of dying as I had been in my childhood, when the horrible abuse was being inflicted. I found our place of connection.

Bill asked me what I needed to do. I told him I needed to go to this woman, this self in a past life and embrace her. I needed to tell her that I am she in a future life, that her spirit did not die and that it was now time to release her attachment to that body, and to allow it to return to the Earth. In the moment that I spoke these words, I felt my vision expand beyond the remains of this starvation victim to the whole of Africa and then to the whole world. A powerful wave of astonished insight washed through me as I exclaimed:

This is it, Bill—this is what I was supposed to see. When people die, their bodies are intended to decompose and surrender to the Earth while their spirits return to the Mystery. When people hold on to their bodies and turn inward in an attempt to clutch to life, instead of surrendering into the release of the body, they create an energy that does not allow the Earth to transform the remains into useful nutrients. The Earth is robbed; the soil cannot give to humankind what humans have not surrendered to the Earth. The soil is stagnant, nothing moves as it was intended in the living and dying and living again process.

It felt as if my awareness went into the Earth where the remains of my former African-self had died. I watched waves of awareness wash through the ground as if a pebble had been dropped and produced reverberating ripples across the land, through the oceans and to all the continents of the world.

Again, I said, *"This is it, Bill!"*—Now, almost shouting those words— *"This is why I have had to be on the edge. If I hadn't been on the edge and felt the discomfort of not being able to really let go and rest, I would have never been able to understand this. This is so important. It is important to me, but it is important to the whole world. This is another important level of my holding on to my weight. My body believed it would never have to go through starvation again if it could just hold on to the weight. It has held on just as hard as the African woman's thin muscles held on to the bones, and the holding on is what has robbed the earth and our world of what it needs to sustain itself. We have developed entire industries based on trying to stop death, even though we know death wins and we do what we can to distract ourselves from this winding down and dying that is part of the whole process of the circle of life.*

The tears, the fears, the holding on were finally released in the surrender. I became aware of how deeply relaxed my body felt. Bill asked me what I could do to change the messages that had been attached to the body. *"Frightened to the bone"* became *"relaxed to the bone"* and *"I am not free to run"* changed to *"I can run freely without fear trapping me."* *"I cannot rest"* became *"I can completely let go and rest in peaceful comfort"* and *"I must always walk on the edge"* became *"I can walk anywhere I choose to walk and know I am safe, even if it is on the edge."* I know something important happened that night.

***

The next day, as I stood over the earth-child, I invited the child that was represented by the form in the dirt to release the dirt and allow the form to re-enter the ground. I invited the energy of the child who might have felt as if she were dirt to come into the *heart of my heart* to join me in the present and release the past allowing the old energies to return to the earth for cleansing. And then I sent an invitation to all the past selves in all the lives I have ever lived, through all time, to release any attachment to the bodies in former lifetimes and come to the present to be reunited with me. It seemed more clear, in that moment, that just as trauma in earlier times in our lives causes parts of us to remain stuck in the event and not move past it until we come back for them, our souls can, also, be traumatized by the death experience and aspects of our souls can feel as if they are stuck in that past lifetime at the time of a death that was so strongly resisted.

Instead of making the healing sound as I did the day before, I stood beside what remained of the earth-form and took in a deep breath in all the directions, which felt like a metaphor that represented drawing back to me any scattered parts of my soul that may have been trapped by attachment to previous lives or previous events. I invited all of me to fill my whole body-mind, soul, and spirit. All of who I have been, who I am, and will be…I invited to come together into my wholeness and oneness. In that moment, I understood how important it was that I had not scattered the dirt or dumped it into the river the day before for fear that someone might find it. I wonder how much of what we do in our lives is from fear, and as a result we erase chances to go deeper into experiences that can expand our awareness of our being, our consciousness, and our experience of life.

***

Another realization that came to me during the ceremony, was that my answering that job inquiry for a position in Africa, so many years before, was important, not because I was to take that job, but because it opened me to the energy of Africa. After I applied and was accepted, but before I found out that the violence had caused the outposts in Sierra Leone and Kosovo to be closed indefinitely, I bought several CDs with African music. They were filled with sounds that seemed to resonate with my soul, and I bought books about Africa to get a feel for the land I would be entering. I just didn't know that my entrance would be in non-ordinary reality. By submerging in African energy, I opened my consciousness to that part of me that remained un-surrendered and stuck in death on the Dark Continent. This whole experience, which included my earth-child from this lifetime and the aspect of my soul-self in Africa, became a conduit through which I could begin to embrace more and more of my self and in doing so, allowed me to feel more alive and present in this life, which also meant embracing my own power.

***

After experiencing that beautiful ritual, I scheduled a body therapy session for the next day. Following the oncologist appointment scheduled for early the next week, I made an appointment with an EMDR therapist in Denver, just in case there were still remnants of pain or anger inside me. The following day, the body therapy session was among the most profound I had experienced since I came to the mountains. Because of my trips to Florida and Connecticut, almost a month had passed between sessions, so I had no idea what might surface, especially with all that had been going on related to the diagnosis of cancer. Cyndi, the therapist I'd been working with since coming to Colorado, thought I would be really tight, but, instead, found that my body had not only maintained the releases from previous months, it was even more open than usual. Normally, my sessions were long, and significant releases occurred several times during a session, but this time, 2-hours had gone by without any emotional releases, not even minimal ones. It seemed as if all the emotional tension from my own work in the previous days had freed me.

As she was winding down the session, Cyndi asked if I felt like there was anything left inside that wanted to come out. It didn't feel like it, but knowing that anger had been difficult for me to access in the past, I mentioned that if there was still any anger or rage deeply buried, I wanted to get to it so I could be free of its power over me in the more subtle and unconscious ways. The therapist asked how I release anger... like if I hit pillows, or punched something. I explained that I have tried to do the "baseball bat thing" but it never felt very real. That kind of expression seemed more like I was play-acting, just doing what I was supposed to do, instead of experiencing something authentic, and it didn't feel like it was connected to the core of me in spite of the fact that I have supported clients who used bats and pillows that resulted in deeply significant and transformational releases.

Just about the time she started working with my left hand, I told her that I have done powerful releases with breath work. Cyndi worked with each finger, and though she was ready to move on and finish up with the session, something in my left hand ring finger seemed disturbed, so I asked if she would check it out more thoroughly. When she focused her attention on that finger, I took in a very deep breath and felt enormous pain. My finger began to swell and felt like something powerful was moving through me. The pain shot up my arm and into my shoulder. She moved to my left shoulder and began working the muscles between the shoulder and sternum. I kept seeing flashes of the drunken man from my childhood, the one who sexually violated me, dripping his body fluids on me that, in my way of looking at it, all led to the cancer on my face and vulva.

When I stayed with the images that were coming into my mind, I became aware that my finger had been caught in the man's clothing, causing it to be twisted back as he lunged forward. My child-self tried to push him off with her shoulder, but a child cannot easily counter the weight of an adult man. A guttural scream exploded that sounded like someone was dying. I am sure people who were many offices away and on the other floors must have heard the piercing sound. When the scream subsided, it felt as if I had released something so very deep. My body was on fire. Cyndi told me that she could feel the energy that had been trapped in a loop between my ring finger and left shoulder, and that loop had an energy line that went into my pelvic area, as well, and it was all related. I could already feel that too, as it seemed to all be releasing simultaneously.

After all of this was finished, I asked Cyndi what she sensed was going on. She told me that normally energy flows through a body from Source through the top of the head, through the Chakras (along the spine) down to the root Chakra at the sacral area and from the root Chakra down into the Earth, for grounding and connection to Spirit. This was no new information; but for me, she said a significant amount of my energy was trapped in a circle from my finger to my shoulder and it remained trapped there, instead of accessing the main energy flow. This side circle had been trapped in a fierce struggle that was no longer happening, but felt like it when I entered this energy pattern. The therapist I worked with for a long time in Florida told me that she could not sense that central energy flow and grid that is formed from the flow in my body, but in all the work we did, we never were able to address it. I had the impression that this work Cyndi did with me, may well have finally gotten to it.

Cyndi explained that the energy flow from finger to shoulder and shoulder back to finger couldn't release on its own for some reason.

After she worked with that ring finger and then moved to my shoulder, she said she could literally feel a powerful shaking energy coming out of my shoulder and then when the scream erupted, the circle was broken and everything let go. Huge waves of heat poured out of me for nearly 8-hours after that session. I know that this was a very important part of why I came to the mountains to finally release this trapped energy to allow it to return to my spine so that I could reclaim my backbone, my strength and power.

Chapter Twenty-Eight
THE MOUNTAIN LIONESS

Anger is a powerful emotion that seeks to stop something from happening that is not wanted or to make something happen that is not happening. It can be used to heal or to destroy. If our focus is on inflicting pain, we will become caught in destruction, which produces more of what we don't want or prevents us from experiencing what we do want. But if our focus is on changing a pattern in which we have been caught, we will become free of the pattern and find that we are manifesting our heart's wishes.

After having completed this whole process, I wrote an email to Oregon David sharing with him what had happened. I felt so good about the progress and the understanding that came out of this experience and was not prepared for his response:

Sandy. This is good work. I'm glad you're getting some of this finished. Play with this .... maybe something important....... part of Sandy, a little girl, is angry that "you" aren't angry about what was done to her........... you're not angry at those who did it to you..............you're too damn understanding about both the perpetrators and too damn understanding of how you "created" this to go ahead and be pissed at the things that were done to her regardless of their source and regardless of who created the Universe...........

Her anger at your lack of anger may be having some important consequences. Smashing some wood or hitting a pillow is theatrical if you aren't willing to feel and express the anger at what was done.....the willingness and desire to feel the anger has to come before getting better at expressing it..... Expressing it without feeling it is just going through the motions.....

Although going through the actions might help you gain willingness and desire to have the anger and express it..... around and around..........

And maybe discover you and the Universe can survive your expression of anger........... so much more willing to express sadness, hurt and loss............ being " f-----" pissed, enraged, livid at what was done to the little girl..... by mean hurt people. Where is that mother lion anger? Isn't that a needed piece?

This is wondering that comes from what you have sent me...... take it or leave it. Clearly a loving mom should have been angry at a man, men, or husband who did bad things to little girl Sandy........... and a father husband should have been mad at any men or women or wife who allowed little girl Sandy to be harmed. Lots of angers not being expressed, right? Maybe try expressing it and acting it out until you sound like you really mean it, until you are believable. And if you really mean it; practice, until it seems like you do. Lots of love and healing to all of you. David

As I started reading David's message, I felt a shock wave move through my body comparable to the time I picked up the wrong end of a soldering iron when I was about 11 years old. It had been plugged in and was extremely hot. I was in such a frozen state of shock to my system that I couldn't release it for a moment. I held the hot iron until my right hand became numb and my left hand removed the burning tool from my right. The inside of me felt as burned by Oregon David's email as my hand felt so long ago. After a number of deep breaths, with tears still pouring down my cheeks and pain filling my heart, I wrote a message back to David. I knew he was telling me something I needed to hear, though hearing it was hard. I truly believed I had moved to a magnificent place of healing when I first told him about that body therapy experience, and it felt like David had pointed out that something was missing in the experience... Something *very important* was missing.

I decided I would work with my response the next morning, so, I went to bed after sending off the message, and when I woke, I went on the Internet to retrieve my email. When the *Sent* mailbox opened, I saw the message from the previous night, and in an instant, it disappeared from the screen, as if it had been erased. I went to the recently deleted file, but found that it was empty, even though I had deleted a number of new messages the previous night without emptying the folder. The *recently deleted file* shouldn't have been empty.

When I looked at my Old Mail file, I saw the message David had sent to me, and it was still there with a curved arrow next to it, which indicated that a return message had been sent. So I sent him another message:

David, Did you get my response to your comments about anger last night? I was deeply moved by what you wrote, and sent you a message while I was in the middle of the pain of realization that came from reading your words. I wanted to look at what I wrote you and though my system shows that a message has been sent, it does not show an actual message. Could you let me know if you did receive it, and if you did, could you forward it back to me? There were feelings in it that went really deep and it helps to see the words I wrote at the time to work more deeply with what was stirred.

Very soon, following my request, David answered:

Hi.... yes, I appreciated your response. .... Be gentle and firm, love. And then he attached what I had written the night before.

David... This was hard to read... My throat is tight, stomach hurts. I know you are right and I am not sure how to do this, yet. I will let myself feel what you have written. I am sure an angry part that is angry because I am not angry, may well see me as if I were my mother who saw and knew and didn't do anything. This angry one must see me as someone not doing anything, just like my mother did nothing. I realize I have separated myself from what happened and risen above the mother lion feelings and the wounded little girl and look down on the atrocities from an evolved spirituality to a place of forgiveness of the abusers, not so unlike my mother who separated herself from seeing the atrocities from a devoted Christian wife position and she refused to see what her husband was doing and forsook her mother lion job. She saw no forgiveness needed because she made herself believe that nothing happened to Sandy. We both abandoned the little girl,

319

even though we did it from opposite places. This is painful for me to see... and the little girl deserved a very angry mother lion...I will find the anger and I will express it. Many, many tears right now...I will find my way. It is no accident that as I was reading your message, a CSI program was on the TV...about a mother who killed her little girl and was let off by a judge who didn't think a good looking, well educated woman would do that sort of thing to her child, when, in fact, she did...and the prosecutors became angry...the anger fueled a case against the judge. They stood up for the little girl, because she died. I will do this for little Sandy, because she lived, and she deserves to know that she didn't die. Thank you. S

I found it interesting that I wrote about my commitment to expressing anger and it was deleted from my computer system as it had been deleted from my internal system...what a great metaphor! I thanked David for holding the anger for me, when I had lost my connection to it, and then sending it back to me so I could reconnect with it. Expressing that anger was something that I committed to doing, but at the same time, I needed to protect my body as a mother lion would protect her cub. Part of that protection was to get the best advice I could from a medical perspective.

***

With all of this on my heart and mind, I drove to Denver for my appointment with the oncologist for the consultation regarding the carcinoma that had developed in the part of my body that had been attacked so long ago. It didn't seem like an accident that the appointment was scheduled for September 11. The date was the anniversary of the attack on the twin towers on 9-11, which led to a world and a nation in explosive anger and division, but it, also, contained 11:11, since my appointment was on the 11th at 11 AM. These were numbers that have been so very special to me; mystical and magical, they represent wholeness, the very opposite of 9-11. For so long, I have loved the number 11 and even more so, the number 11:11. So often, I just happen to glance at the clock when it is displaying 11:11 and so many days, I would see that time both morning and night. The number 1, especially when I see it as 111 or 11:11, connects me to Spirit aware-ness, to the feeling of flow and love.

I began to notice 11's many years ago and for some unexplained rea-son, seeing them—whether on a clock, a sign, a freeway exit, a page in a book, or any other place where numbers might appear—caused something very profound to happen inside me. When these numbers cross my path or come into my awareness I feel connected to the world, to the Universe; I would feel what I can only describe as abundant love for everything and everyone, and I am filled with a confidence that everything is well...all is as it is supposed to be and I am safe, no matter what outer circumstances might be occurring. And...I have no idea why this happens.

However, for many years of my life, I did not feel connected to anything or anyone. Most of my life, I felt as if I had been dropped onto the wrong planet and I would never belong here, wherever *here* happened to be. I felt as if I was living in my waking life, what that dream self who was first torpedoed, experienced and then spent her life running from war to war, never finding her home, never finding rest. In fear and resistance to being here, I held my breath more than I breathed. And though from the outside, it might have looked like my life was flowing, at times with magnificent strength and direction, my experience of my life felt more like it was a product of thrashing about in the water, taking gasps of air to sustain me during the long periods of time that felt like I was caught in the under currents of *the ocean of life*. This was an ocean that seemed life threatening rather than life giving, and was something over which I had no control.

So the experience of connection and flow was a welcome relief to my struggling self, and something in me believed that I would someday find the way to feel 11:11 all the time, or at least most of the time. With what felt like cancer exploding in my body as my personal 9-11, and the deepest awareness of love and connection to the Universe in 11:11, I couldn't have choreographed the energies of the appointment with such perfection had I been in control of the doctor's schedule and arranged it with intention.

I left my mountain hideaway in plenty of time to drive the 30 some miles to the doctor's office. I had to laugh, time after time, as I looked at my Magellan guidance system to see how long until the next turn or see how many miles were left. The first time I looked, I had 11 miles to the next turn, and again 1.1 miles…I, also, just happened to look at the system when I had 11 miles left in the trip. I was even directed to go to 11th street to get to the hospital. It seemed as if the Universe was expressing its love, as well as its sense of humor.

Shortly after 11:00, maybe about 11 minutes, I was ushered into the conference room to discuss options with the head of the oncology department of Rocky Mountain Cancer Center, followed by an exam. The initial response was that the skin looked pre-cancerous, not cancerous as it had been diagnosed earlier, but to be sure, he informed me that whether it was cancer or pre-cancer, the tissue would have to be removed under anesthesia in a hospital. My belief was that the work I had done the week before had given permission for the cells to begin the process of going in reverse, and that is what they were doing at the time he looked at them.

Following the RMCC appointment, I had several errands to run, and again I smiled; when I finished up with the first errand, it was 1:11, and when I completed the second it was 2:11. And again, as before, each time I looked at how far I was from the next turn, every number included 11. At one point, while driving down Interstate 25, the Magellan voice informed me that I had to take a right turn in 1.1 miles. Normally it sends the turn message at 2 miles and .5 miles. That one brought laugh out loud laughter!

I arrived at the EMDR therapist's office a few minutes early, and we began the session, for which she charged $110 per hour. I didn't notice the 11 in that figure until this writing. I explained that I selected her from the long list of EMDR therapists in the Denver area because she was one of four facilitators, which, for me, meant that she knew what she was doing, and that she was not a conventional therapist who would want to spend hours talking about the issue rather than letting me deal with what was at hand.

***

Traditional EMDR sessions have the client provide an image of the issue and the belief that is attached to it and then what belief is the desired outcome. This sets the person's internal system on a course towards healing. For me, the image was the stinking man who raped me when I was about six years old. He had been in my thoughts for sometime…so I had a fairly clear picture to describe him in the setting, which was an ugly dark place that my father had taken me to in the night. The man was wearing a filthy undershirt, the kind without arms and with a low cut front and back. Those tank top shirts were the kind my father wore, too, and I hated them. The rapist smelled of alcohol, was unshaven, and un-bathed. And when he abused me, his stink dripped on me, as I wrote about earlier.

Laura asked me what belief I held about all of this…and to my surprise, the words that spontaneously came out of my mouth, were *"Now I stink!"* I explained to the therapist that after I got married, it was not uncommon for me to take at least two baths a day, and when I began therapy in the mid 1980s, far before this memory ever arose, I began taking four or more baths a day, often in scalding hot water, so hot I looked burned when I got out of the tub. Laura asked me what I would prefer to be true instead of, *"Now, I stink."* And the phrase that came to my mind immediately was, *"I am fresh, and beautiful."* The former feeling-belief held a 10, on a scale of 1 – 10 where 10 is 100% belief. The *"Now, I stink"* belief was what had been pushed to the surface, and from my perspective, the fuming anger that was attached to this whole experience had turned places on my skin into cancer. The feelings that were attached to the negative belief were sadness, hopeless, and helplessness, all felt in my throat as extreme tightness and in my pelvic area as sensitive and burning pain.

Before we got started on the process, I asked Laura if people in nearby offices would hear me if loud sounds came out and suggested that she could go to the ones that could possibly hear, to let them know that there might be loud sounds. I wanted to feel free to deal with whatever came up without having to hold back the sound to protect others from becoming afraid or calling 911. She took care of it and returned to begin the session. It was obvious that in that short time out, I had disconnected from the emotion that had arisen a few minutes before, so she asked what I needed to return to that place. An image of the stinking man came to me…and instantly, I was back there.

I could tell that I was in the room alone with this man; I was sitting on a bed, wearing only underpants. A rough wool blanket was under me, making my legs feel very irritated. Everything went black. I could no longer see anything, though I was aware that the man was still in the room and I could sense he was moving toward me. Through the darkness, I could see that he was unzipping his pants, I began to cry…I knew what would be coming next…and I couldn't see anything anymore. My teeth began to hurt, especially the top teeth on the left side, and then my left side went away. My right side was still in the dark and felt exceedingly heavy. And then it went into a deeper dark and quiet place…all of me, both left and right sides were in the quiet place. I had disconnected from whatever was happening someplace else.

Laura reminded me to return to my body and be aware of what was happening. I could feel the man coming closer and became aware of my bones hurting. I felt myself waiting…just waiting for it to get over, and I went away again. I knew he had crawled on top of me, and I wanted it to just get over.

Tears had been falling since the beginning of this part of the session, but they became more pronounced…lots of tears covered my cheeks as I felt the man moving on me…*His undershirt stinks…his body stinks, his mouth stinks. I try to move away from him. I begin to cry out that I don't want him to touch my skin…his filthy skin…and my left hand reaches up to stop him from touching my skin.*

I try to move away from the stench; I turn my head to avoid having to smell his skin, his clothes, his breath. I can see his black chest hair...and I go away again.

Laura asked if I wanted to take a break for a moment. She suggested that perhaps I was avoiding going to that moment when his cold wet sweat touched me and his saliva dropped on me in such a way that brought me back into my body and I felt what had been happening instead of being in the protection of dissociation. I explained to her that after the first shocking rape when I was 4, I had learned to dissociate, so there was never a connection between my thoughts and my body feelings; they could be two separate things but this event brought these two aspects of myself together. I knew that I had learned how to observe what was happening to me rather than experience it...and in the observation, I had learned to understand the rapist, for whom I could feel compassion, sort of a detached compassion. The problem was this was the same detached compassion I felt for the little girl who was getting raped. I knew that I had to find a way to break this wall of separation between my thinking-observing self and the child being raped.

As I was explaining this to Laura, I began to cry. I went into another deep place, and with what felt like the voice of a child, I said, *"If I don't do this right, if I can't find the anger, I will..."* and the words stopped. I could hear the conflict inside my head. One part of me wanted, more than anything, to be able to get angry, to release all of this that had a hold of me for so long, and another part of me understood that all of us are connected, the rapist and the raped...to become angry is to disconnect from the truth that we all hold all that is human, including each other. I couldn't find a way to bring these conflicting thoughts together. On another level, I knew that we draw to us what we need for our soul's journey, and even though I was a little child, my soul drew this...so how could I become angry...ragingly angry when I contributed to the creation of this whole drama.

More tears fell, I felt so trapped. I heard myself say, *"I want to get angry. If I don't do it right...if I don't do it right.... if I don't do it right...ahhh-*

hhh...I will get cancer all over my body." In that moment, I felt utterly hopeless. Because in my head I knew that we are all one, I could not be angry and if my head would not let me be angry, the anger that I knew was in my body would create more cancer.

With all the people I have worked with over the years with cancer, there was such a high correlation between the cancer site in their bodies, and an emotional or physical trauma related to that function of the body that originated in some childhood event, though it might have been triggered by an experience in adulthood. The hardest thing for many men was to connect with the hurt and let themselves cry, and for women to connect to anger and explode in rage, because our culture teaches us that only certain emotions are acceptable for each gender. Patients who judged the feelings, just as I was doing, didn't heal. Even if they were cured of cancer but didn't heal the original trauma, they were vulnerable to becoming sick again, with another bout of cancer or some other illness, maybe depression or some other mental disorder. And what irony that the one who reflected so much of this to patients and supported them in connecting their thoughts and feelings, was unable to find a way to bring thoughts and feelings together and allow the expression of the anger. I was devastated.

Laura asked if I would be willing to go back into the experience again, and stay with it. When I returned to my body experience, I could see the thick black chest hair and feel it scratching my skin. I hated him touching my skin. I felt myself as the little child, and spoke to no one, to everyone... *"I don't want him to touch my skin...I don't understand why no one will throw this man off me."* And the comment became a plea... *"Why won't someone throw this man off me?"* I felt my voice become more childlike as I cried out, *"If it was my little girl, I know I could throw him against the wall. I know I could...but nobody is throwing him against the wall for me..."* I told Laura that I understood why my mother and father would not do that, but then the child re-surfaced and then asked through her screaming tears... *"Why won't God throw him off for me?"* and then she pleaded directly to God... *"Why won't you throw him off for me?"*

Everything went silent inside and I heard an answer... *"Because this is supposed to be happening. This is what made you break open, and without breaking open, you could not have learned all you learned about yourself and about spirituality. It was necessary for your deep understanding."* And with that explanation, I felt my child-self slip into another dissociative state to find a way to not let what was "supposed to happen" hurt so bad. Almost as soon as I went into dissociation, I saw my mother's face in front of me, telling me that we all must suffer as Christ suffered. We deserve to suffer.

I could hear something from very deep inside me speaking clearly against the thoughts that had come forward. It let me know that I didn't need this horrible treatment to know the spiritual truths that I have come to know in the years it has taken to heal from the damage because I came into this world with this knowing. Through streaming tears, I told Laura that I had already known all of this...I didn't need this, and I didn't deserve to suffer.

Immediately, upon speaking these words, I was back into the time with the rapist and experienced myself as little Sandy. I could see the man's face and I began to speak... *"He is so ugly...his eyes are ugly, he is so stinky, he is crawling over me, I have to touch him to push him away...I don't want to touch him. I don't want his stinky skin to touch me. His wool shirt scratches me. I try to push him away but my finger is caught in a hole in his stinky undershirt. His weight...ah...I am trying not to smell him. He smells so bad."*

And in that horrible moment, I am aware that his penis is pushing between my legs, and the child's voice returns, *"It is sticky, it is pushing...I don't want to be here"*—sweat, saliva, sticky liquid—*"I don't want to be here!"*

While my child self was screaming, I felt myself as an adult, or perhaps that part of myself that separates and leaves to become the observer, actually seeing what was happening to my little Sandy, and feeling her distress in a way that I had never felt it before...I directed my words towards the child who kept escaping. And in escaping, she remained trapped there in that horrible, ugly raping incident. I told her that I needed to help her because she has been stuck. I spoke directly to her, *"I am coming to get you. I will throw the stinking man off of you."* And my child-self let out a wailing cry. Then I turned to the man who was raping my little child-self, my little girl. I said with raging anger, *"Filthy Man!"*

I felt my left hand raise into the air without being in conscious control of it, much like when that same hand raised to do healing, and then my fingernails sank into his skin. I was aware that blood was coming from him as my fingers sank deeper and deeper into his back. He would not let go of his hold on little Sandy so my fingers penetrated even deeper and wrapped around his spine; feeling more like claws, they grabbed his spine and pulled him off little Sandy. I felt my head begin to sway back and forth as a guttural sound came out of my belly, which sounded more animal-like than human. My teeth were bared as if they were ready to tear him apart should he fight back in any way.

I swung the man away from the little girl as if he were a rag doll, and he fell into a bloody pile on the floor, and then I noticed it was a forest floor. I felt myself as the lioness, the mother lion that had just saved her cub. Half lioness, half woman, I lifted the child in my arms and caressed her tiny body. She sobbed in my arms and I held her. I told her that I would never allow anyone to ever hurt her again. Something so very important happened inside, as my child-self knew for the very first time that I was capable of protecting her, and I cried for her, and I cried for me.

I took the child to a beautiful waterfall where pure water spilled over her body, washing all of the remnants of the man from her…from me, and we bathed together in cool refreshing water. I looked at the child and realized how beautiful she is. I turned my head for a moment and was so surprised to see what was happening. I was stunned to find myself laughing, not a wicked laugh, but a deep humorous laugh that communicates that everything is all right. I saw a pride of lions tearing at the flesh of the very dead stinky man.

I had not even thought of killing him, I simply wanted him off my child-self. But as the lioness wrapped her claws around his backbone and threw him because he would not release the child, he must have died and now he was food for the lions. It seemed appropriate. I wasn't feeling vindictive for what was happening; it was more like a natural event, and as I shared what I was seeing with Laura, I explained that now the man's soul is free to discover what he needed to learn from that lifetime. There was so much for all of us to learn.

My attention returned to the child and the waterfall, as little Sandy stood next to me and I invited her to leave the place where she had spent far too many decades and come with me into her future, which is my present. She flowed into me and seems to have settled along my backbone, where she feels safe. Deep from the inside of me, I felt fresh and beautiful, as if I was radiating from the inside out. I felt that I had reclaimed what was stolen from me, which was myself.

I opened my eyes and felt that I had completed the work I needed to do that day. So much made sense on a much deeper level because I allowed myself to experience what had trapped me for far too long a time. My need to feel clean came from that deeply buried feeling that I had become the filth of that man. My fear of being seen came from a belief that if anyone got to know me, they would see what I had tried to cover up since I was six years old when my wise spiritual awareness knew that we are all one, a thought that felt unbearable to accept when my skin was touched by the filthy man...who on some level, I believed was me. Being one meant being him.

What I didn't understand was that though we are all one, we are, also, all unique, and both are true. And what took years for me to realize was that though we are all one, in our uniqueness, we each make choices...and some of us make choices that others of us would not choose, choices that have devastating consequences. To understand part of the truth of our oneness—without understanding uniqueness, choices and consequences—would lead us to incorrect conclusions, one being, we all deserve to suffer, or none of us deserves to experience suffering from the consequences of our actions. Mother Lion had no problem being able to see the truth and when she joined me, I finally was able to feel the truth… to experience it in my DNA…something that transformed me.

Until that vulnerable part of me could count on me to protect her, she would not give up her defenses, one of which was to focus her energy on struggling with whatever seemed to be on top of her and another was to invite fat to cover her body to keep people from noticing her, which from her perspective meant that she would not be hurt like her daddy hurt her, like the stinking man hurt her, or all the other men in her childhood. Another important part of all this, is that until she experienced for herself that I was willing to use my power and strength to protect her, she would do whatever she could to prevent me from making connection with people out there in the world.

***

In all of this, I continue to be amazed at how everything fits together exactly as is necessary for transformation to happen; and all that happened to support this experience was no exception. The week before my appointment with Laura, I got an unusual call from my landlady, asking if it would be possible for me to use the Internet to find out what mountain lion dung looks like. She is an avid hiker and was interested in knowing if she has been hiking near these wild animals. I did a search and came across the Colorado Division of Wildlife site with a 5-page Mountain Lion Education Course. On the first page was a photo of a most beautiful and ferocious lioness, and page 3 had a photograph of the mountain lion's waste, something it usually hides so as to not call attention to itself. I downloaded the article and printed a copy of a photo of the dung for my landlady and copied the first page showing this magnificent animal for myself. The lioness, with her powerful jaws extended and teeth exposed, had her nose snarled back in that pose that dares anyone to even think about challenging her. I put the photo in the folder that I had brought with me to the doctors office, to remind me of that beautiful strength that I needed to access.

When I returned to that recent event as the adult who had finally come to throw the man off the little girl, without knowing it, I had come as that lioness with her fangs exposed and her nose snarled ready to attack. In shamanic terms, I experienced what is called *shape shifting*, and energetically became the lioness to rescue the little girl who had been trapped under a wicked, stinking man for decades. Though I didn't know it at the time, when my head was swaying back and forth, and the guttural sound came out of my belly, that sounded more animal-like than human, I had already taken on the energetic form of the lioness. My teeth were bared as if they were ready to tear him apart should the man fight back in any way, because I *was* the lioness.

Laura told me afterward, that I looked like a wild beast, an animal in attack with teeth exposed and jaw extended; I actually looked like a lioness, something that she could see from the outside. Without knowing what I was experiencing, she knew that something monumentally important had happened. And it had! Now, my child self knows that she is safe in me, and I know I have the ability to embody the mountain lioness with all her power, her strength, and beauty. This was a magnificent transformation, with repercussions that will likely change my life dramatically, now and in the future, as well.

***

My normal process in writing is to allow the flow of whatever is being formed in my mind and transferred on my computer, to be uninterrupted by editing, and after I have completed a section, I let it rest for a day or two, and then go back to edit. Then, when the writing project is finished, I go back and read it again to be sure all parts fit together into a whole that flows. When I re-read this passage about the little girl and the stinking man, I was shocked to realize that there were *two* events in this one experience. There was the event when I was about 6, when my father took me to the hell hole and left me with the stinking drunken man who raped me, but buried within the lines of what I wrote was another incident, and that was the first rape when I was only 4. That one took place in the woods outside my family home, in what I called the forest. That was the first act of sexual violence that my little child-self experienced, a rape that was committed by my father. He, too, was drunk and he wore the same kind of tank undershirt as that man when I was 6. That is why the man who the lioness pulled off of little Sandy and threw against the wall, fell to the forest floor, not the floor in the room.

When the drunk man's body fluids fell on the 6-year-old, which brought her back into her body where she felt his skin touching hers and could feel the hair on his chest touching her, she could tell that the stinking man's hair was not like father's chest hair. She not only had to face the pain of what that horrible man was doing to her, but also, the pain of her dissociated memory of that first rape that came to the surface of her consciousness. The differences between the two men's chest hair allowed her mind to recognize her father apart from the drunken man. This awareness made her experience a double trauma as she became conscious of what was happening in that moment and, also, remembered what her father had done to her two years earlier.

Though my 6-year-old self dissociated both events, by burying them even deeper inside her unconscious, every time I saw my father wearing an open undershirt, I felt sickened without knowing why. I hated those tank-style undershirts, and I hated any shirts that had holes in them, even more. Even though my former husband wore the T-shirt kind of undershirts, I made sure he didn't wear ones with holes in them. That may have been one of the unconscious reasons why I took over the job of laying out his clothes every day.

The part of me that hated the tank shirts was stuck in the past, trapped in the struggle of trying to dissociate from what was happening, but was being brought back by the stinking drips. She was trapped in that filthy hellhole where her father took her decades ago, struggling to stay alive, believing if she allowed herself to remember, she would die.

She was the one who gave me the dream in a dream in a dream, I wrote about in chapter 11. She escaped in her mind, but found herself in strange hotels, in boats where wars were going on around her, on back streets where wars had torn apart everything. She spent her life escaping attacks and believed she was alone and, so, so desperately lost in foreign war-torn lands, terrified of everyone who came near her. Trapped in the struggle to survive, she didn't get to know the outcome. She deserved to know that she did live and that she grew up into a woman who became powerful enough to travel through space and time to throw that horrible man against the wall, just like she said she would do if she had a little girl who was being hurt by a man like that. And she deserved to know that the war was over and that she finally found her way home. And she did. Life is amazing!

***

Another important piece of the puzzle came together in this complicated expression of patterns within a life, between lives, and in the dreams that integrate lives and worlds; this was something I hadn't seen until most of what is in *The Meaning of Three* was finished. In chapter 18, I had commented that *an event and our experience of it in adult life can find its origin in childhood... and...when we are willing to dig deeper, we can find roots that go into past lives.* It was so very clear to me that my adult struggle with cancer on my face and in my pelvic area was connected to the drunken man who raped me when I was six years old. But a more subtle connection went much deeper to that lifetime I wrote about in chapter 5, when I was the drunken man who stumbled and caused the death of the "wench." As she died in the fire, I vowed to make it up to her, and lifetime after lifetime I became her slave, her servant, or someone she could make suffer, but none of that could resolve my own self-punishment for what I had done.

My hatred of myself as a drunk in that lifetime drew a drunken man to my 6-year-old who was so much like I had been many, many lifetimes ago. And the rage I felt that was buried by my fear must have been similar to the rage the woman felt when she fell into the fire. I believe the vow I had made to make up for what I had done *was* the contract that Bill helped me to end by leading me through the ritual of burning the contract I had with Jake. And when I signed the Akashic divorce degree, it ended the centuries old agreement that required me to remain married to Jake as a way to pay for that night I was drunk and stumbled into my beloved causing her to fall into the fire and burn to death. But it, also, ended the centuries old energy pattern that drew painful, dark energy to me, as in the form of the drunken man when I was so little.

Part of the reason I had such a hard time getting in touch with the anger toward the stinking man who so cruelly invaded me as a child, was that I had been too much like that man in a past life. But when all of that was separated out, I finally was able to forgive myself, to rage at the man who violated my child-self, and finally to forgive all of us for having been trapped in such ugly patterns.

Chapter Twenty-Nine
THE TWO DAVIDS
AND
THE RELUCTANT REVOLUTIONARY

Do not be afraid to own who you are. You have come into this life to live into your being. If you are afraid, ask your future self who is not afraid to help you go back to whatever made you afraid in the past, face your fear, and let go of what was frightening by bringing truth to that past experience. In doing so, you will set yourself free to be who you came here to be in the present.

Many years before this current writing, Oregon David and I were having dinner at the Hurricane Restaurant in Pass-a-grill, Florida sharing our thoughts and our philosophies. In the course of a deep, yet playful conversation, David called me a powerful woman, an identity I refused to take on, to which he replied, with an intensity that surprised me, telling me that I had to stop pretending to be all, *"sweetness and light."* If I didn't know him better, I would have thought he was angry with me. He told me I was someone seeking to turn the world on its ear and that would make lots of people angry. He became almost stern as he spoke about my unwillingness to notice the revolutionary views I held about the world and how it is organized, about the meanings of life, and the direction we ought to go as collective human beings.

David chastised me when he said I had no right to be a revolutionary who pretended not to be one. He wanted me to own what I was doing with my writing, with my spiritual stance and the potential effects of that view on the status quo, effects that would not be felt lightly. He told me that I had to look at myself in the world in a way I wouldn't like, *as a determined revolutionary who could and would make enemies,* and such acknowledgment would be necessary for my survival.

David pushed me until I finally acknowledged that my worldview was one I really did want to prevail over the worldview that has held the Western world captive for at least the last four hundred, and the entire world for at least this last century, but on a deeper level has held humanity captive, perhaps from the very beginning of time. I had to acknowledge that those in power would not let go easily, but that in my view, if they did not let go, none of us would survive.

He told me that I had to accept that in pressing for my worldview I was accepting the potential for a confrontation with those who were dedicated to maintaining the current view. He reminded me that there would be those whose intent would be to stop or perhaps destroy me. David told me that if the worldview that I hold is to prevail, it would do so because I choose not to enter the battle naively.

I had forgotten I had written that passage expressing Oregon David's pushing me towards my power in 1997 and "accidentally" found what I had written when I was searching for something else. This bigger story that would turn the world on its ear is the one I have wanted to tell for a very long time. So in a very real way, as I began to write this book a few hundred pages or so ago, this greater human story that I have wanted to tell for a long time holds my life story, and my life story holds one small event that was really not so small, and that was my visit to Alanza. And from another perspective the story of my meeting Alanza holds my life story, and my life story contains this greater human story. Perhaps each holds the others because, on some level, they are all the same story.

So over a decade ago, Oregon David called me a revolutionary, and now, 11 years later, I acknowledge that I am. And there is another eleven.

***

Another piece of writing that I did in 1997, a passage that I, also, had completely forgotten about until the search that uncovered Oregon David's comments, had to do with the whole concept of past, present, and future being the same. In that piece, I had written about a body therapy appointment I had with Clearwater David because I was feeling very disconnected. At that time, I wrote about the work we did that day:

David quietly stood beside me, gathering information about my state of being as I lay on the therapy table. After a moment, he commented that my energy was noticeably scattered, perhaps more than he had experienced from me in a long while. His assessment was correct; I did feel as if I had splintered into billions of pieces and all the pieces were floating in some internal spherical ocean; the pieces were not only unaware of themselves in the ocean, but had no idea that I was watching them or feeling anguish over the sense of their disconnection. The pieces didn't even know that they were all connected with each other and with me. This made me feel deeply sad.

Though I can't tell you how I knew it, while I was looking within myself seeing this scattered state of disconnected aspects of myself, I could see that I was, also, looking at the Universe, and all the pieces were the galaxies, the star systems and solar systems. If I allowed my awareness to drop into any point within the sphere I could experience the events occurring within that point in sequential order in three-dimensional time-space. I found my awareness moving into the space of Earth looking for myself and began flowing through shadowed equestrian battles not sure if I was the one on the stallion holding the lance or the one on the ground pinned by the weight of my fallen horse. I could feel myself as villagers, as raiders, armies, as nations and I watched migrations and expulsions, funerals and births. Everything that ever occurred throughout the entire history of the Earth was contained within the space of Earth and everything within the Universe was contained within the sphere. It was overwhelming to see how much pain and conflict still existed within the sphere of Earth. I began to cry because I knew I was looking at the Universe, but I was, also, looking at the universe that is me within myself. I, Sandy, contained the battles, the dark swirling places, the ignorance, and the pain of my own history and present. My heart ached since I believed I had evolved beyond what I was seeing, but obviously, had not.

David asked what I thought I needed to do to bring my conflicting and scattered energy together. Without hesitation, I told him I needed to feel like *one*, not billions of scattered pieces. When he asked what this kind of one would look like, I saw a perfect, beautiful iridescent sphere suspended in space in front of me. As before, I could see every-thing playing out simultaneously, yet I could see what was happening sequentially by focusing on one spot. It was as if each spot was centered on a particular event and within that spot was the past and present of that spot. I could see that spot's connection with all the other spots, three dimensionally, and then multi-dimensionally. There were shadow swirls and dark places as well as bright rivers and oceans of light, brighter than sunlight but not painful to my eyes. It was hard to know when I was looking into me or when I shifted and was looking into the Universe.

I felt as if I were some gigantic awareness peering in on all that is and ever has been, wanting to let all the factions know they were all a part of me and they didn't have to be afraid, but I didn't know how to gain their attention to let them know. The sphere seemed to be made of such a thin bubble that if I tried to move into it, it would explode and all that was inside would drift off into the ever-expanding Universe, disconnected forever.

David asked me if I were to search for a way to communicate, how might I do that. I decided to take on the form of the bubble, very gently merge with it, and then I began a search among all the people in all the times for the Sandy in 1997 to connect with her; I knew she would know me. On one level I was looking into my own self and the billions of cells of awareness that make up the whole of who I am, searching for the inner me under the mask, and on another level, I was looking at the whole of the Universe and all who have populated it for all time. I felt my awareness shift from the me on the Earth, searching the heavens for connection with the Self-Aware-I-Am, and then found myself being that greater Sandy-Self searching through time and space for the Sandy on Earth searching the heavens for me. I lost conscious awareness of Clearwater David, the room, and the therapy session, as I became entranced by the two-fold search.

In one magnificent moment, the Sandy in time connected with the Sandy above time; a cry of agony braided with relief and joy emerged from every cell of my body. The feelings in the sound were like the simultaneous cries of both a mother and lost child reunited after an unholy separation. I felt the recognition, the embrace, the integration, and the transformation that was accompanied by a profound upward flow of an energy of ecstasy in every level and every cell of me. My heart opened beyond any opening I had ever felt in this or any lifetime. The tears that filled my eyes were the only means of communicating to David that something profound was happening inside me. And then, I dropped into a quiet state for several minutes.

After a time, David asked if the sphere contained the future as well as the past, and immediately I knew that it did contain the future. I don't know if his question created the future in the sphere, or simply brought my attention to it. As I investigated the sphere, seeing past, present, and future simultaneously in the moment of my observation, I saw the presence of a magnificent transformation akin to what happened in me when the great Sandy-Self and small Sandy-self found each other and embraced. Somehow I knew that what I experienced on the personal level was, also, contained in the Universe, and would happen sometime in the future in linear time, though from above time, it is happening. I saw this embrace of the great and the small taking place on the transpersonal level, and the ecstasy was universal. I allowed my awareness to take me to a time when the human species would experience its connection; the vision was spectacular with no words to describe it, only the fullness of joyful tears. I knew something important had happened during that therapy session, but I wasn't sure what it all meant.

***

As I write these words in the latter part of the first decade of the twenty-first century in human history, I can understand Oregon David's concern back in 1997 about what he called my revolutionary perspective, and how there would be people who would want to attack all of this, and perhaps destroy me. If we could actually discover that we are all connected, all part of the Great Spirit, the One, like the cells within us are all a part of one body, then we would realize that when we declare war on another group of people, we are attacking part of ourselves, like a cancer that attacks and kills the body, and in the process, kills itself. If we really understood this, we would release armies and weapons development; we would focus our resources on what would make the entire body of humanity and the world we live in, healthy and empowered, recognizing that if one part of our body is without nutrition and care, that part can die, and in doing so the entire body would suffer, and eventually die. But those who believe that they gain their livelihood from the supply of armies and development of weapons would feel threatened if they didn't have an awakening that the new planet would be one that allowed them to thrive by focusing their awareness and productivity on something that allows healing and thriving, not killing.

My understanding of how all of this works, is that as long as we experience wars within ourselves, as long as parts of us are running and running through war torn territory in our own bodies, where parts of us attempt to control or suppress other parts of us or where our minds use force to overcome our bodies, or our spirits attempt to separate from the body and mind disowning thoughts and feeling experiences, where deeply buried experiences in our past continue to create tornadic patterns in our present, we will continue to create the outer reflection of wars, of famine, of oppression, and all the other external conditions we face in our world today.

I am no longer the reluctant revolutionary, but I am a revolutionary without armies; I am a revolutionary without any need to attack or declare war on anyone or anything. I am a change agent, a scout, a shaman that has had the privilege of having gone ahead and has seen the world from a place where all of us know our connection to the

One...where all of us recognize that we are sparks of God, like the essence that flows into all the cells of our bodies that continues to exist when the body no longer houses us and reorganizes itself into the dust of the earth providing nutrition to all that pass through it. This place I have seen knows that we are eternal parts of the whole moving through time and eternity experiencing being in physical form, reaching out to touch the hand of God and finding the hand that is reaching back contains the hand of our higher Self.

So many things in living in my second story, from the Sandy-self that focuses on my lived life in this three-dimensional reality, drew my attention away from the discoveries I made when I was with the two Davids in 1997. But a decade later, my focus was drawn back to it by way of a psychic telling me about three books I was going to write, three books that would eventually bring together decades of writing and a lifetime of experience to create an understanding of the meaning of three. In the third story, the future self draws the present self to her to allow the present self to discover that she must go into the past to rescue some aspect that has been stuck, waiting for the present self to learn enough to return to heal the past. All of this must happen to allow the past self to survive, which then allows the present and the future to exist. Though none of that makes any logical sense, it made perfect sense to me.

Chapter Thirty
ENDING AND BEGINNING WITH THREE

We can spend our lives searching for someone outside ourselves to make us feel complete. But completeness can come only when we discover that the one we have been searching for has been our own Self.

After weeks of missed connections, on the last day of summer, 2007, Bill, my Atlanta friend, and I finally scheduled an exchange session. He had been hoping to work on a personal issue for some time, but our schedules had just not come together, and by the appointed time, I believed that I had basically completed the work that was reflected in my completion of *The Meaning of Three*. The reason I first contacted him seemed resolved with the EMDR work I did with Laura when I became the protective lion; I didn't feel compelled to jump into anything new.

When Bill called, I suggested that we begin with what he wanted to work on, and he was willing to accept my invitation. Sometimes the sessions can go for several hours, so I felt fine about offering him the time should he need it. To my surprise, Bill's work took just a bit over an hour, so there was plenty of time to do a session for me. I was ready to tell my dear friend that I didn't need to work with anything, but instead, mentioned that I wasn't sure what to work on since it felt as if I had already worked through my concerns about cancer.

Sensing that there might be one little unfinished spot, Bill asked me what I do when I work with cancer patients, and immediately I responded that I ask if they would be willing to talk with the part of their body that is carrying the cancer. And as soon as I spoke those

343

words, I heard my pelvic area say, *"I need you to not hate me,"* followed by another voice that said, *"I need you to accept me."* The first felt as if it were coming from a very young part of me, and the second seemed to come from a part of me that was a little older, perhaps a teenage part. My first response to my own question was that I don't hate my vagina or any parts of me that had been stuck in the pain there. But I did sense that the little girl hated it, and, as soon as I thought those words, I heard the child say that if she didn't have a vagina, she would not have been raped. Instantly, I saw the image of little boys being brutally raped, and realized that it wasn't because I was a girl that I was treated like that, but simply because I was a child who was not strong enough to fight off wickedly abusing adults.

The little girl who hated her vagina seemed to finally understand that it didn't make sense to hate this part of her body any longer. She did see, though, that many of the men who hurt her, including my father, did hate women and hated her as a woman-child. They had the power to inflict that hatred on her because she had turned against her own vagina and blamed it for what happened. By turning against her own body, she opened a space where their destructive energies could lodge inside her.

Bill asked the child if she would be willing to give back the hate energy, wherever she stored it in her body...and both she and I began the process of releasing the energy from us by inviting love energy to come in to take the place where the hate energy used to be. I felt warmth throughout my body as the release began happening.

Then Bill asked me if I would be willing to give back the fear and the pain that had been connected to the hate energy. As soon as he said those words, I felt myself contract and my throat wanted to cry. As much pain as I had released over the years, I was surprised to see how much was still in me. Bill asked about the size of the pain...as big as a building? And instantly I saw a huge mountain, and Bill said next, *"A mountain?"* He asked what color were the energies, and I saw the fear as a blue-black energy...that had permeated every cell and this fear energy had caused huge tension in my body; it was even in the intricate muscles in my spine that I had been working to release for decades. I remember as a pre-teen, I often curled around a coffee table, back side down and pulled myself into a backbend clutching my feet with my hands under the table and pulled so very hard to release something in my back...something that my little dissociated girl self didn't know, but felt all the time. I was aware that I have released so much in my back in the past, like when the African woman released the tension and surrendered to her death. But this was another energy. I released the blue-black energy by breathing into it and allowing oxygen to loosen the tension and release the fear.

The pain energy looked like red lightening bolts that pierced into my body, into tissues, everywhere. I gave permission for the fear, the tension, and the pain to go into the huge mountain and when Bill said, *"Give it to all those men,"* I saw the weight of the mountain falling onto their backs...after all, it was their energy. But then Bill completed his statement by saying, *"Even Jake."* And tears came to my eyes.

Through the tears, I told Bill a story about Jake that had broken my heart when I first heard it. I explained to Bill that when Jake was a little boy, his older cousin brought her newborn infant to Jake's parents' home for a first visit. Jake offered to watch the baby while the two mothers prepared lunch in the kitchen. The little boy crawled up on the couch and began to study the infant. Apparently he was talking to her and then began to very gently touch the baby's hands and then her face. His little fingers carefully caressed the tiny eyebrows and ears, the delicate little nose and mouth...He was fascinated with this miniature human being, when he heard the sounds of muffled laughter, and he looked up from the infant to see his mother and cousin laughing from the kitchen doorway. He looked embarrassed and scooted off the couch and said, "Stupid Baby!" which brought out even more laughter, now not concealed.

Jake didn't tell me this story. His mother did. Twenty years later, when she told me what had happened, she still thought it was a cute story, completely unaware of how Jake experienced the event, but when I heard it, my heart broke. For the first time, I understood why Jake had expressed no interest in children, and actually acted as if he disliked them. For the nearly five years of our engagement, we had never talked about children. When the minister who was going to conduct our wedding ceremony asked me how many children I wanted, I answered four, and Jake's answer was, *"I'm not marrying her to be a baby factory."* He didn't want children, and I had five miscarriages. His gentle side, his inner feminine, a part that is in all of us—men and women, little girls and little boys, alike—was the part of him that was so curious, so carefully touching the baby when he heard the laughter and felt it as ridicule. His feminine self was crushed and his masculine self came out with *"Stupid Baby"* comment, expressing an attitude he carried all his life. He must have been so humiliated by the incident that he became a macho-man who could turn the woman that he loved into a wench, a servant, a dog-faced pig, or slug bait. I suspect that was his way to make sure he didn't become too gentle or too tender for fear he would feel the pain of that ridicule he believed was coming to him from two women who were completely unaware of the effects of their laughter.

Because I knew the story and understood the lifetime of damage, from well meaning family, from peers, from friends and enemies, from persons in authority and his time in the military and Vietnam, and what all of that had done to *my knight in a tweed coat*, my heart didn't want to give him back the pain, the fear, and the hate that he had given to me so many times in our lives together. But I knew that if I didn't give it back, not only would I keep the energy that was doing harm to my body, he would not experience being responsible for the rage he held for women, and for himself for having a gentle, tender, feminine side, who could see the preciousness of an infant…and the preciousness of a wife. He was drawn to me when we were teenagers because he could see the gentleness that was in me, just like the gentleness that was in him when he touched the baby. But after we became close, he turned against the gentleness in me, just as he had turned on that part of him and he tried to toughen me up, to make me strong. Being around the vulnerable Sandy unconsciously reminded him of his own vulnerable self, so he had to shock it out of me by teaching me not to trust even him…something he achieved when he brought out my trusting vulnerable self by asking me to stick out my tongue, and when I did, he tried to hurt me, as much as he had been hurt when his mother and cousin laughed, an act that sent shock waves through a little boy who protected himself by calling a baby stupid and years later calling his wife dumb for sticking out her tongue.

I took in a deep breath, and, with tears in my eyes I gave back the energy to Jake, as well. I told all the men who had ever done harm to me, that they could give back whatever pain, fear, anger, and hate they received to whomever gave it to them if they chose to let it go. I was ready to say good-bye to them when Bill said he had one more question. He asked me if the men were willing to say they were sorry to Sandy for what they had done to her. Jake immediately answered that he was very willing to say he was sorry, but the rest of the men had no response at all...they seemed to be totally uninterested.

Bill asked me what I thought would be necessary to get them to apologize to little Sandy, and I thought that since it was their energy that they had given to me, perhaps they needed to not just take it back, but to feel what they had given to me, to feel what their energy had done to my body. And in the moment I said that, I saw their energy eating them as if it was in the form of millions of microbial piranha. I was in shock to see the men nearly dissolving in front of me, and I was deeply saddened to see the shock and fear that was visible on their faces. But even with this horror happening to them, they would not apologize. They stood like macho-men, unwilling to acknowledge the pain they had caused the child and all the damage that followed in her life. They seemed to be able to ignore the fact that they were being eaten and were dissolving. They remained in their self-deception, holding tightly to their *macho-man* perception of themselves.

In that moment, Bill intervened, as one man to other men. He said, *"Such men! You would give this pain to a little girl. Not man enough to carry it, so you dump it on a little kid."* And instantly the men realized that they were false men; they were terrified little boys, afraid of the pain and not at all powerful. They exhibited such shame and collectively asked the child for forgiveness. But before she could answer, Bill asked me what they did with Sandy's feminine energy...and I knew instantly that they had taken it to support their weakened masculine energy. Since we all need both an empowered masculine and vibrant feminine energy in order to be strong and powerful people, and their feminine had been damaged in their families of origin. In their growing up, they believed they needed to defeat women to steal the women's feminine energy to feel strong. Without a doubt, I believe that this is a core wound that has plagued humankind for eons. As a side note, I believe the opposite is, also, true, that women who have a wounded masculine energy within them, emasculate the men in their lives, and pull in their masculine energy to support their weakened state.

Bill took a momentary side step, and asked my teenager if she had anything she needed to say to these men before she released them. I felt myself transform into the young teen, the beautiful girl who looked stunning in the black bathing suit, but had the joy of coming of age stolen from her. She was noticeably angry with them for how destructive they were of her sense of self-worth. She was obviously in agony when she said that she hated them for robbing her joy of womanhood. She lamented having spent her youth covering up her womanly shape with bulky clothes, with loose sweaters and big jackets to hide her femininity. And she spent her adult life putting on weight as a body-mask to cover her feminine body, as well, working hard to put more weight on every time I worked hard at taking it off. She wanted to reclaim her right to be a woman and to feel the sensuality of her shapeliness, without having it invaded by disrespectful, weak men pretending to be strong.

Bill suggested that maybe it was time now to take back my feminine, which I did without any hesitation, and in the moment I did that, the men completely collapsed under the weight of the mountain of energy that I had given back to them. Now, it was up to them to give back the energy they received from the people in their lives that crushed their inner feminine and caused their masculine energy to become aggressive and destructive to little girls and women as their way to feel strong, while underneath they were broken and weak. With that, the child, the teenager, and my adult self released all the men and let them drift away.

Then, we three—little Sandy, teen Sandy, and adult-Sandy—said good-bye to Jake, wishing him God speed in his healing and the reclaiming of his inner-feminine. With all of this, my child self knew that I didn't hate her vagina and my teen self knew that I accepted her femininity. Finally, perhaps for the first time in my entire life, I felt free and whole, and fully accepting of my feminine self. Something very deep seemed to have transformed. Somehow, there was, also, a thread in all of this connected to myself in that past lifetime when in the drunken state, the man that I was then, ran towards the woman I loved but stumbled into her, instead, with that shockingly horrible outcome. From that experience, one of my energy patterns as a soul was to hold myself back from running free, fully feeling the flowing energies inside me. It was time to let all of that go! And finally, I felt free to run in fields with the wind blowing in my hair.

Bill asked me if I would be willing to invite my inner mate, Jon-Luke, to come and as soon as Bill had spoken the words, he was there; in fact, he had never been gone from me…I just wasn't aware of him very often. The child, the teen, and I were so glad to see him. Jon-Luke kneeled down and hugged the little girl, who was so happy that he had come back, and he kissed the teenage Sandy on her forehead and told her that she is an amazing and beautiful spark of God. She seemed to glow from the inside out…and he embraced me with a tenderness that I had never allowed myself to feel before.

Bill asked if I would be willing to let Jon-Luke touch me, and my amazingly wonderful inner mate began to trace his fingers over my face, my ears, my eyebrows, my nose, my lips, stopping to send extra tenderness to the places were the pre-cancer cells had been frozen off. My face received the love that his fingers sent into me. He touched my entire body, and gently kissed the spot on the external part of my vulva where the biopsy had left a wound. For a moment I was self-conscious of my heavy body, and without him saying a single word, I knew that he loved me as I was, as I am, and as I will be. I felt his energy create a grid of protection around me, and for the first time ever, all of me knew I was safe and didn't have to hide inside all these pounds of fat to be safe. His protection, which allowed me to feel safe, was the gift he gave to me.

With tears of joy, I watched the little child reach her arms up to Jon-Luke, who helped her climb up on his shoulders, and her small legs hung over his chest. Then she wrapped her arms around his head to hang on as she beamed with delight at being up so very high. Jon-Luke then beckoned for the teenager to come as he put his right arm over her shoulder, like a proud father of his powerful daughter. Then he called to his beloved as he wrapped his left arm around my shoulders and I wrapped my arm around his waist. The four of us turned and began to walk along a path into the sunset...this was the family I had always dreamed of, and it was now, truly mine. Though I was experiencing this from the place of Sandy, the mate of Jon-Luke, I was, also, observing the four of them, each separate, yet together...all aspects of me. I told Bill what I was seeing, and reminded him of the work we had done years ago, when the little girl that had been buried in the garbage had finally been unburied. In that piece of our work, I saw the child and the fat lady walking along a path into the distant sunset...and then I realized something that quaked through my entire body. I said to my very dear friend, *"Oh, Bill. I am not fat. Jon-Luke and the two girls are walking with adult Sandy and she is beautiful and slender!"* I began to cry...tears, so many tears, because I not only saw that I was not fat, but I could feel it, and I knew in all of my being that I will walk into the sunset with my inner mate as a slender women...I knew it in my body-mind, my soul, and my spirit. And I know that what I create on the outside is a reflection of what is on the inside. And so it is!

Chapter Thirty-One
INCOMPLETE COMPLETIONS

Allow yourself to see the synchronicities that bring together exactly what needs to happen for you to take the next step in your life. There is so, so much more to this Universe than we could imagine, and you are an integral part of the ever evolving and eternal Universe.

There are times when we believe that something is completely finished, polished and showroom ready, and then we discover that there is still one little spot that we missed. What follows in this chapter was one of those times. Just a few days after this significant work with Bill, I received an email message from Anne, my dear psychic friend from Seattle who helped me through so many difficult times. The message was actually sent by her son in her name, announcing that Anne's husband, Frank had died and they had planned a life-celebration on the following Monday. I knew I wanted to be there to support my wonderful friend, a great spiritual guide, and a truly beautiful person, as an expression of gratitude for all the support she had given me.

I left that Monday morning for the Denver airport driving down from the mountains of Colorado into the glare of the morning sun, and as I drove, I asked Frank if there was any message he might want me to bring to the funeral, and all I got was a message saying yellow daisies... several times...the answer was the same. I wondered if I was getting in the way because of the work I did a couple of weeks before with the yellow daisies for little Sandy—an event that seemed like a lifetime ago—but the answer didn't change. I decided I'd buy a card for Anne with daisies on it and maybe buy her a bouquet, if there was time before the celebration of Frank's life.

This was to be a very short trip, up on Monday, back on Tuesday, and the only person I told I was coming was my eldest sister, because I could stay at her house, which was only 10 minutes from where the memorial for Frank was to be held. I didn't want to deal with anyone else, or try to figure out how to make times match and schedules work when this was about supporting Anne in her loss, being there to celebrate a life, and saying good-bye to Frank.

I arrived in Seattle about 12:30, and rented a yellow-orange convertible and drove to the North end of the city where I had planned to meet my sister at her office near Northgate. As I approached her building, I called her and then I pulled up in front of her office tower about 1:30, expecting that she would be down in a minute or two. Because I wasn't used to the car, and I remembered that these kinds of cars have a wide turning radius, I decided not to try to park in a very narrow space that was available, and instead, parked parallel to the building.

Just as I turned off the engine, I looked around to be sure I wasn't blocking anyone from backing out of a space, when I saw a maroon truck drive past me...the driver was my former husband, Jake ...or at least I was very sure it was. The driver pulled into that space I didn't take, and when the man stepped out, I saw that it was, in fact, Jake. In total dismay, I got out of my car, and called to him. He walked toward me, with a questioning look on his face, gave me a hug and asked me what I was doing there. All I could say in the moment, was, *"Oh, my gracious! What are the chances that of all the times and places you would be here just at the very moment that I got here."* I seemed so much more amazed at the situation than was Jake...His response was, well, there are about 1 million people in this area, so I guess it is a one in a million chance that this could happen. He saw it as just "chance" while I wondered about all the work someone... or something...had done to make sure that Jake and Sandy were in exactly that particular place at that precise moment, in such a way that not a single mistimed event would happen to prevent us from running into each other. If I had parked in the empty space instead of along the side of the building, Jake would have driven past me and I would not have been in a position to notice him driving by. I wondered what was so important that would cause this encounter to take place. To say I was stunned would be an understatement for what was going on inside me.

I explained that I had just arrived from the airport, picked up the rental car and came to go to lunch with my sister, who works in the building where, it was clear, that he had come to do an estimate for a job. He then said, *"I wondered who that old lady was in that car that was blocking the drive."* Of course, I commented, with near indignation, that I am not an old lady!

I told him that I was in town for a funeral and was going back the next day, and I invited him to join my sister and me for lunch, but he had his meeting. So I suggested that if there was a convenient time, perhaps we could meet for breakfast or lunch before my departure the next day. Moments later, my sister came out of the building, and was as surprised to see Jake as I had been. He and I hugged good-bye as the man he was to meet approached, and my sister and I got into my car to find a place to eat.

As we drove to Northgate Mall to get lunch, I was obviously still in a state of surprised shock at the synchronous event that had just taken place...And every so often during lunch, I would shake my head and say, *"I just don't understand! What are the chances? What meaning could this possibly have?"*

Before I saw Jake, I actually had two thoughts about my time in Seattle; one was that I would see if I could get on a 9 am flight instead of the 2 pm flight that I had scheduled, and the other was that possibly before heading to the airport, I might drive to West Seattle to see my mother for an hour or two. I couldn't understand why I had opted for the later flight at the time I made the reservation when I could have taken the earlier one at booking. Whenever that happens, I wonder what is underneath plans that I am unaware of at the time.

***

The funeral was a celebration of a man I didn't know very well, as I only saw Frank on the few occasions I had sessions with Anne in her home. He seemed a bit shy, but was very kind to me. On one occasion, he offered me soup he had made from the vegetables in his garden, and another time he picked me a huge basket of raspberries that grew near his house. Once he showed me the wooden boat he was building, something that was obviously a work from his heart. And he walked me through the amazing back yard that he had created, that turned what must have previously been ordinary into a paradise garden.

He had hollowed out the land and created a feeling of dropping into another world, a forested jungle of huge plants, gigantic trees, mountain-like rocks, a waterfall and a stream that actually made me feel as if I was in another time and place. On more than one occasion, I walked through this amazing garden and sat in a swing chair to overlook the stream and pond. What was remarkable was that though he created this place, it didn't feel the least bit artificial. It felt as if it was intended to be exactly that way...sort of like it was the true energy of the land, and Frank just helped transform it into its true nature, as Michelangelo found the true essence in marble and simply carved out what didn't belong. I remember how at peace I felt when I entered this world carved into being by this man I knew only from his creation.

The ceremony was quite simple...after a potluck dinner, the 100 or so people were invited to take a piece of yarn and hold it through the time we were together. Then, those who wanted to do so, could tell about their memories of the man who was there, and is now gone. People talked about him being a Renaissance man, and how much his being impacted their lives. What seemed to be a common thread was how connected to the outdoors he was. I really didn't know Frank, so I couldn't give a meaningful story and thought this was more a time for the others to speak. Then a woman stood up and read a most beautiful poem that Frank had written about a place that lives in his heart. It was a profound poem, so descriptive of a place in the outer world that he had visited sometime in his past, and loved so much. He wrote about the mountains, the waterfalls, the trees, the animals, the stones, and *the beautiful yellow daisies.* The only flower he mentioned in his poem were the yellow daisies...I was astounded.

After the woman sat down, I leaned over to Anne to be sure I heard it right, that he had written that poem. When she said, yes, I felt compelled to say something. When I approached the microphone, I told the others that I didn't think I really knew Frank, certainly not like the others had, but that after hearing that poem, I knew that Frank's heart opened to the place he had visited and written about, so long ago, and he carried that place in his heart. I told the others that as I listened to his words, I knew that he had created his heart's place in his back yard. That is why a visitor, sensitive to heart, would feel such peace, because they were actually experiencing being in Frank's peace-filled heart when they walked the paths and sat quietly beside the waterfall or by the pond or stream. He had created himself in the land, as it created itself in him. What a profound experience! After the ceremony, Anne told me that she plans to plant many, many yellow daisies in the garden of Frank's heart. I was so profoundly moved by the love that was expressed for this quiet man...and by the love that he expressed in what he created.

Chapter Thirty-Two
SAYING GOOD-BYE

Transformation requires that we say good-buy to what was and open to where our path is leading us, just as summer lets go to create fall, and fall lets go to create winter. With each step in the process, who you thought you were erodes more and more until who you truly are becomes your experience.

I called Jake the morning after the celebration for Frank's life, and we planned to meet at the car rental agency at 11:30, an hour earlier than I had originally scheduled to drop off the car before catching my flight back to Colorado. That way he and I could visit for an hour and then he could take me to the airport.

Instead of us having lunch, he drove us to a small park beside a lake very near the airport. We sat and talked for a little over an hour. For me, it was the most meaningful conversation the two of us ever had. For the first time since he stood on the porch when we were 17, on Christmas Eve, when he brought me the blue blanket so I would be warm, I felt like we touched each other's hearts, but this time, after all of the years, all of the pain, all of the growth, we could experience heart touch with a deeper consciousness.

The conversation began lightly as we drove toward the park. I made a comment about him calling me *"an old lady who was in his way"* the day before. And he defended himself by saying he really couldn't see into the car, but could see only that it was a woman. He said if he had really been able to see me, he would have recognized me, but the way cars are made today, you really can't see in... What a metaphor, for my being so defended, hidden behind a glass darkly, and not being seen!

After a few superficial comments, Jake asked how my health had been…and I responded automatically, saying I was very fine. But, then I decided to tell him the truth. I explained about the 24 pre-cancer spots on my face (17 from the first doctor and 7 from the second) that were frozen off, and that they were all gone, but for the one on my brow…and I told him about the one in my vaginal area that hadn't been dealt with, yet.

I told him I had been working with the emotional aspects of cancer, and was very sure that the actual cancer in my vulva was in process of shifting, explaining that the first biopsy came back as cancer but the second doctor believed it was pre cancer. My interpretation was that the emotional work I had done that was connected to childhood trauma was setting the healing process in motion. Jake acknowledged that he understood stress was a cause of cancer, but expressed concern that I might not be taking its removal seriously, and I assured him that I would do what was necessary.

He, like most people, related the sun to cancer, reminding me that I really loved being in the sun…as if the sun caused me to get cancer. But I explained that I believed that it was the heat of the sun that brought out the internal heat from stored up pain and anger, and was about to tell him about that childhood experience, when I was 6 and about the man who dripped on me, but stopped myself and I asked if he wanted me to tell him about what I had discovered, since I knew in the past that such things disturbed him. After he said, yes, I explained about the drunken man and that I had cancer spots on those places in the front where his body fluids had splashed on me, not on my back, which had been in the sun as much, if not more than the front of my body.

The mention of the man who raped me when I was 6, moved the conversation about men abusing children, and how that was something he could never understand. How could a man be "turned on" by a little body, a child? I explained that people wounded as children in areas of sexuality could become stunted in their development at whatever age the trauma occurred, and they would then spend the rest of their lives trying to regain power over a situation where they felt powerless as a child. It might even be that they were so traumatized by having their innocence robbed from them at such an early age, that they sought the innocence of young children to try to regain their own. It is, also, possible that men who feel emasculated, have such rage for women but feel powerless in front of them, so they turn on little girls to express the rage that they can't express toward women or more specifically, to the woman who hurt them so deeply, usually when they were young.

The conversation shifted to our sexual relationship, and Jake told me that he was so very sorry that he didn't support me the way I needed to be supported in all that happened to me. He remembered things he had done, and things he didn't do, and was obviously so remorseful, so sad. He asked for forgiveness, saying that he believes we could have found a way, and it was a shame that we didn't. Of course, I told him I forgave him, and I asked him to forgive me for not knowing how to be there for him, either.

But no one knew about all of these things 20 years ago; it took those of us who had suffered from abuse to go to therapists who could then write books until more people learned what was necessary to do for people injured in this way to heal. So it took our going through the pain, the agony, and the growth to get us to a place where we can now pass on the information. I told him that I had nearly finished writing a book, one of three that I knew had to be written and my purpose was just that, to help others not have to go through the pain that we went through.

He then shifted just a bit and said that he has never been the same since I left him. With tears in his eyes, he said, *"You never love again like the first love. A little piece of me is missing…that I can never get back."* If this had been a therapy session, I could have done a process to help him bring that part back to him, but it wasn't therapy, and I was feeling the same sadness. There was some of that *"Grow old with me, the best is yet to be"* in my heart toward him, and I told him I understood.

I asked him how things were going with his wife, and he said they are working on their relationship...that everything hasn't been worked out, but it is better. I wished him the very best, because, he deserves to be happy in his marriage; he deserves to be happy inside himself.

He dropped me off at the airport, and we hugged and gave each other a kiss as I got out of the truck to check in. I felt so deeply happy for the "chance" meeting at Northgate and the decision to get together for an hour or so before I left. It felt like there was a profound healing that had happened, an ending of a chapter, or possibly the completion of a book.

Or maybe it was the physical expression of the ending of the contract I had symbolically done on the ethereal plane when Bill asked me if I was ready to end the contract and sign the divorce decree. Somehow, that "chance" meeting, felt like something that absolutely had to happen to free Jake and me from what had held us captive for far too long. That sense of freedom from some heavy burden allowed me to feel love for Jake, as I had never felt it before. It was a love that could respect who he is without needing to change him to fit my needs, as well as a love for myself that recognized that who he is and who I am are so very different. It was simply love!

***

The TSA agent checked my driver's license with my boarding pass and told me that I was so much prettier than my license, and I smiled. I really did feel beautiful; I know the glow that the agent saw was the product of my feeling fully connected to me, fully in harmony, aware that something bigger than me had worked wonders to get Jake and me together so we could have this conversation, one that really did say good-bye to what had been, with full consciousness and awareness. And then I stopped off at Ivar's at the gate and got fish for lunch...the young man who served me told me that I had a most beautiful smile. I thanked him, and knew that he saw the radiance, too.

Something very important happened in those 24 hours when I made a quick trip to a funeral. I think I experienced a funeral of my own, a funeral for a marriage that ended a very long time ago…but while the marriage died, the love has continued.

***

As a side note, I have always appreciated the meanings of names. And for some reason, after that trip to Seattle, I decided to look up the meaning of Jake, which I discovered means *Supplanter,* or someone who takes the place of another and causes another to stumble. When I read this, I was stunned by the discovery that the one that tried to get even with me for so many lifetimes for my stumbling into her, causing her to fall into the fire so long ago became my mate in this lifetime, with the name, Jake, who, on so many levels, caused me to stumble in countless lives. I believe he was the supplanter of Jon, my inner mate. And it was a wonderful surprise to discover that the name of my inner mate, Jon, means *God Given* connected to Luke, which means *Outgoing, Strong Light.* My dearest inner mate is the masculine part of me that gives to me and to the world, God-given strong light. So, all of my life, when I was searching for eyes that had light shining from the inside, I was really looking for my inner-mate, the God-given light and strength in my own eyes. Life is a mystical, magical miracle, available to us when we awaken from the dream. I am very sure that this light was what was shining from the man on the bus in Washington, DC and what the TSA agent and the server at Ivar's saw in my eyes just before I boarded the plane for Colorado.

***

By the time I arrived in Denver, it was dark, and darkness has a way of drawing up feelings that are unaddressed in the daylight. As I was driving back up into the mountains, I was feeling so very depressed, so alone in the world, so without a home. I wanted to feel my home welcoming me, people turning lights on for me and asking how my trip went. I wanted love, and felt so lonely, without it. I love the mountains, but they are not people with open arms. And I cried as I drove up to the gate and looked down on a very dark, dark house. My throat was tight, and though I was very tired, I couldn't go to sleep that night. I realized that I was acknowledging a death, too...but there was no one to share this with. I was deeply sad.

The next morning, I needed to pick up Jenny and Rachael from the kennels, and as I drove through the fall colored roads, it occurred to me how much we celebrate the coming of fall, the beautiful colors, without realizing that the changing of the colors is a dying. Leaves have lost the green of life...and in their dying they create a beauty that we photograph and are inspired by...but we don't do that for ourselves or for the changes and deaths in our lives.

My heart seemed to open in this realization, and I welcomed Jenny and Rachael back into my arms. I came home and received a call from my landlady...she wanted to welcome me home even though she was in Utah and would be gone another couple of weeks. She asked how I was, and I told her about the day...and as I spoke about everything, I began to cry. But it was more a healing cry of acknowledgment that I finally released *my knight in a tweed coat* from decades ago. The truth is that I will always love Jake, and that if I had never known him before, but just met him today, I would most likely not be drawn to him, or him to me because something important had changed in me, and I suspect in him, as well. During the hour we spent by the lake, Jake acknowledged that he sees everything in black and white, and I see things in gray tones. I wouldn't even say that about me. I would say that he sees things in black and white, and I see things in colors, multiple shades and hues of myriad colors. He believes in a one in a million chance and I have come to believe in synchronicity and all of what that means about the Universe we inhabit.

My landlady seemed touched by what I told her and that I would share something so personal with her. For so long I had longed to have people in my life who love me and welcome me home, people with whom I could share anything in my life, but I had been too afraid to let my real self out and be vulnerable enough to share myself as I did with her on the phone that night. Maybe that old pattern had a funeral, too…with all the other funerals that this trip represented. It seemed to be a time for funerals, letting go of people who were alive in the flesh, but have died, without letting go of the love… Letting go of people who are still alive, but are no longer in relationship, as it was or might have been, without letting go of the love… Letting go of wishes for what is not…and accepting what is, and letting go of lies and patterns that keep us attached to lies, especially the lie that there is really no one under the mask.

***

When I look back over my life, I realize how much I have transformed in the process of taking off the mask that I began wearing, likely, even before I was born. I, also, realize how the mask removal process has been in a dragonfly's pattern instead of a butterfly's way of transforming. A butterfly goes into its cocoon as a caterpillar and the process begins to liquefy the crawling creature, leaving all but a tiny cluster of cells that feed on the liquid and these cells grow into the magnificent butterfly. But the patterning of the dragonfly moves through about 16 smaller transformations, each time making smaller changes on its path from being a larva until it finally emerges from muddy water and takes flight as a beautiful 4-winged creature. And from what I can tell, most of us go through our lives making changes and transformations in dragonfly stages. What must dissolve is the mask that covers the most beautiful "winged-being" that lives within us. Who I am at the core of me, is not transformed, for who I am, is eternal…who I am, is the unique mystery in magnificent union with the universal mystery. What transforms is the identity of who I believe myself to be.

The transformation process is one that shifts identity from the mask to the mystery. With each step in the process, who we thought we were erodes more and more until our unique consciousness takes the quantum leap that requires finally releasing identity with the mask and returns its identity to the mystery. The self that we have come to cherish is not the mystery. This can be a difficult and frightening concept to embrace for the cherished self, which is, most likely, the reason that the majority of us make these changes in stages.

363

When the magnificent being that I am, who in her unique form had come into the world to be a healer, a shaman, a guide to my fellow human beings into new and different worlds was still in the womb, I experienced the energetic vibrations of my parents that let me know that my father didn't want me and my mother wanted me only if I could be a boy. My father's not wanting children was never spoken in words, until I was an adult, and in one revealing conversation on the front porch, he told me that he resented having sex with my mother because he didn't want children and learned to hate it when she approached him "like an animal" for sex, which resulted in another child. Apparently after the fifth child, the boy, she stopped the behavior, and he stopped having sex with her. And except for that one time, he didn't tell me he didn't want us; instead, he spent his entire life shouting it in his actions, and in his most cruel treatment of his third daughter that shattered her life.

My mother wanting a boy, and her disappointment with each girl was clearly spoken all through our lives, and demonstrated in her treatment of us. Every year on my birthday, she told me how disappointed she was that I came three days before my older sister's first birthday, because I ruined that special day for my sister. Even now, as she approaches 92, she tells me that same story of her disappointment at every family gathering, or whenever I speak to her on the phone if there is any mention of my older sister.

Over the years, the messages of my parents were very clear. So a part of me turned on another part of me for having made a terrible mistake in opening to a sperm that would make me a girl. In great fear for my survival in a family that didn't want me, my focus shifted away from my magnificence and turned toward my parents' energy fields to try to figure out what I needed to do to be safe. I put on a mask that I believed would protect me, and I took on the vibration of the third child…the family peacemaker, the one who sacrifices herself for peace among the warring parties. I was good at pleasing people and learned how to become invisible when being seen was too dangerous.

As more and more darts were thrown my way, and attacking the dart thrower was not possible, I turned into a dartboard, first in my family of origin and then in my marriage. I was too frightened to question my identity during that first time of questioning, and over time, more layers of masks covered the magnificence that lay beneath. In my 40s, as Carl Jung pointed out, I entered the time of second questioning when I knew something was missing. That was when I began the meta-morphosis process that has been evolving over the past two decades. Each step gave me more strength to remove the next layer of the mask, and every now and then, I was given a glimpse into the magnificence that was deep within that provides the courage to continue to become conscious of masks, and the courage to finally remove them.

Now I can say with certainty that I am a being who can live as a shaman; but, this is not a mask that I wear, it is the name given to something my unique spark does in the world as an expression of itself. I can say with certainty that I am eternal…not the "I" that we all identify as Sandy Sela-Smith, who one day, perhaps on March 08, 2037 will pass away, but the "I" that is under the mask and may well return to the physical world on November 1, of 2039. I can say with certainty that the "I" within Sandy that contains the mystery, which is my true self, is love; I can say I know I am safe; I am free to be open and to express myself in whatever magnificent ways I choose. And I know with certainty that all of the identities, which have formed around the unique being that I am in the mystery, through all time, have provided the way for the final transformation. At that time, the being that I am, in essence, will be fully expressed in physical form creating the marriage between the spiritual and the material in such a way that the mystery of the All is equally yoked and in union with the unique mystery. My true self will experience the flow between the whole and the part of the whole, neither pushing nor resisting the rhythmic pulse of the flow, and both are who I am.

Every life through which I have expressed myself has been absolutely necessary and eternally valuable in the completion of the transforma-tion, and every event, which has occurred in this life I am living as Sandy, has been valuable in the journey toward wholeness. And I honor the masks that were worn, the masks that have been removed, the ones that are in the process of being released, and even the ones that are put back on as I and the "I that is cherished" work our way through to the final transformation.

Chapter Thirty-Three
THE MEANING OF THREE

You are so much more than you have thought. Embrace your whole self in all the magical, mystical meanings of three that are within you.

As this book was coming to a close, I noticed something that seemed very important. In that long ago lifetime when I was a rowdy, drinking man, self-centered and not respectful to the woman that I loved, I knew that my carelessness cost her life. When I pledged to her soul that I would find a way to make up for what I had done, I had, without knowing it, signed a contract in the Akashic records. Lifetime after lifetime, I tried to make it up to her by coming back as someone she could treat as disrespectfully as I had treated her, but none of the lifetimes seemed to free me of my contract.

Becoming her servant, her slave, her wench during incarnations when she was a man, as she demonstrated similar qualities that I held back in that long ago lifetime, was not enough to ease the guilt my soul carried. Being raped as a tiny child in Nanking and buried alive underneath the murdered bodies of my fellow countrymen was not even enough. The only punishment my soul-self believed would be sufficient would be if I died the same way I made her die, and that happened in that most painful life as a tiny child in Hitler's Third Reich, when finally I, too, was burned alive. The terror of going into the blackness of the abyss, into the death by fire led me into this life and its terror. And my soul continued to believe the lie that I still had to be punished for what I had done, so I created this life, one that would be able to lead me to the truth that I am free.

But to be truly free, I had to become conscious of the beliefs that created those lifetimes, and I couldn't do that without finding a way to become far more spiritually aware than my soul had become up to that time. In this dragonfly transformation, I was born into a family that guaranteed to either kill me or allow me to grow spiritually enough to set myself free. What I discovered in my editing was that when I was 21, and ready to get married to a man with whom I had already completed that contract from so long ago, but didn't know it, I developed hives that I described as *"hot, red irritated skin with tiny white bumps all over me that made me feel as if I was on fire."* My skin was telling me what my soul had experienced in the previous life, which was the completion of the contract. It was not necessary for me to marry someone because of a contract to make up for what I had done, a contract that was rooted in love, but, also, in guilt. However, at 21, I didn't know about contracts. It took decades of discovery to learn to recognize what held me captive was already dissolved.

When I had the heart attack in 2000, the one I had learned how to heal because of the work I did with my mother, it was the *fire* in my apartment complex that *"seemed to push me over the edge."* On one level, it looked like it pushed me into near death, but on another, it forced me to let go of any of those last remnants of belief that seem to indicate that "things happen to us, over which we have no control and no choice." I chose to live, and I created the healing of my heart. I chose to *know* that I had the choice to live, and the Sandy on the higher planes created the synchronous circumstances that could teach me how to heal my heart.

***

When the man on the bus told me that the contract had ended, the Sandy of the mid 1980s had no idea what he meant; but after bringing all of the writing from the past together into this volume, now I do know. I believe that the most significant understanding I have gained from all of this, is that all the lives I have lived, I created based on the beliefs I held to be true, and I created so many lifetimes based on a belief that I had to fulfill a contract to make up for what I had done, so long ago. True freedom came when I understood that both that woman and I created that life and the fiery death and there was no way to make up for what was done.

Fulfilling a contract to "make it up to her" would not erase what I had done; such a contract is based on false assumptions that she had nothing to do with what we created together, and that a wrong can be "made up." Nothing in all the Universe can change what I did in that life, but now I understand the soul of a drunken man who uses his addiction to cover up his own pain, and I understand the soul of a woman who allows herself to be treated like a wench to cover up her pain...I played both roles. I have learned that true healing comes when the pain is allowed to be, when it is not resisted, when I do not try to make up for it or erase it, but when I surrender into it and let it pass through me, which then, allows me to see truth. In facing the pain, I know that I do not choose to remain confined by a contract, and I do not need to try to strive for pain to make up for pain, or strive for pleasure to distract me from pain. I can simply choose what I prefer, what brings me joy, what makes my life feel complete as it is connected to and in harmony with the mystery.

When I was a little child, my soul drew to me a drunken man, one who disregarded the person of my child-self, who used his size as power over me and hurt my little girl-self without caring what effect it had on her. In that past lifetime, I was like that drunken man from this life, who so long ago disregarded the woman I called my wench without caring what effect it had on her. When I grew up in this lifetime, I married a man, who treated me like I treated the woman lifetimes before, and even called me his wench. I accepted being called the wench and accepted being treated without care. And, now, I can understand and forgive him and me in this life, as well as both of us in the past.

Knowing what I know now, I could say that all those pain riddled life-times were such a horrible waste of lives, so very unnecessary and such a loss, but it took living those lives and reconnecting with them in this one, for me to discover that I didn't have to live with the suffering that I experienced...the basic premise was a lie. So it did take all of it, those lives and this one for me to get to the place where I am now...where I can live from truth as much as I can and teach a revolutionary truth to any who is willing to consider another way of looking. The deepest truth is that each of those lives was necessary to get me to a place where I could go back and free the drunken man, free the wenches, the slaves, the servants, all the ones who died with remorse for what they did and didn't do, the ones who lived with broken hearts, the ones in hiding and the ones found, the ones sacrificed, raped and murdered, and burned in the fiery furnace.

And it took all those lives to create this one; the one that began in such terror in the land of the midnight sun, and the land of six months of night, where both light and dark existed with such intensity. It took all those lives and the beginning of this one for me to experience such treachery filled with internal and external wars, with struggle and pain to finally crack open the mask that I had been wearing, which allowed me to uncover the hidden parts who believed that the mask would save them. It took all those lives to bring healing to those hidden parts so that I could reconnect with the mystery, to the true being that has lived within me for all those lifetimes and for all the lifetimes that will come. It took those lives to lead me to Sela, who gave me her name and has been drawing me to her, lovingly and carefully, through each life until I could finally recognize her. She is the authentic self, the "me" who lived under the mask, not to hide, but to be with the masked self, and all the hiding selves, directing them, leading them, and drawing them in, until I was finally ready to risk taking off the mask.

***

When Jake and I talked by the lake before my plane left from that amazing one day trip to Seattle and after he said how sorry he was for how he treated me, he told me that he had forgiven me for the pain I had caused him, and that he didn't hold what I had done to him against me. On some level, I believe that he was talking, not just about this lifetime when I had the affair near the end of our marriage, but I believe he was forgiving me for what I had done in that lifetime so long ago, as well. I believe his forgiveness for the pain I caused him was, also, for all the lifetimes in between. In that beautiful moment, we both experienced freedom from being trapped in painful roles with each other, that unless we are set free from them, the roles never end. On some deep and, perhaps unconscious level, we both set ourselves free to live our lives from our true selves instead of playing roles and wearing masks, at least with each other. And that is why I believe our souls, that are eternally connected and flow in the mystery, created the unbelievably synchronous meeting outside an office building in North Seattle so that we could bring into the physical, three dimensional plane, what occurred on the higher planes when I signed the divorce degree and was so surprised to see his signature appear next to mine.

With this understanding, I can now choose to create life experiences without being entangled in all the drama and trauma of the past. All I need to do is to decide what I would prefer to experience and choose whatever that may be, in all its purity, all its wonder, and all its joy. And that is what I go about creating. If I find anything blocking the creation of what I prefer or if I find that I experience sadness, anger, pain, rage, depression or fear, in what I create, I know that I have work to do inside me, because all I experience is what I create.

In all of its multiple dimensions, I am the creator of this three-dimensional experience I call my life. In my universe, I am the one that creates a place for any other that I draw to me just as that other is the creator of his or her universe and creates a place for me in that universe, as well. Together we create our shared experience in the three dimensions of this world…and from the three—you and me, and what we create—all else is formed. And the amazing thing is that there is something that exists in all of us and in all of what we create, that contains it all. Though most people have written or adopted a story about it, whatever it is remains a mystery.

Joseph Campbell, mythology professor, writer, and orator, spent decades of his life studying what he called the mystery as seen in the creation of myths—the stories people tell to explain life—as expressed in the writings, art, and religions of the world. He pointed out that this mystery is in every person. In fact, as he addressed his readers, he said the mystery is you. But he was quick to add that this mystery was not the "you" with whom you identify. He called this you, the "cherished" you, or what I, like others before me have identified as your "personal-

371

ity." However, as I have expressed in the preceding pages, I found the mystery through studying my personal stories, as well as those stories held by hundreds of clients. In my internal inquiry I have discovered not two—the mystery and the cherished you—but, at the very least, three aspects that can be called "you": the first is *the mask* that I, also, call the false self, the second is the *self behind the mask*, which I identify as the hidden self, and third, *the one under the mask*, which I call the authentic self.

The Mask or false self is like Campbell's cherished self, the one we present to the world and to ourselves as a way to be accepted by the world or as way that will make us feel safer in the world, whether accepted or not. For most of us there is generally one identifiable personality mask that remains fairly consistent through a lifetime with some minor alterations or changes as we move through developmental stages and significant life-changing events. This personality mask contains the behaviors we develop, the responses we make, the roles we play and the myriad patterns we create or assume throughout our lives. This mask is what most of us point to when we identify who we are or when we identify who other people are. It is what our conscious awareness attaches to and lives from, as if the mask is really who we are. I agree with Campbell when he says about the mystery that "you are it," but not the "you" that you cherish.

Behind the mask is the unaccepted, frightened, angry, or repressed self that hides because it feels unsafe to show itself in the outer world, and at times it is even afraid to reveal itself to the consciousness that has attached itself to the mask that covers it. Most of us know there is a part of ourselves that we don't want the outside to know. However, some people identify completely with the mask and are altogether unaware that this hidden self even exists or only now and then become aware of its presence when what is hidden leaks through the mask into the outer world. Those who don't know, or don't want to know the part that is behind the mask can disown the hidden self by saying, "That was the alcohol talking, I was just tired and didn't mean it, or I have no idea where that came from; you know that is not like me," and dismiss whatever leaked out until the next time.

A strong personality can control the hidden self behind the mask so tightly and with such pressure in an attempt to prevent any leaking at all, but what is behind the mask usually leaks through in subtle ways or in more noticeable ways when resistance is down. However, when something catastrophic happens that causes the mask to crack open, the compressed and hidden self can explode into the outer world, taking over the mask position, at least for a while.

Though we may be unaware of it, most of us have multiple masks as well as multiple hidden selves behind the mask. We can present the mask that is most appropriate to the external world, like the roles we play and at times we might be unaware that we are putting on separate masks. We can also have many hidden parts, some of which are in a struggle with other parts of ourselves or with our masked selves. As a result, we can feel torn or can feel like there is a war going on inside us. At times, hidden parts can sabotage what our personality mask wants to present to the world and those parts might get in our own way of accomplishing what the mask has set out to accomplish.

What is under the mask is what I call the authentic self. This is not a thing that can be pointed to or a set of patterns that can be defined; it can only be known through experience. The authentic self is not defined by what it does; rather it is known by what we experience when we are in it and what others experience when they are in its presence. It is the eternal essence of you that has never been disconnected from the mystery. It is your personal experience of the mystery breathed into being within you. The authentic self is a state of being; your unique and pure being *in union* with the mystery. The "authentic you" knows you are complete; it knows nothing is missing, and what it uniquely does in this world flows from this being formed from the union of the universal mystery and the unique mystery that is you. When you are experiencing yourself in the authentic self, there is no mask that needs to be worn; there is no self that needs to be hidden. There is no reason to fear anything because you and the mystery are one in physical form. You are a being capable of creating what you imagine and what you prefer because you and the mystery are one. When this lifetime is complete, this authentic you, this essence that flows in every cell releases its attachment to the body, and returns to the One. It may choose to return through agreement and incarnation into another lifetime to continue the dragonfly process of transformation that will allow the unique spirit that is you, to experience life in physical form.

Some people can go through an entire lifetime never experiencing their authentic self. Others discover it after major catastrophic or near-death events that allow them to connect with the mystery and feel the union, making masks and hiding no longer useful. And others seem to never have disconnected from knowing the existence of the union, even if the knowing is clouded for a time awaiting the moment consciousness is able to fully connect with it.

For most of us, it seems that early on something external that acts as if it is separated from the mystery—such as an angry, abusing, or judging parent; a terrifying sibling or peer, or an incident that causes an infant or child to feel unsafe—and the attention of the authentic self becomes distracted from the mystery and focuses on whatever appears to be separated. As consciousness shifts attention from experiencing the mystery to what is feared, as being something other than the mystery, it is as if the authentic self goes to sleep and the distracted self goes into a waking-dream state, which experiences itself as hiding. This hiding self creates a mask to reestablish the safety that it believes was lost. Consciousness attaches to the hidden self behind the mask or the false self in the mask. This focus on what seems frightening leads consciousness into believing what it sees and the creative power of consciousness goes about creating experiences that match the focus. What is created can cause consciousness to believe even more in separation. The experience of life lived from separation of the false or hidden self is a life that feels empty, as if something very important is missing. Like the tiny child, who crawls away from mother and, not seeing her, believes that mother is gone, consciousness turns its focus from the experience of the union and believes mystery is gone and feels abandoned.

Over time, the false self in the mask is what we come to believe we are. The false self that we cherish must be released if we are to experience the union in which our unique being is connected with the mystery. The problem is that the consciousness residing in false self believes it will die if the mask is released and the hidden self resists such a release because it believes that the mask is the only protection from its destruction. If we remove the mask without bringing truth to the hidden self, the likelihood is that when one mask is removed, another will take its place, and the false self will shift its identity to a new, more acceptable mask, and we continue to experience a disconnected life.

However, the mystery that moves in us continues to create experiences that provide opportunities for the hidden self and the self that is attached to the mask to return focus to the mystery and the union with the mystery. While the deepest truth is that there are no separate selves, there are no masks, there is no hiding and no life with something missing, the *experience* we have while we are in a metaphoric dream state, that we call being awake, is that there are separations, masks, and things missing. Like the knight on a white horse that kisses sleeping beauty into wakefulness, the mystery seeks to awaken the being of the authentic self in each of us. The unique being—the eternal essence that flows in each of us, unfettered by fear, free to be and free to express that being—is both the mystery and the reflection of the mystery in the union.

The discovery of this mystery within us, and our union with it, is the central message presented in *The Meaning of Three*. From all that I have learned in my journey, I believe that the *union* of Campbell's mystery with the unique mystery within you *is* the "you" under the mask.

***

So we come full circle, here. I have lived through *The Meaning of Three* and now I have brought it to you, offering the opportunity to choose to allow the meanings you have gained in the reading to transform your understanding of yourself. You can decide if you want to look behind your mask to find the parts of you that have been hidden there so long, for whatever reasons you believed made it necessary to hide yourself, to reconnect with those hidden and frightened parts to let them know they are a part of your whole self. And then you can find the "eternal you" that has been drawing you to risk removing the mask. Will you allow yourself to get to know the amazing being that is there inside you, who is right now, reading along with you and wondering what choice you will make?

If you want to look, but just don't know how, you can remember the passages in this book that resonated with you as you read them. Let yourself remember and feel the feelings that were associated with what you read and ask the feelings to take you to whatever it was that caused parts of you to go into hiding behind the mask. Bring love to the parts of you that are in pain, allow the anger to be expressed in a healing way that does not add to more fear energy, as revealed in many passages in *The Meaning of Three.* If the feelings seem overwhelming to you, know that the eternal you, the mystery that moves in you can lead you to the right support system to help you release the lies and let go of the beliefs that have kept you covered by the mask. The mystery will lead you, but it is your responsibility to make the choice.

You are an incredible spark of God, a magical being, a unique light-ray of the Great I Am, in union with the mystery and capable of experiencing a life filled with joy, with peace, with light. You can live in, with, and from what your spirit prefers. However, like my little fetus self, you might have discovered that who you are was not wanted, so you turned away from your true self and became who they wanted you to be, or perhaps, like my 4-year-old self who was so shocked by the painful betrayal in the forest, you experienced your own version of betrayal and pain and learned to push away what you know in order to live into what you hoped could be. Or perhaps you might be like my 6-year-old self, you may feel as if you have a lot of garbage piled on top of you that you have come to believe you are the garbage. Don't forget that your true self is capable of helping you to know that you are wanted, that you are safe and that you are not garbage. Your true self is leading you to the inner places to rescue any lost part of you and to a mystical healing pond that washes away all that needs to be cleansed—whatever needs to be cleansed away isn't you, even if you created it.

You, like my 21-year-old self, might have made decisions for many reasons that were not in your best interest, though you thought you were supposed to make them, and later you tried to make those decisions work, despite the fact that they could never work. You may believe that you have to prove your worth, but no matter how hard you try, you never feel good enough despite what everyone else believes about you. Or others may have decided for you that you have no worth and you have been struggling to prove to them, or to yourself, that you do. You know that what they are seeing is not really you, so you never feel satisfied. It is, also, possible that you might have given up and accepted the negative assessment as your own self-judgment and have felt hopeless to change what now seems true.

You might be caught in the mid-life crisis, wanting so much to find what is missing, but afraid you don't have the courage to risk losing everything, yet, what you have does not fill the empty space that keeps calling to you to be filled. Or you might have moved into your later years, feeling like somehow you missed what your life should have been, and you have lost all of the years you focused on what didn't matter. This could make you feel like it is too late, and your life has been wasted. It is never too late. Whatever was necessary to get you to the point where you can risk taking off your mask to allow your true self to be known, is exactly what had to happen…and now you can decide to be who you truly are. My wish for you is that you take at least the first step to release whatever it was that caused, and may still be causing you to believe that you are anything less than who you truly are. You are a magnificent spirit, incarnated into an equally magnificent 3-dimensional being, intricately formed from the interflow of mind, body, and spirit, living in the multi-dimensions of the unconscious, the conscious, and the infinite—or as the ancients called the underworld, the physical world, and the spiritual world—formed from the interconnections of past, present, and future. You are so much more than you have ever thought you are…and by reading *The Meaning of Three: The Mask,* you may well have begun the process of removing your mask, and finding your true self.

God-speed on your journey.

EPILOGUE
A Deeper Meaning of Three

Everything was finished. The 33 chapters, the forward, the endorsements, were complete and I was ready to send the entire project off to my publisher, when something in me encouraged me to pick up Eckhart Tolle's *A New Age.* I read it from cover to cover while traveling to Florida to arrange for an operation to finally deal with the cancer that had decreased in size considerably from the first diagnosis—I believe because of the work I had done—but still remained in a smaller version. As I read Tolle's book, I saw another very significant meaning of three.

Though I had written about the three aspects of mind, body, and spirit that make up who we are as in the many meanings of three, it wasn't until after I had read *A New Earth* that I finally understood the significance of what I had written in *The Mask* in relationship to Tolle's book and another book that I read in 2007, *The Secret,* by Rhonda Byrne. Together these three books represent the wholeness of a single message that seems to jell magnificently when all three are connected, a message that is absolutely necessary for us to "*really get*" if we are to survive as a species. Though all three of us touched on the aspects presented by the others, there is value in reading all three to understand the depth and breadth of mind/body/spirit wholeness.

We are living in a world that is rapidly approaching a time of unstoppable revolutionary change. How we humans have lived for centuries, if not millennia, is no longer sustainable, and many of us are, finally, beginning to understand this. What the change is going to look like will depend on whether or not humanity chooses to become conscious of its self and begins the process of living from our highest nature or if, in the end, we choose to remain unconscious. Living *with* a belief in separation brings about living *out* of the disconnected dark energies, such as fear, anger, greed, revenge, jealousy, hate and more, inflicting damage on each other—individually and collectively—a perspective that will destroy ourselves and our planet.

Throughout history, a few profoundly wise individuals have entered the stream of humanity bringing truths about our highest nature. However, most of our ancestors did not have the ears to hear or the ability to understand the messages, resulting in distortions that made the messages unheard or unrecognizable, often using the distorted messages to defend living from the disconnected energies. Sprinkled throughout the more recent centuries, individuals who sought deeper understandings were able to discern original messages and integrate the profound truths from the past, bringing light into the world; but for the most part, the light was available only to the small number of learned people, while not available to the masses.

Over the past several decades, a growing number of individuals have been "waking up" to see the world and themselves, in a new way. Many of these people shed light from their perspectives, allowing greater numbers to wake up to the fact that we are so much more than what was once believed. As people are waking, they are becoming aware that we are at a crossroads; one path leads to transformation and the other leads to annihilation. The former requires that we choose to become conscious and learn to live from our highest nature, while the latter path to destruction would result from our decision, even if unconsciously chosen, to live from the fearful energies.

Most recently, among many other fine authors, two, Rhonda Byrne and Eckhart Tolle, brought the truths of the ages to a world audience, made possible by great advances in technology and the access to world-communication systems. Though few of the ideas they presented were new, the messages were offered in a way that could be understood by so many at a time when people were opening to hear these profound ideas in such huge numbers, and the means to present these ideas were globally available.

In 2007, millions of people around the world read *The Secret* by Rhonda Byrne and many viewed the DVD or watched presentations explaining the transformative concepts that were in that book and film. In the last few years, millions more have read Eckhart Tolle's, *The Power of Now* and *A New Earth* and millions of people logged on to Oprah.com on Monday nights for 10 weeks to participate in a world-wide class with students from 139 or more nations and all 50 states in the US to have a glimpse into a new way of experiencing themselves and our world.

Both authors reflect what is possible when we experience and live from connection with who we truly are: unique beings, eternally connected to the Originating Principle. Both authors support the idea that we have the ability to live in joy, in health, in abundance, and in peace, which emanate from us when we live from our true self. And, both concur that our true self is a part of the whole, called by many names, including: The Force, One, The Great Spirit, Universal Consciousness, the Universe, the All, the Great I Am, Spirit, Yahweh, Krishna, Allah, Brahman, Buddha, God, and more. As long as we remain disconnected from our true self that is in relationship with the One, we live in the struggles related to the negative dark energies.

But, what do we do when we know the truths presented to us by Byrne and Tolle, and still cannot seem to create joy; but, instead we struggle with anxiety and depression and our lives seem to be filled with fear, conflict, violence, illness, or exhaustion? Or, despite what we have come to believe, we remain trapped in addictions and distractions that we use to keep from dealing with what seems too overwhelming. We know that we can experience abundance in all areas of our lives, but we seem to be living in lack on too many levels, and even if we have abundance, we do not feel peace.

We are aware that peace is something that can be ours if we learn to surrender and be present in the now, but how do we stop resisting surrender? How do we accept what feels so unacceptable and how can we stay in the present when we keep being triggered by fear, pain, and agony of the past, or keep longing for what used to be that no longer exists, or longing for what we wished could have been but never was? If we become powerful teachers of these truths, or devoted follow-ers, we might continue to experience a sense that something is not working, but find that we need to distract ourselves from the gnawing awareness that something is still missing, or we feel as if we have to pretend to the world that everything is working when it isn't, and there is no struggle when there is. How do we experience the awareness of who we are and what we can create from our being when we continue to live our lives feeling separated from what we *know* and who we are? Tolle refers to the magnificent awareness of the power of the breath as a way to reconnect when we have disconnected; however, the fact that we have to keep connecting and have to remain *vigilant*—to be sure that the ego or what he calls the pain body do not distract us from the stillness that is our highest nature—suggests that something within makes us disconnect; something in us remains outside the stillness and it possesses the power to take us away from the truth of who we are. By separating from the ego, which is related to mind, and the pain-body, which is related to our physical body, two of the three aspects of our wholeness are dissociated and we cannot experience wholeness.

Byrne suggests that we must become the master of our minds by controlling our thoughts, and that meditation is a way that we can learn to be that master. But if we have to be a master, a controller of something within, there is something in us that needs to be controlled, which points out that something in us remains disconnected from our higher nature. Even if we have good intensions of living in connection, as long as we experience separation inside ourselves, and part of us remains disconnected from our true self, we will experience a world that reflects separation back to us, with all the pain and destruction that exist on that path.

Despite how much our awareness expands and how much we know about the power of attraction and our magnificent ability to create what is our focus as described by Byrne in *The Secret*, or how spiritually evolved we become in being able to touch our essence in relationship with universal consciousness, as presented by Tolle in *A New Earth*, many of us fail to continuously experience the wonders presented by these two authors. The reason we do not experience the power of our Oneness and are left feeling that our lives lack authenticity—as if something very important is still missing regardless of all our awakenings and understandings—is that we continue to bypass the third part of the three aspects of ourselves...our bodies.

In my study of these two transformative books, I interpreted the message in Byrne's work as a message about the mind, and Tolle's book as a message about the spirit. What I found missing in both messages was the honoring of the body as a profoundly significant component of who we are in mind/body/spirit. Without the physical world as represented by the body, the mind would have nothing to envision and nothing to create; without the physical, spirit, or what Tolle calls the life that we are, would have no venue to experience itself or become conscious of itself. It is the body, the physical aspect of ourselves, which contains, experiences, and directs the pulse of life, and through the body the pulse of life experiences its own being.

I believe that there are three aspects to the pulse or breath of life that moves in the wholeness of the universe and indwells everything that is manifest, including us. These aspects, reflected in the breath of life, include the **In-Breath**, the **Out-Breath** and the **Still Point Between the Breaths**. Byrne addressed the In-Breath, where as unique beings flowing in the essence of God, we open ourselves up, we extend ourselves into the world and take in what is out there, which can expand ourselves in the process of interacting with the world. This is the part of the pulse of life that envisions and creates. It is active and interactive and it experiences relationship with what is out there. When we understand the *Secret,* and finally accept who we are, we can become powerful creators of our own lives by what we draw to us. But to use this powerful energy that is in us—that is us—to create what is good for all of us rather than to destroy goodness, we need to connect with the other two aspects of who we are in spirit and body to become aware of unconscious thoughts that counter the intention of our conscious thoughts.

Tolle provides a profound and transformative perspective of the third aspect of the pulse of life, and that is the Still Point, which contains that quiet place between the breaths. When we become conscious of this stillness we become present with the essence of ourselves in relation to the essence of the universe, and experience union with the profound Universal Consciousness. This place of union is what Joseph Campbell called *The Mystery,* and what I have called the *You Under the Mask.* But stillness and the experience of Universal Consciousness in this quiet place is not enough on its own. It needs to be integrated with mind and body.

As much as we know about the beginning of the pulse as presented by *The Secret*, or the completion of the pulse in stillness, as revealed in *A New Earth,* if we fail to connect the alpha and omega—the beginning and the end—with the middle aspect of the pulse, and bring consciousness to the physical aspect of who we are, we will find that what we create is filled with shadows and darkness and we will not remain in awareness of the peace of universal consciousness. If we don't deal with the middle aspect, we will not bring the *awareness within the stillness* into the aspects of our lives represented by the in and out breaths.

It is in this middle aspect—in the out-breath—where we go within ourselves and respond to what we have taken in during the in-breath. Whatever we take in—whether it is air, food, water, ideas, experiences with whatever or whoever is out there—we transform it into what we need or believe we need, or we are transformed by it. The physical expression of our being offers the energy field, within which integration of mind and spirit can take place. But for most, if not all of us, there is far too much pain from a lifetime of wounds to remain connected to consciousness of our selves within our bodies. When we are caught in the experience of the pain, we lose connection with the mystery of Universal Consciousness and with the knowledge of who we truly are. And as Tolle suggests, the pain-body becomes our focus.

If we have gained the understandings that these two authors have so eloquently given to us, but have not brought as deep an understanding to the middle part of the three aspects, we disconnect from the truths represented by the work of Byrne and Tolle, no matter how diligent we focus on our "creative powers" or on the "stillness." The body needs understanding as much as the mind and spirit need it; to stand in vigilant guard against the body or to maintain control is not the answer. The significance of focusing on this middle aspect of bringing truth to the body, to the physical aspect of us, is what I have presented in *The Meaning of Three: The Mask*.

This middle aspect of the pulse of life is where God and man entwine, where the Universal Mystery unites with the unique mystery that resides in each of us. This is the place where being and doing can become one…and God experiences life in the physical, material world as man experiences God in life, and in this experience, the two become one. However, human trauma, usually occurring very early in life, causes our awareness to disconnect from the stillness and our thoughts to disconnect from the knowledge of who we truly are, as we franticly attempt to recreate the safety we believe we lost in the trauma. We try to use our doing to recreate safety instead of allowing our doing to become a creative expression of our being. And, we put on a mask in a futile attempt to create what appears to be a more acceptable being than our false conclusion of who we believe we are behind the mask.

On that significant plane trip to Florida, reading the little yellow-orange book, that calls us to awaken to our life's purpose, I realized that *The Meaning of Three: The Mask*, completes the work of Byrne and Tolle, by presenting the middle aspect of the wholeness, and connects this middle piece to first and third aspects of the pulse of life. I have used my personal journey to provide a glimpse into the worlds of pain our bodies carry, worlds formed out of the beliefs we hold, and too often, that separate us from who we are. I wrote about my journey to offer a way of bringing truth and healing to the painful wounds and resultant beliefs carried by the body that disconnect us from our true selves. The *thoughts and feelings* of the body that disconnect us from the truths, also, *contain the pathways to* those beliefs that, when accessed with love—rather than controlled or vigilantly avoided—allow *our whole self* to become integrated within. This internal integration then leads to the fullness of the experience of union with the wholeness of the universe. Universal consciousness

385

and unique individual consciousness become one, as expressed in an integrated and whole body, mind, and spirit. Nothing in us is fearfully avoided or controlled; all that is in us is integrated within and integrated with Wholeness.

What is contained in the pages of *The Meaning of Three: The Mask* about the struggle and pain that needed to be faced and healed provides ample reasons why humanity has avoided taking this healing path. We can understand why, instead, most of us have chosen unconsciousness over facing the pain that we all hold in our bodies, pain not just from our personal past, but also, pain passed on to us through the patterns of our ancestors, from being marinated in pain of our cultures, our family systems, and humanity, and from the journey of our souls through time.

So instead of allowing ourselves to be aware that we create our lives and aware that the pain in us creates the pain that comes to us in the outer world, we become unconscious of the truths of who we are and what we do. Instead, we project our pain onto those around us as a way to stop feeling what we don't want to feel, or we distract ourselves or numb ourselves as a way to escape, but we must remain on watch, for fear our distractions will not distract us enough, and we tremble at the thought that we will fall back into our pain. The problem is that sending it out doesn't work, because what we send out comes back, and after the distractions or numbing attempts are over, the pain remains, usually demanding more distraction and greater numbing. If we don't face the pain internally we will draw more of it to us. Rather than interpreting this returning pain as a judgment from the Universe, my work has taught me that it is the loving Universe providing opportunities for us to see what we are holding onto and giving us another chance to let go of the pain-causing beliefs.

After millennia of projection, humanity faces a world filled and overflowing with pain. We can no longer continue this pattern of being unconscious and projecting the pain outward, and survive. The world has reached the satiation point with pain, which means it can take no more without imploding or exploding; if we are willing to see, we can look around and notice the signs of the cracks and the crumbling in every layer of our human systems, which, by the way, are reflecting the cracking and crumbling of our defended and false selves protected by the mask.

Humanity can choose to become conscious of the truths represented in *The Secret* and *A New Earth,* and can choose to take the personal journey toward healing as presented in *The Meaning of Three: The Mask.* In doing this we, as individuals and, ultimately, as a species, can connect with the truths that are presented in these three books, or our species can choose to remain unconscious, struggling with the inhumane responses to pain that have placed us at this crossroads between transformation and destruction. We can no longer go on pretending that all is well, or that in time, all this darkness will just swing back, like the proverbial pendulum, to becoming light again. We have arrived at the point in human history where we must decide what we will do with our consciousness and with truth. It is time to choose whether or not we will face the fear to bring healing to ourselves, and in the process, bring healing to the planet. Though the problem is universal, the decision to find your true self is personal. It is up to you to decide.

***

About the Author

Dr. Sandy Sela-Smith conducts workshops on topics covered in *The Meaning of Three: The Mask,* intended to offer ways to release the mask, bring healing to what is hiding behind the mask, and connect with the authentic self under the mask. For more information or to make requests, log onto her web site at http://www.infiniteconnections.us or use the website for this book, which is http://www.53251.authorworld.com. Either site will keep you updated about Dr. Sela-Smith's workshops, presentations, healing CDs, and speaking engagements, and you can order additional books from the authorworld site.

If you would like to be placed on a notification list when her other two books, *Behind the Mask, and Under the Mask,* are in print, send an email stating that request to: themeaningof3@aol.com

Printed in the United States
135500LV00004B/1/P